**Standard Grade | General | Credit**

# History

---

**General Level 2006**

**Credit Level 2006**

**General Level 2007**

**Credit Level 2007**

**General Level 2008**

**Credit Level 2008**

Leckie×Leckie

© Scottish Qualifications Authority
All rights reserved. Copying prohibited. No part of this publication may be reproduced, stored in a retrieval system, or transmitted in any form or by any means, electronic, mechanical, photocopying, recording or otherwise.

First exam published in 2006.
Published by Leckie & Leckie Ltd, 3rd Floor, 4 Queen Street, Edinburgh EH2 1JE
tel: 0131 220 6831 fax: 0131 225 9987 enquiries@leckieandleckie.co.uk www.leckieandleckie.co.uk

ISBN 978-1-84372-635-7

A CIP Catalogue record for this book is available from the British Library.

Leckie & Leckie is a division of Huveaux plc.

Leckie & Leckie is grateful to the copyright holders, as credited at the back of the book, for permission to use their material.
Every effort has been made to trace the copyright holders and to obtain their permission for the use of copyright material.
Leckie & Leckie will gladly receive information enabling them to rectify any error or omission in subsequent editions.

2006 | General

[BLANK PAGE]

# 1540/402

| NATIONAL QUALIFICATIONS 2006 | MONDAY, 15 MAY 10.20 AM – 11.50 AM | HISTORY STANDARD GRADE General Level |
|---|---|---|

Answer questions from Unit I **and** Unit II **and** Unit III.

Choose only **one** Context from each Unit and answer Sections A **and** B. The Contexts chosen should be those you have studied.

The Contexts in each Unit are:

Unit I— Changing Life in Scotland and Britain
  Context A: 1750s–1850s .............................. Pages 2–3
  Context B: 1830s–1930s .............................. Pages 4–5
  Context C: 1880s–Present Day .................... Pages 6–7

Unit II— International Cooperation and Conflict
  Context A: 1790s–1820s ............................. Pages 8–10
  Context B: 1890s–1920s ............................. Pages 11–13
  Context C: 1930s–1960s ............................. Pages 15–17

Unit III— People and Power
  Context A: USA 1850–1880 ......................... Pages 18–19
  Context B: India 1917–1947 ........................ Pages 20–21
  Context C: Russia 1914–1941 ..................... Pages 22–23
  Context D: Germany 1918–1939 ................. Pages 24–25

Use the information in the sources, and your own knowledge, to answer the questions.

Number the questions as shown in the question paper.

Some sources have been adapted or translated.

# UNIT I—CHANGING LIFE IN SCOTLAND AND BRITAIN

## CONTEXT A: 1750s–1850s

### SECTION A: KNOWLEDGE AND UNDERSTANDING

Study the information in the sources. You must also use your own knowledge in your answers.

**Source A** is from the New Statistical Account for Auchtertool in Fife, written in 1845.

**Source A**

> The state of farming is now very different to what it was 50 years ago. The new iron ploughs are generally used and the effects of these are visible in the state of the land when it receives the seed—now sown by machine. The progress of growth is greater—right up until the reaping. After the grain is ready for the barn, the use of threshing machines makes its preparation for the market speedy and easy.

1. Describe some new methods of farming the land in use by 1845. **3**

**Source B** is from "The Oxford Companion to Scottish History".

**Source B**

> The famine of 1695–1699, when crops failed three years running, may have reduced the population of Scotland by 13%. Although it was the last nationwide famine, it was not the last period of hunger. With the coming of better farming however, such food shortages became rarer and the numbers dying of starvation dropped. People ate better and Scotland's population increased from about 1·25 million in 1755 to 2·9 million in 1851.

2. How important was a better food supply in causing Scotland's population to increase in the period 1750 to the 1850s? **4**

## SECTION B: ENQUIRY SKILLS

**The issue for investigating is:**

> The government was wrong to use force against the Radicals in Britain.

**Study the sources carefully and answer the questions which follow.**

**You should use your own knowledge where appropriate.**

**Source C** was written by Henry Cockburn, an Edinburgh lawyer, in his book "Memorials of Our Time".

**Source C**

> I remember the disturbances in 1819 and 1820 called "The Radical War". The whole country was suffering under great distress and many were out of work. This was taken advantage of by a few radicals who began to demand changes. There was a lot of excitement and some fighting. It was all exaggerated, however. The government said it was the start of a revolution and that the actions of some unhappy, unemployed weavers should be considered as a civil war. The government ordered soldiers to use force to stop the Radicals.

3. How useful is **Source C** for investigating government action against Radicals in the nineteenth century? **3**

**Source D** is from "A History of the Scottish People" by T.C. Smout.

**Source D**

> In 1820 soldiers arrested 27 members of a Glasgow Radical Committee on suspicion that they were planning a revolution. On April 5th, the streets of Glasgow were lined with troops and there was a clash between 300 angry Radicals and some soldiers on horseback. A party of fifty Radicals left the town and marched towards Carron hoping to meet up with others and seize guns at the iron works. They were attacked by a group of soldiers and fled after a short fight in which four were wounded.

4. What evidence is there in **Source C** that the government should **not** have used force against the Radicals?

   What evidence in **Source D** suggests that the government were right to use force against the Radicals? **5**

5. How far do you agree that the government was wrong to use force against the Radicals in Britain?

   You must use evidence **from the sources** and **your own knowledge** to come to a conclusion. **4**

[END OF CONTEXT IA]

**Now turn to the Context you have chosen in Unit II.**

# UNIT I—CHANGING LIFE IN SCOTLAND AND BRITAIN

## CONTEXT B: 1830s–1930s

### SECTION A: KNOWLEDGE AND UNDERSTANDING

Study the information in the sources. You must also use your own knowledge in your answers.

**Source A** was written by the historian Richard Fenton.

**Source A**

> By 1850 the shape of the fields as we know them today was established. Underground drains in use after 1850 replaced the need for surface drainage. The surfaces were now more level in the enclosed fields. This led to further crop improvements such as potatoes. It was also now easier to manage the different kinds of livestock. This made possible the quick adoption of new equipment with a resulting growth in farming toolmakers. These changes mainly took place in the Lowlands.

1. Describe some new methods of farming the land in use by the 1930s. **3**

**Source B** is from "The Scottish Nation" by T.M. Devine.

**Source B**

> The increase in Scotland's urban population happened very quickly in the nineteenth century. The main reason for this growth was the revolution in agriculture. Population increase could not have taken place without a substantial increase in food production. The workers in the towns did not cultivate their own supplies. The urban working class relied on grain, milk, potatoes and meat supplied from Scottish farms. People ate better and the population increased from 2·3 million in 1831 to 4 million by 1891.

2. How important was an improved food supply in causing Scotland's population to increase in the period 1830–1930? **4**

## SECTION B: ENQUIRY SKILLS

**The issue for investigating is:**

> The government was right to use forceful action against the Suffragettes in Britain.

**Study the sources carefully and answer the questions which follow.**

**You should use your own knowledge where appropriate.**

**Source C** is from the "Daily Express" written in 1909.

**Source C**

> The Suffragettes' militant actions have gone too far. Politicians have been interrupted while making speeches. The Prime Minister has had his windows broken. Last year, we warned the government that the time for dealing gently with these mischievous women had ended. Those who call themselves militant Suffragettes need to be halted. These women who unite to create disorder deserve to be forcibly arrested. It is good to see the government now using its full force against the WSPU.

3. How useful is **Source C** for investigating government action against the Suffragettes? **3**

**Source D** is from "Scotland and Britain 1830–1980" by S. Chalmers and L. Cheyne.

**Source D**

> In response to Suffragettes going on hunger strike, the government introduced force feeding, as they argued they could not let women die. Many people were horrified at the cruelty of the government. The government was condemned for its brutality to women. Force feeding was a dreadful, painful business. The bravery and determination of the women being force fed gained them the admiration of many people. It caused many men to take them more seriously. The General Election of 1910 showed the Liberal Government had lost a lot of support.

4. What evidence in **Source C** agrees with the government's use of forceful action against the Suffragettes?

   What evidence in **Source D** disagrees with the government's use of forceful action against the Suffragettes? **5**

5. How far do you agree that the British government was right to use forceful action against the Suffragettes in Britain?

   You must use evidence **from the sources** and **your own knowledge** to come to a conclusion. **4**

[END OF CONTEXT IB]

**Now turn to the Context you have chosen in Unit II.**

# UNIT I—CHANGING LIFE IN SCOTLAND AND BRITAIN

**CONTEXT C: 1880s–Present Day**

*SECTION A: KNOWLEDGE AND UNDERSTANDING*

**Study the information in the sources. You must also use your own knowledge in your answers.**

**Source A** is about changes in women's employment since the Second World War.

**Source A**

> The development of a number of household gadgets that became more widely available from the 1950s greatly eased the burden of housework for women. Men increasingly have helped with household tasks, although in many households women are still expected to run the home and hold down a full-time job. Changes in industry created more jobs for women. Part-time work was increasingly available, which suited many women with young children.

1. Describe the changes which made it easier for women to go out to work after 1945. **3**

**Source B** is from "British Social and Economic History" by Ben Walsh.

**Source B**

> By the 1880s, improvements in farming meant people enjoyed a better diet. Clean water helped to wipe out many of the killer diseases such as cholera and typhoid fever. By the 1930s, people were spending more money on fruit than on bread, which improved their health. A healthier diet increased people's resistance to disease. In more modern times, the risk of cancer and heart disease has been reduced through an improved diet.

2. How important was better diet as a reason for Scotland's population increasing after 1880? **4**

## SECTION B: ENQUIRY SKILLS

The issue for investigating is:

> The government was right to use forceful action against the Suffragettes in Britain.

**Study the sources carefully and answer the questions which follow.**

**You should use your own knowledge where appropriate.**

**Source C** is from the "Daily Express" written in 1909.

**Source C**

> The Suffragettes' militant action have gone too far. Politicians have been interrupted while making speeches. The Prime Minister has had his windows broken. Last year, we warned the government that the time for dealing gently with these mischievous women had ended. Those who call themselves militant Suffragettes need to be halted. These women who unite to create disorder deserve to be forcibly arrested. It is good to see the government now using its full force against the WSPU.

3. How useful is **Source C** for investigating government action against the Suffragettes?   **3**

**Source D** is from "Scotland and Britain 1830–1980" by S. Chalmers and L. Cheyne.

**Source D**

> In response to Suffragettes going on hunger strike, the government introduced force feeding, as they argued they could not let women die. Many people were horrified at the cruelty of the government. The government was condemned for its brutality to women. Force feeding was a dreadful, painful business. The bravery and determination of the women being force fed gained them the admiration of many people. It caused many men to take them more seriously. The General Election of 1910 showed the Liberal Government had lost a lot of support.

4. What evidence in **Source C** agrees with the government's use of forceful action against the Suffragettes?

   What evidence in **Source D** disagrees with the government's use of forceful action against the Suffragettes?   **5**

5. How far do you agree that the British government was right to use forceful action against the Suffragettes in Britain?

   You must use evidence **from the sources** and **your own knowledge** to come to a conclusion.   **4**

[END OF CONTEXT IC]

**Now turn to the Context you have chosen in Unit II.**

*Marks*

## UNIT II—INTERNATIONAL COOPERATION AND CONFLICT

CONTEXT A: 1790s–1820s

SECTION A: KNOWLEDGE AND UNDERSTANDING

Study the information in the sources. You must also use your own knowledge in your answers.

**Source A** gives information about the Battle of Leipzig in October 1813.

**Source A**

|  | France | Allies of the Fourth Coalition |
|---|---|---|
| Commanded by | Napoleon | Schwarzenberg, Blucher, Bernadotte |
| Soldiers from | France, Poland, Germany | Austria, Russia, Prussia, Sweden |
| Size of armies | 177,500 | 332,000 |
| Losses | 68,000 | 54,000 |

1. Describe the strengths of the Fourth Coalition in October 1813.     **3**

**Source B** is from a letter written by Bernard Coleridge, aged 11, from his ship at sea, to his father.

**Source B**

> We live on beef which has been ten or eleven years stored in corn and on biscuits which quite make your throat cold owing to the maggots which are very cold when you eat them. We drink water of the colour of the bark of a tree and there are plenty of little weevils in it. Our wine is exactly like bullock's blood and sawdust mixed together. I hope I shall not learn to swear like the other sailors, and, with God's help, I shall not.

2. How important was poor diet as a cause of complaint on board ships in Nelson's navy?     **3**

## SECTION B: ENQUIRY SKILLS

The following sources are about Spain and the Congress System.

**Study the sources carefully and answer the questions which follow.**

**You should use your own knowledge where appropriate.**

**Source C** is part of a note sent by Metternich to the government of Spain in December 1822.

**Source C**

> The rulers of Austria, Prussia, Russia and France were unwilling to interfere in the internal affairs of Spain—if revolution could be kept inside Spanish territory. But this is not the case. The Revolution in Spain has been the cause of great disasters in other states. It was the Revolution which set the example for others in Naples and Piedmont. If the Congress powers had not become involved there would have been uprisings throughout Italy. France and Germany would also have been threatened.

3. How fully does **Source C** explain why the Congress powers interfered in events in Spain in the 1820s?

   You must use evidence **from the source** and **from your own knowledge** and give reasons for your answer.  **4**

**Source D** is a modern cartoon about the Congress System.

**Source D**

### A FATAL TUG-OF-WAR.

**Divisions among powers will spell the end of the Congress System.**

*[Cartoon: Divisions Among Powers. Greek Independence. TURKEY AUSTRIA PRUSSIA GREECE FRANCE RUSSIA BRITAIN. BREAKDOWN OF CONGRESS SYSTEM.]*

4. What is the attitude of the author of **Source D** towards the Congress System?  **3**

[Turn over

*Marks*

**Source E** is from "Mastering Modern History" by Norman Lowe.

**Source E**

> One result of the Greek revolt was that it marked the end of the Congress System as an instrument for crushing revolutions. For the first time Russia was acting with Britain and France in opposition to Austria. There could be no further pretence that Europe was united. This suited British Foreign Secretary Canning who wanted to break up the Congress System for a number of reasons but mainly to further Britain's trading interests.

5. To what extent do **Sources D** and **E** agree about the problems facing the Congress System?

4

*[END OF CONTEXT IIA]*

**Now turn to the Context you have chosen in Unit III.**

# UNIT II—INTERNATIONAL COOPERATION AND CONFLICT

## CONTEXT B: 1890s–1920s

### SECTION A: KNOWLEDGE AND UNDERSTANDING

Study the information in the sources. You must also use your own knowledge in your answers.

**Source A** shows the strengths of the British and German navies in 1914.

**Source A**

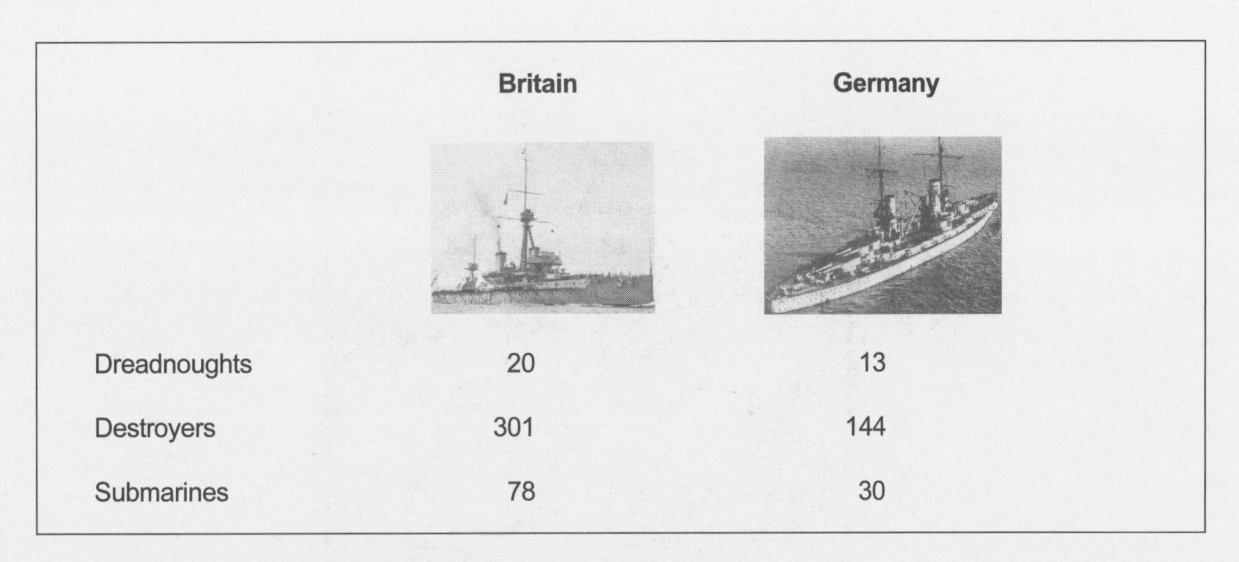

|  | Britain | Germany |
|---|---|---|
| Dreadnoughts | 20 | 13 |
| Destroyers | 301 | 144 |
| Submarines | 78 | 30 |

1. Describe the Arms Race in Europe in the years 1900–1914. — 3

**Source B** is taken from "World History from 1914 to the Present Day" by C. Culpin.

**Source B**

> Aircraft were still new inventions in 1914, and the part they could play in war had not really been thought out. At first they were used for reconnaissance, to find out what the enemy was doing. The light spotter planes could fly over enemy lines to take photographs. Later, fighter planes were designed to shoot down enemy aircraft and protect the troops in the trenches. The Royal Flying Corps, which had been founded in April 1912, became the basis of the Royal Air Force.

2. How important a role did air technology play on the Western Front during the First World War? — 3

[Turn over

*Marks*

## SECTION B: ENQUIRY SKILLS

The following sources are about the League of Nations during the 1920s.

**Study the sources carefully and answer the questions which follow.**

**You should use your own knowledge where appropriate.**

**Source C** is a 1920s cartoon showing the League of Nations taking steps towards world peace across "shark-infested waters."

**Source C**

*[Cartoon captioned "—AND NOW—THE NEXT STEP!" showing a figure labelled "THE LEAGUE" stepping across stones labelled "LOCARNO", "KELLOGG-BRIAND PACT" and "DISARMAMENT", with sharks labelled "DICTATORS" and "ECONOMIC CRISIS" in the water.]*

3. What is the attitude of the author of **Source C** towards the League of Nations' progress in achieving world peace?   **3**

**Source D** is taken from "The Struggle for Peace, 1918–1989" by J. Traynor.

**Source D**

> By 1928, ten years had gone by without a major war. Over sixty nations had sworn not to go to war as a means of settling their disputes. The next step forward would be disarmament. In such conditions of economic depression and suspicion, countries were less likely to work together on behalf of the League. A further problem was the rise of dictators in Europe, such as Mussolini in Italy. Dictators who had seized power by force were not likely to work with others to prevent war and for the peaceful ideals of the League.

4. How far do **Sources C** and **D** agree about the problems faced by the League of Nations in the 1920s?   **4**

Source E is taken from "Modern World History".

**Source E**

> The setting up of the League of Nations was written into the Treaty of Versailles. Refugees fleeing from conflicts were given vital help. A famous Norwegian explorer, Fridjof Nansen, worked for the League on the problems of prisoners of war stranded in Russia and he helped half a million men to return safely home. The Health Organisation organised work on health matters, especially in poorer countries. It worked successfully to reduce the number of cases of leprosy. The absence of the USA, however, greatly weakened the authority of the League.

5. How fully does **Source E** show the successes of the League of Nations during the 1920s?

   You must use evidence **from the source** and **from your own knowledge** and give reasons for your answer. **4**

[END OF CONTEXT IIB]

**Now turn to the Context you have chosen in Unit III.**

[BLANK PAGE]

Marks

# UNIT II—INTERNATIONAL COOPERATION AND CONFLICT

## CONTEXT C: 1930s–1960s

### SECTION A: KNOWLEDGE AND UNDERSTANDING

**Study the information in the sources. You must also use your own knowledge in your answers.**

**Source A** shows the growth of the German navy and air force in the 1930s.

**Source A**

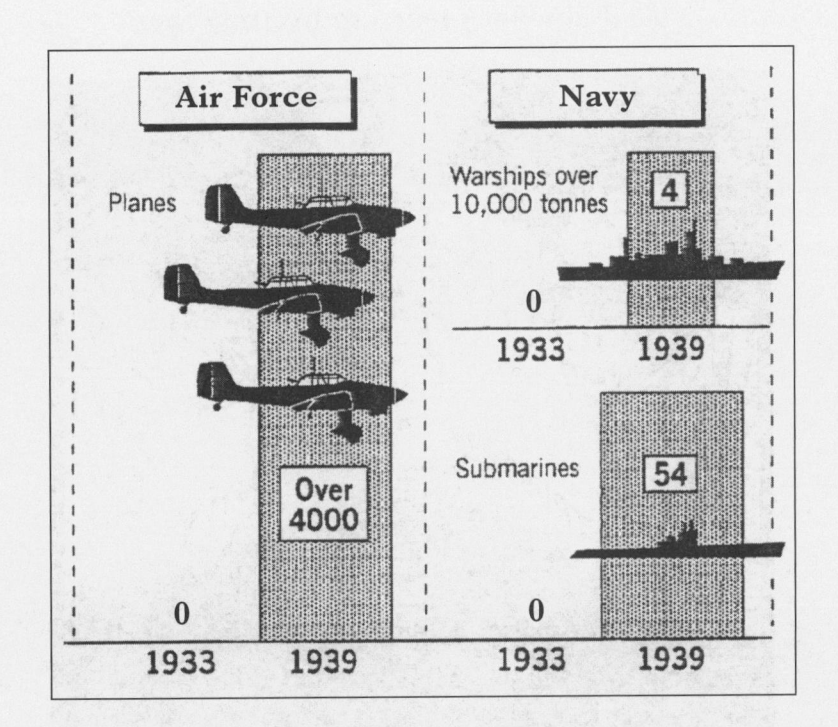

*[Bar chart showing Air Force: Planes 0 in 1933, Over 4000 in 1939; Navy: Warships over 10,000 tonnes 0 in 1933, 4 in 1939; Submarines 0 in 1933, 54 in 1939]*

1. In what ways did Hitler increase Germany's military strength between 1933 and 1939?  3

**Source B** is from "International Cooperation and Conflict" by W. Doran and R. Dargie.

**Source B**

> In 1956 there was a revolution in Cuba where Fidel Castro became the new President. In 1962 United States spy-planes took photographs of Soviet missile launchers in Cuba. President Kennedy thought the Soviet Union was preparing to attack the USA and his advisers urged him to bomb the bases in Cuba.

2. How important was the Cuban Missile Crisis in causing international tension in the early 1960s?  3

[Turn over

*Marks*

## SECTION B: ENQUIRY SKILLS

The following sources are about the United Nations.

**Study the sources carefully and answer the questions which follow.**

**You should use your own knowledge where appropriate.**

**Source C** is a cartoon about the United Nations. The three soldiers are from the UN's biggest members—USA, Britain and the Soviet Union.

**Source C**

"And now let's learn to live together"

*[Cartoon showing three soldiers labelled "THE TRUSTEES OF HUMANITY" standing over a graveyard of crosses and helmets. Signed ZEC.]*

3. What is the attitude of the author of **Source C** towards the role of the United Nations? **3**

Source D is from the Charter of the United Nations.

Source D

> We, the peoples of the United Nations, are determined to save succeeding generations from the scourge of war. Twice in our lifetime it has brought untold sorrow to mankind. We aim to develop friendly relations among nations and settle disputes peacefully. We aim to promote better standards of living everywhere in the world. We promise to practise tolerance and live together in peace with one another as good neighbours.

4. How far do **Sources C** and **D** agree about the role of the United Nations? **4**

Source E is from "Our World Today" by Derek Heater.

Source E

> Although it has tried to live up to the proud aims of its Charter, since the United Nations was formed in 1945, the world has become a much more dangerous place. Many wars have been fought and there are thousands of nuclear weapons now in the world. The UN has been powerless to stop all of this. Some reports also claim that some officials are inefficient and waste a lot of money.

5. How fully does **Source E** describe the problems of the United Nations?

   You must use evidence **from the source** and **from your own knowledge** and give reasons for your answer. **4**

[END OF CONTEXT IIC]

**Now turn to the Context you have chosen in Unit III.**

## UNIT III—PEOPLE AND POWER

### CONTEXT A: USA 1850–1880

*SECTION A: KNOWLEDGE AND UNDERSTANDING*

Study the information in the sources. You must also use your own knowledge in your answers.

**Source A** describes what happened when Abraham Lincoln was elected president.

**Source A**

> The Southern reaction to Lincoln's election was quick and decisive. Within three months of the election—before Lincoln was even sworn in—seven Southern states seceded from the Union and formed the Confederate States of America. In all, eleven states would eventually join the Confederacy.

1. Describe the events that happened after Lincoln's election as President. **3**

**Source B** is about the Mormons.

**Source B**

> The Mormons went West to escape persecution. Ordinary people were irritated by the Mormons' hard work and carefulness. Rumours of the existence of a Mormon secret society called the Danites added to their fears. Most of the Mormon leaders were imprisoned. Non-Mormons were disgusted when they found out Mormon men could have more than one wife at the same time. This led to fears that there would be a Mormon population explosion and they would be outnumbered.

2. Explain why many Americans disliked the Mormons in the period 1850–1880. **4**

*Marks*

## SECTION B: ENQUIRY SKILLS

The following sources are about the Freedmen's Bureau.

**Study the sources carefully and answer the questions which follow.**

**You should use your own knowledge where appropriate.**

**Source C** was written by the historian, Hugh Brogan.

**Source C**

> The Freedmen's Bureau was set up by Congress in 1865 and did heroic work in providing homes and food for former slaves. Despite much opposition in the South, it succeeded in establishing 4,000 schools. It also improved health facilities by setting up 100 hospitals. The Freedmen's Bureau also protected ex-slaves by supervising the terms under which they were hired as free men. However, its officials were resented by the Ku Klux Klan particularly when the Bureau took plantation owners to court for breaking new labour contracts.

3. What is the attitude of the author of **Source C** towards the work of the Freedmen's Bureau? **3**

**Source D** is taken from "Black Peoples of the Americas" by Bob Rees and Marika Sherwood.

**Source D**

> In 1865 Congress set up Freedmen's Bureau to help Blacks get employment and civil rights after the Civil War ended. It had opened 100 hospitals and operated over 4,000 primary schools. Food was given to the poorest Blacks and Whites. The Freedmen's Bank was also opened. Such new opportunities were quickly seized by ex-slaves but alarmed Southern Whites in organisations like the Ku Klux Klan.

4. How far do **Sources C** and **D** agree about the work of the Freedmen's Bureau? **4**

[*END OF CONTEXT IIIA*]

*Marks*

# UNIT III—PEOPLE AND POWER

### CONTEXT B: INDIA 1917–1947

## SECTION A: KNOWLEDGE AND UNDERSTANDING

**Study the information in the sources. You must also use your own knowledge in your answers.**

**Source A** was written by Professor Niall Ferguson.

**Source A**

> General Dyer's actions in the Amritsar massacre were harsh. The event produced martyrs for the Indian nationalist cause. It also created a crisis of confidence in Britain. Nationalist grievances were growing strongly in India. The British Empire had been shaken. In previous centuries the British had felt no concerns about shooting to kill. That had started to change. The ruthless determination to defend the Empire seemed to have vanished.

1. Describe the results of the Amritsar massacre of April 1919.  3

**Source B** is from the Indian politician Nehru's autobiography written in 1941.

**Source B**

> I returned to India after some travels in Europe. When I first read about Gandhi's Satyaghraha (non violence) in the newspapers, I was very relieved. Here at last was a way out of our difficulties with the British. This was a method of action which was open and possibly effective. When we later saw the organised enthusiasm of the people during the Salt Campaign, we felt ashamed for doubting Gandhi. We marvelled at the ways in which salt making was spreading.

2. Explain why Gandhi's campaign tactics for independence attracted support from Indians.  4

*Marks*

## SECTION B: ENQUIRY SKILLS

The following sources are views on Indian independence.

**Study the sources carefully and answer the questions which follow.**

**You should use your own knowledge where appropriate.**

**Source C** shows the views of Hugh Dalton, an important member of the Labour Government after World War Two.

**Source C**

> The Congress Party and Gandhi have been for many years pushing hard for Indian independence. Indians have supported the war effort in huge numbers. We have not given a great deal to the Indian people. We are in a place where Indians shout aloud that we are not wanted. We do not have the military force to squash those Indians who don't want us ruling India. The only thing to do is to get out.

3. What are Hugh Dalton's views, as shown in **Source C**, on Indian independence?     **3**

**Source D** is from "Britain in the World since 1945" by John Ray.

**Source D**

> There had been many difficult times since 1939. There were some people in Britain who said that India should never be given up. Trade with India had brought so much wealth to Britain. India had been called "the brightest jewel in the British crown". The British had ruled there for two centuries during which time they had built roads and railways. They had taken education and medicine to Indians. The British Empire still had the power to control millions of people across all continents.

4. How far do **Sources C** and **D** disagree on whether Britain should have given India its independence?     **4**

*[END OF CONTEXT IIIB]*

## UNIT III—PEOPLE AND POWER

### CONTEXT C: RUSSIA 1914–1941

*SECTION A: KNOWLEDGE AND UNDERSTANDING*

**Study the information in the sources. You must also use your own knowledge in your answers.**

**Source A** is from "Romanov to Gorbachev" by Peter Mantin and Colin Lankester.

**Source A**

> The main feature of the revolution in February 1917, was that it was not planned but took everyone by surprise. It had no leaders and therefore there was no one ready to take the leadership of the country. As a result, the leaders of the Duma were forced to take charge of the country. The leader of the Petrograd Soviet, Alexander Kerensky, became Minister of Justice. This gave the Soviet some direct say in the running of the country. In effect, the Provisional Government and the Petrograd Soviet formed a "Dual Government" which ruled Russia.

1. Describe the results of the February Revolution in 1917.   3

**Source B** is from "Reaction and Revolutions: Russia 1881–1924" by Michael Lynch.

**Source B**

> In the final assessment, the outstanding factor explaining the success of the Reds in the Civil War was their clear sense of purpose. By contrast, the Whites were an uncoordinated collection of separate forces, whose morale was never high. Since they were without a common cause, other than hatred of Reds, the Whites lacked effective leadership. This was a problem they were unable to resolve. No White leader emerged of the ability of Trotsky or Lenin.

2. Explain why the Whites lost the Civil War.   4

*Marks*

## SECTION B: ENQUIRY SKILLS

The following sources are about the treatment of the Kulaks.

**Study the sources carefully and answer the questions which follow.**

**You should use your own knowledge where appropriate.**

**Source C** is from a speech made by Joseph Stalin in December 1929.

**Source C**

> Now we are able to carry on a determined offensive against the Kulaks, break their resistance to collectivisation, eliminate them as a class and replace their output by the output of the collective farms. Now, the elimination of the Kulaks is being carried out by the masses of poor and middle peasants themselves. They are putting complete collectivisation into practice. There is another question: whether the Kulaks should be allowed to join the collective farms? Of course not, for they are the sworn enemies of the collective farm movement.

3. What is the attitude of Stalin in **Source C** towards the Kulaks?      3

**Source D** is from Y. Kukushkin, a Soviet historian.

**Source D**

> The Kulaks were resisting the collective farm movement in a bid to retain their positions, cost what it might. The Kulaks began to wage a campaign of terror against those who supported and worked for collectivisation. In late 1927 and early 1928, the Kulaks everywhere began to refuse to sell their produce at state-fixed prices. They hid grain and sabotaged the grain trade in a bid to destabilise the socialist economy. The increasingly serious class struggle in the countryside made the liquidation of the Kulaks as a class a top priority task.

4. How far do **Sources C** and **D** agree about the Kulaks and collectivisation?      4

*[END OF CONTEXT IIIC]*

UNIT III—PEOPLE AND POWER

CONTEXT D: GERMANY 1918–1939

SECTION A: KNOWLEDGE AND UNDERSTANDING

Study the information in the sources. You must also use your own knowledge in your answers.

Source A is from "Germany 1918–39" by John Kerr.

Source A

> In 1923, the Nazis attempted to seize power in Munich and overthrow the Bavarian Government. With the collapse of this Beer Hall Putsch, most people believed that Hitler and the Nazis were finished. But the trial gave Hitler much needed national publicity. He was photographed standing beside Ludendorff which made people think that Hitler was an important person. When he was found guilty, Hitler was given a short prison sentence.

1. Describe the results of the Beer Hall Putsch, 1923.     3

Source B is a modern historian's view of the "Night of the Long Knives".

Source B

> By 1934, the SA "bully boys" had outlived their usefulness to Hitler. He acted swiftly and without warning. On June 30th, SA leaders were arrested and immediately shot. Ernst Roehm, the SA leader, was among the many victims. Hitler justified his actions on the grounds that Roehm was plotting to overthrow the government. The episode not only removed some of Hitler's opponents, it also showed would-be opponents that Hitler was ready to act ruthlessly whenever threatened.

2. Explain why Hitler was able to defeat his opponents in the 1930s.     4

## SECTION B: ENQUIRY SKILLS

The following sources are about attitudes in Germany towards National Socialism.

**Study the sources carefully and answer the questions which follow.**

**You should use your own knowledge where appropriate.**

**Source C** is from the memories of Karl Billinger, a German Communist, published in 1935.

**Source C**

> For three months after the Nazis came to power, I managed to avoid saluting the swastika flag. You could always steer clear of SA parades and demonstrations by turning off into a side street. I tried it once too often, however. I caught sight of an approaching procession and without thinking I turned my back on it and walked away. Four Brown Shirt thugs crossed towards me and one said. "Are you trying to get out of it? Salute! Now!" I did this and said "Heil Hitler". I could have spat at myself as I walked past the procession with my arm in the air.

3. What was the attitude of the author of **Source C** towards the Nazis? **3**

**Source D** was written by historians G. Lacey and K. Shepherd.

**Source D**

> At first many people refused to join the Nazi Party. Some did not give the "Heil Hitler" salute. All the evidence suggests that ordinary Germans greatly resented many aspects of the Nazi regime such as the strong-arm tactics of the SA. As for the endless meetings and parades, even by the end of the 1933 these were treated with indifference by many. People attended because their jobs might depend on it. Grumbling became a national pastime—but it was rarely done in public.

4. How far do **Sources C** and **D** agree on attitudes in Germany towards the Nazis? **4**

[END OF CONTEXT IIID]

[END OF QUESTION PAPER]

[BLANK PAGE]

2006 | Credit

[BLANK PAGE]

# 1540/403

NATIONAL
QUALIFICATIONS
2006

MONDAY, 15 MAY
1.00 PM – 2.45 PM

HISTORY
STANDARD GRADE
Credit Level

Answer questions from Unit I **and** Unit II **and** Unit III.

Choose only **one** Context from each Unit and answer Sections A **and** B. The Contexts chosen should be those you have studied.

The Contexts in each Unit are:

Unit I— Changing Life in Scotland and Britain
- Context A: 1750s–1850s .............................. Pages 2–3
- Context B: 1830s–1930s .............................. Pages 4–5
- Context C: 1880s–Present Day..................... Pages 6–7

Unit II— International Cooperation and Conflict
- Context A: 1790s–1820s .............................. Pages 8–9
- Context B: 1890s–1920s .............................. Pages 10–11
- Context C: 1930s–1960s .............................. Pages 12–13

Unit III— People and Power
- Context A: USA 1850–1880 ......................... Pages 14–15
- Context B: India 1917–1947......................... Pages 16–17
- Context C: Russia 1914–1941 ..................... Pages 18–19
- Context D: Germany 1918–1939.................. Pages 20–21

Number the questions as shown in the question paper.

Some sources have been adapted or translated.

## UNIT I—CHANGING LIFE IN SCOTLAND AND BRITAIN

**CONTEXT A: 1750s–1850s**

### SECTION A: KNOWLEDGE AND UNDERSTANDING

> The inhabitants of Edinburgh chose to build houses close to the protection of the Castle and this resulted in high tenement buildings.

1. Describe some of the problems of living in high rise accommodation in the early nineteenth century. **3**

> By the late eighteenth century, as a result of the new technology, successful mills had been established in places like New Lanark and Blantyre.

2. Explain some of the ways in which new technology affected the textile industry in the late eighteenth century. **4**

### SECTION B: ENQUIRY SKILLS

**The issue for investigating is:**

> Emigration from the Highlands and Islands of Scotland in the nineteenth century was beneficial for the emigrants.

**Study the sources carefully and answer the questions which follow.**
**You should use your own knowledge where appropriate.**

**Source A** was written in 1851 by Francis Clark, the owner of the Island of Ulva, in a report on Highland poverty.

**Source A**

> When it no longer became profitable to collect kelp (seaweed) I still paid my tenants to collect it — or they would have had no money at all. Farming cannot be well done on the island as the soil is poor and the weather uncertain. To make some money for myself I have been converting some crofts into farms for sheep. I have increased my sheep stock as the removal of crofters gave me more space. The population of Ulva was 500; it is now 150. Some went to other parts of Scotland but most went to America, Australia or Canada where they are doing well.

3. How useful is **Source A** for investigating emigration from the Highlands and Islands of Scotland in the nineteenth century? **4**

**Source B** is from an eyewitness account from Catherine MacPhee of Barra in 1836.

**Source B**

> I saw our houses swept away and the people being driven out of the countryside to the streets of Glasgow and to the wilds of Canada, such as them that did not die of hunger and smallpox while going across the ocean. I have seen the women putting their children in the carts which were being sent from Benbecula to board an emigrant ship on Loch Boisdale. Almost everyone was crying. Bailiffs and constables gathered behind them and made sure they boarded the ship. Some men showed boldness and looked for adventure but for most it was a loathsome day.

**Source C** is from a letter written by John Scott in Ontario, Canada, to his uncle in Scotland in 1835.

**Source C**

> We had a good journey out on a new ship with few passengers. I am building a new house and a barn. This is a wild country but we have managed with great difficulty to chop down about seven acres of trees. We ripped out the stumps using levers as we had no oxen to pull them out. All the livestock we have now is a sow and a male pig but we are hoping to do well in this new land.

**Look at Sources A, B and C.**

4. What evidence is there in the sources to support the view that emigration was beneficial for emigrants from the Highlands and Islands of Scotland?

   What evidence in the sources disagrees with the view that emigration was beneficial for emigrants from the Highlands and Islands of Scotland? **6**

5. How far do you agree that emigration from the Highlands and Islands of Scotland in the nineteenth century was beneficial for the emigrants?

   You must use evidence **from the sources** and **your own knowledge** to reach a **balanced conclusion**. **5**

*[END OF CONTEXT IA]*

Marks

# UNIT I—CHANGING LIFE IN SCOTLAND AND BRITAIN

CONTEXT B: 1830s–1930s

## SECTION A: KNOWLEDGE AND UNDERSTANDING

> In many Scottish towns tenement buildings were built as it was cheaper to build upwards rather than outwards.

1. Describe some of the problems of living in tenement accommodation before 1914. **3**

> By the 1930s coal production in some Scottish areas had improved as a result of technological changes.

2. Explain some of the ways in which new technology affected the coal industry before the 1930s. **4**

## SECTION B: ENQUIRY SKILLS

**The issue for investigating is:**

> Emigration from the Highlands and Islands of Scotland between 1830 and 1930 was beneficial for the emigrants.

**Study the sources carefully and answer the questions which follow.**
**You should use your own knowledge where appropriate.**

**Source A** was written by a journalist from Fife in his "Notes of a Winter Tour of the Highlands" in 1847.

**Source A**

> The most vivid description would not do justice to the extraordinary and disgusting filth of Roag near Dunvegan. The people barricade themselves up behind their cows in the farthest and smallest end of the hut. There the whole family sits in dirt, and smoke, and darkness. They stare from morning to night into a peat fire. They appear quite contented to have no clean air or clean water. They must be instructed, and assisted to escape these conditions, and encouraged to emigrate.

3. How useful is **Source A** for investigating emigration from the Highlands and Islands of Scotland in the period 1830–1930? **4**

**Source B** is from an eyewitness account from Catherine MacPhee of Barra in 1836.

**Source B**

> I saw our houses swept away and the people being driven out of the countryside to the streets of Glasgow and to the wilds of Canada, such as them that did not die of hunger and smallpox while going across the ocean. I have seen the women putting their children in the carts which were being sent from Benbecula to board an emigrant ship on Loch Boisdale. Almost everyone was crying. Bailiffs and constables gathered behind them and made sure they boarded the ship. Some men showed boldness and looked for adventure but for most it was a loathsome day.

**Source C** is from the memoirs of John MacDonald who emigrated from Uist to Canada in 1912.

**Source C**

> We settled in British Columbia, on the west coast of Canada. Many Scots emigrated because of the better living prospects that life in Canada offered them. Unlike some emigrants, we had no difficulty settling down as we had two uncles and an aunt to welcome us. Scottish emigrants received a special warm welcome from the Canadians. I met hundreds of Scottish, mainly Highland, emigrants in Vancouver. All of our family in Canada stayed on at school till they were fourteen. None of us regretted leaving Uist.

**Look at Sources A, B and C.**

4. What evidence is there in the sources to support the view that emigration was beneficial for emigrants from the Highlands and Islands of Scotland?

   What evidence in the sources disagrees with the view that emigration was beneficial for emigrants from the Highlands and Islands of Scotland? **6**

5. How far do you agree that emigration from the Highlands and Islands of Scotland between 1830 and 1930 was beneficial for the emigrants?

   You must use evidence **from the sources** and **your own knowledge** to reach a **balanced conclusion**. **5**

[*END OF CONTEXT IB*]

# UNIT I—CHANGING LIFE IN SCOTLAND AND BRITAIN

## CONTEXT C: 1880s–Present Day

### SECTION A: KNOWLEDGE AND UNDERSTANDING

> All the cities began to build blocks of high-rise flats. Glasgow, especially, developed this form of housing.

1. Describe some of the problems of living in high-rise flats after 1950. **3**

> Car ownership in Scotland increased but there were different views on whether this was really an improvement.

2. Explain some of the ways in which motor transport affected the lives of people in Scotland in the twentieth century. **4**

### SECTION B: ENQUIRY SKILLS

**The issue for investigating is:**

> Emigration from Scotland after 1880 was beneficial for the emigrants.

Study the sources carefully and answer the questions which follow.
You should use your own knowledge where appropriate.

**Source A** is from the memoirs of John MacDonald, a Highlander who emigrated from Uist to Canada in 1912.

**Source A**

> We settled in British Columbia, on the west coast of Canada. Many Scots emigrated because of the better living prospects that life in Canada offered them. Unlike some emigrants, we had no difficulty settling down as we had two uncles and an aunt to welcome us. Scottish emigrants received a special warm welcome from the Canadians. I met hundreds of Scottish, mainly Highland, emigrants in Vancouver. All of our family in Canada stayed on at school till they were fourteen. None of us regretted leaving Uist.

3. How useful is **Source A** for investigating emigration from Scotland after 1880? **4**

*Marks*

**Source B** is from Bibby's Quarterly, a magazine for British farmers, published in May 1899.

**Source B**

> Many people have been persuaded to leave by the exaggerated claims of emigration agents. They contrast the poverty and hardship in Britain with the greater freedom and wealth overseas. By telling such lies, thousands have been encouraged to leave comfortable homes and good friends but at the end of their journey they have found hostile land and crowded cities. We know many individuals and families who have emigrated and who have returned home, after great expense and loss of time.

**Source C** is from "Expansion, Trade and Industry" by Christopher Culpin, published in 1993.

**Source C**

> Huge numbers of people left Britain, some for "push" reasons and others for "pull" reasons. The "push" reasons included the terrible living conditions many workers faced. Poor wages made life a hard struggle to survive. The "pull" reasons were the opportunities for a better future offered by Australia, Canada and America. Some emigrants were attracted by the promise of cheap farmland. Although improvements in ships made the emigrants' journey safer and easier, they still suffered considerable hardships on the long voyages.

**Look at Sources A, B and C**

4. What evidence is there in the sources to support the view that emigration was beneficial for emigrants from Scotland?

    What evidence in the sources disagrees with the view that emigration was beneficial for emigrants from Scotland? **6**

5. How far do you agree that emigration from Scotland after 1880 was beneficial for the emigrants?

    You must use evidence **from the sources** and **your own knowledge** to reach a **balanced conclusion**. **5**

[*END OF CONTEXT IC*]

Marks

## UNIT II—INTERNATIONAL COOPERATION AND CONFLICT

CONTEXT A: 1790s–1820s

### SECTION A: KNOWLEDGE AND UNDERSTANDING

> The execution of Louis XVI was the final challenge to the rest of Europe.

1. How important was the death of Louis XVI as a cause of war between Britain and France? **5**

> There was now, in 1815, the chance of a long and lasting peace with France.

2. Describe how France was treated in the Vienna Settlement, following the Hundred Days. **4**

### SECTION B: ENQUIRY SKILLS

The following sources are about the effects of war on the civilian populations in Britain and in France.

**Study the sources carefully and answer the questions which follow.
You should use your own knowledge where appropriate.**

**Source A** is a French cartoon showing the intended effects of the Continental System upon Britain. It was produced in 1806.

**Source A**

3. How useful is **Source A** as evidence of the effects of war on civilians in Britain? **4**

*Marks*

**Source B** is from an address made by members of the French Senate in December 1813.

**Source B**

> Our ills are now at their height. We are suffering from poverty unexampled in the whole history of the state. Commerce is destroyed; industry is dying. What are the causes of these unutterable miseries? The answer is a government which causes excessive taxes and creates deplorable methods for their collection; a government which practises cruel methods of recruiting for the armies. The barbarous and endless war swallows up the youth of the country and tears them from education, agriculture and commerce.

4. Discuss the attitude of the authors of **Source B** towards the government in France in 1813. **3**

**Source C** is from "Britain 1714–1851" by Denis Richards and Anthony Quick.

**Source C**

> By 1797 Britain had weathered the storm of financial crisis. This was partly due to the introduction of a form of income tax. However, though the country came through its dangers, the distress among the poorer classes was now acute. The war sent food prices soaring but wages made no corresponding advance, especially in country districts in the South. For many, starvation loomed ahead. The main effect of the French Revolution, it seemed, was to involve Britain in a lengthy war which needed vast amounts of young manpower.

5. To what extent do **Sources B** and **C** agree about the effects of the war on civilians in Britain and France? **5**

*[END OF CONTEXT IIA]*

# UNIT II—INTERNATIONAL COOPERATION AND CONFLICT

## CONTEXT B: 1890s–1920s

### SECTION A: KNOWLEDGE AND UNDERSTANDING

> The event which finally triggered war came on 28th June 1914 in Sarajevo, a town in the Austro-Hungarian province of Bosnia.

1. How important were the assassinations of the Archduke Franz Ferdinand and his wife in causing the First World War? **5**

> The disarmament terms of the Treaty of Versailles upset many Germans.

2. Describe the military terms imposed on Germany by the Treaty of Versailles. **4**

### SECTION B: ENQUIRY SKILLS

The following sources are about life in Britain and Germany during the First World War.

**Study the sources carefully and answer the questions which follow.
You should use your own knowledge where appropriate.**

**Source A** is a British government poster produced in 1914.

**Source A**

[Poster: "YOUR COUNTRY'S CALL — Isn't this worth fighting for? ENLIST NOW"]

3. How useful is **Source A** as evidence of methods used by the British government to encourage men to enlist during the First World War? **4**

*Marks*

In **Source B** an eyewitness remembers living in an English village in 1917.

**Source B**

> It was a terrible time, terrible. We were starving. I can remember my mother having to go out to pick dandelion leaves and then washing them and making sandwiches with them. We were forced to pick the greens off the turnips and cook them with potatoes, mashed up with margarine. We never saw a piece of meat for ages. Many days our mother would make a jug of custard for our dinner, and we ate it with bread and butter. I got sick of the sight of custard. I don't know how mother managed. I hated seeing her sitting at the table with an empty plate. "Mummy you're not eating?", I'd say. "I'm not hungry", she'd reply. Whatever she had was for my brother and myself. If it had gone on for many more months, I don't know what would have happened to us.

4. Discuss the attitude of the author of **Source B** towards food supply in Britain during the First World War. 3

**Source C** is the view of a German politician in 1917.

**Source C**

> How long can it go on? The food situation is unbearable. The bread ration was reduced this spring and the potato supply has been insufficient. During the past month most labourers have had to live on dry bread and a little meat. Undernourishment is spreading. These conditions do not make for good health. When we honestly face up to this situation we just have to say "our strength is totally spent".

5. To what extent do **Sources B** and **C** agree that conditions for civilians were difficult during the First World War? 5

[*END OF CONTEXT IIB*]

UNIT II—INTERNATIONAL COOPERATION AND CONFLICT

CONTEXT C: 1930s–1960s

SECTION A: KNOWLEDGE AND UNDERSTANDING

> Hitler wanted the Sudetenland to become part of Germany.

1. How important was the Czech Crisis of 1938 as a cause of growing tension in Europe up to September 1939?   **5**

> In 1945 the British Empire seemed as strong as ever but things had changed.

2. Describe Britain's decline as a world power between 1945 and 1960.   **4**

SECTION B: ENQUIRY SKILLS

The following sources are about the problems faced by the people of Britain and Germany during the Second World War.

**Study the sources carefully and answer the questions which follow.**
**You should use your own knowledge where appropriate.**

Source A is a British government poster from 1939.

Source A

> Hitler will send no warning—
> so always carry your gas mask
>
> ISSUED BY THE MINISTRY OF HOME SECURITY

3. How useful is **Source A** as evidence of how the British government protected civilians from air raids during the Second World War?   **4**

*Marks*

**Source B** was written by a British woman after the Second World War.

**Source B**

> I was working at Wills Tobacco Company in Bristol when war broke out in September 1939. I didn't like the air-raid shelters because they made the noise of the bombs even louder. We often just stayed at home and slept under the table. Food was scarce but I was relieved that it never ran out, and a lot was done to distribute it fairly. Many things were rationed; sugar, tea, eggs and cheese for example. Yet other things like potatoes and carrots were quite plentiful so we ate a lot of them. I was reasonably happy that our diet was healthy but there was not a lot of variety. I didn't like the clothes coupons much. We had to collect coupons to buy a new dress or curtains or something like that.

4. Discuss the attitude of the author of **Source B** to food supplies in Britain during the Second World War.   3

**Source C** is from "Era of the Second World War" by Carole Brown.

**Source C**

> Life was not so easy after 1942 when many German cities were bombed. Some 400,000 Germans were killed in the bombing raids. The German people suffered food shortages and lots of items were rationed. Household goods and clothes were available only on a points system. However, price controls stopped inflation and food was shared out more fairly. As long as Germany remained a fighting force, full employment in essential industries made poorer families better off.

5. To what extent do **Sources B** and **C** agree about shortages in Britain and Germany during the Second World War?   5

[*END OF CONTEXT IIC*]

# UNIT III—PEOPLE AND POWER

### CONTEXT A: USA 1850–1880

*SECTION A: KNOWLEDGE AND UNDERSTANDING*

> Many white men distrusted and feared the Native Americans or despised them, like their Black American slaves, as an inferior race.

**(Note: for this answer you should write a short essay of several paragraphs including an introduction and a conclusion.)**

1. Explain why conflict developed in America as a result of white attitudes towards:

   **EITHER**

   (a) Black American slaves before 1860

   **OR**

   (b) Native Americans after 1865.

*SECTION B: ENQUIRY SKILLS*

The following sources are about the problems facing Black Americans during Reconstruction.

**Study the sources carefully and answer the questions which follow.
You should use your own knowledge where appropriate.**

**Source A** is from "America" by G. Tindall and D. Shi.

**Source A**

> The Black Codes were laws passed by Southern states after the Civil War. Although they gave freed slaves certain rights, these laws imposed such severe restrictions that many people thought slavery was on the way back. The details of the Black Codes varied from state to state but some provisions were the same like prohibiting the right of freedmen to vote. Freed slaves could testify in courts but only when their own race was involved. They were obliged to sign a Labour Contract every year with punishments if the contracts were broken.

2. How fully does **Source A** explain why the Black Codes made life difficult for freed slaves after 1865?

   You must use evidence **from the source** and **from your own knowledge** and give reasons for your answer.

*Marks*

8

8

5

Marks

**Source B** is from "The United States 1850–1880".

**Source B**

> After the Civil War, the new Southern governments passed laws which limited most opportunities for freed slaves. In some cases the Codes left freedmen not much better off than they had been before the 1863 Emancipation Declaration. They were kept from giving evidence against Whites in all court trials. On the work front, they had to sign annual binding agreements with their employers with strict penalties if the terms were breached. Many Northerners believed that the laws were in effect re-establishing slavery.

3. To what extent do **Sources A** and **B** agree about the problems facing Black Americans during Reconstruction? 4

*[END OF CONTEXT IIIA]*

Marks

# UNIT III—PEOPLE AND POWER

## CONTEXT B: INDIA 1917–1947

### SECTION A: KNOWLEDGE AND UNDERSTANDING

> The impact of the British Raj on all aspects of Indian life was far reaching.

(Note: for this answer you should write a short essay of several paragraphs including an introduction and a conclusion.)

1. Explain the effects on India of British control of:

   **EITHER**

   (a) the Indian economy       8

   **OR**

   (b) Indian government and society.       8

### SECTION B: ENQUIRY SKILLS

The following sources relate to Direct Action, 1946–1947.

**Study the sources carefully and answer the questions which follow. You should use your own knowledge where appropriate.**

**Source A** was written by a journalist called Nikhil Chakravartty.

**Source A**

> On that night of 15–16th August, when it all began, it was only the presence of mind of some Muslim journalists which saved my life when I came across the rioting. I had never seen such devastation. Although this was not a war there were hundreds of people lying dead on the roadside, and still the fires burned all over the place. Many shops were being looted and many houses were burned down. On the third day, I came back home where I found to my horror an old Muslim washerman being beaten up; civilised people who knew him were doing it.

2. How fully does **Source A** describe the events during the days of Direct Action?

   You must use evidence **from the source** and **from your own knowledge** and give reasons for your answer.       5

**Source B** was written by Stanley Taylor of the Indian Police.

**Source B**

> The scenes which took place on that night in August were indescribable. The British were no longer the target of the rioters. Armed with every conceivable kind of weapon, the rioters slaughtered the young and the old, men and women without restraint. The streets were piled high with corpses. Shops were looted, houses were burnt and thousands of people rendered homeless. Soon the bazaar areas were ablaze. A pall of smoke from burning houses hung over the city. It will never be known how many were killed.

3. To what extent do **Sources A** and **B** agree about the days of Direct Action?     4

*[END OF CONTEXT IIIB]*

## UNIT III—PEOPLE AND POWER

### CONTEXT C: RUSSIA 1914–1941

*SECTION A: KNOWLEDGE AND UNDERSTANDING*

> The Communists tried several policies to improve the economy of the Soviet Union.

**(Note: for this answer you should write a short essay of several paragraphs including an introduction and a conclusion.)**

1. Explain the effects on Russia of:

**EITHER**

(a) Lenin's New Economic Policy    8

**OR**

(b) Stalin's Five Year Plans.    8

*SECTION B: ENQUIRY SKILLS*

The following sources are about the problems facing Tsar Nicholas between 1914 and 1916.

**Study the sources carefully and answer the questions which follow.
You should use your own knowledge where appropriate.**

**Source A** is from "People and Power: Russia" by David Armstrong.

**Source A**

> In 1914 the First World War was greeted with great enthusiasm in Russia. Discontent with the Tsar's rule seemed to have been forgotten. At first, things went well but the situation became much worse in the next two years. The Tsar decided to take personal command of his retreating army but this made no difference and the soldiers' anger grew. In the cities, discontent arose as food was scarce, prices rose and people found it hard to stay warm. The peasants were growing less food because so many of them had been conscripted into the army.

2. How fully does **Source A** describe the problems facing Tsar Nicholas by 1916?

   You must use evidence **from the source** and **from your own knowledge** and give reasons for your answer.    5

**Source B** is from "Russia in Revolution" by John Taylor.

**Source B**

> By 1916 Russia was not a contented country. With unrest growing in the army, the situation in Russia was rapidly becoming worse. The mobilisation of so many peasants resulted in farms lying derelict when food was in short supply. Shortages of food, clothing and fuel made the cost of living in the cities more than most people could manage. Yet the trams were still running, the theatres were open and horse racing continued. Nevertheless, trouble was brewing and it was to explode the next year.

3. To what extent do **Sources A** and **B** agree about the problems facing the Tsar by 1916? **4**

*[END OF CONTEXT IIIC]*

## UNIT III—PEOPLE AND POWER

### CONTEXT D: GERMANY 1918–1939

SECTION A: KNOWLEDGE AND UNDERSTANDING

> Hitler attempted to transform German society with policies directed at youth and the Jewish people.

**(Note: for this answer you should write a short essay of several paragraphs including an introduction and a conclusion.)**

1. Explain the effects of Nazi policies between 1933 and 1939 towards:

    **EITHER**

    (a) young people

    **OR**

    (b) Jewish people.

*Marks*

8

8

### SECTION B: ENQUIRY SKILLS

The following sources are about the weaknesses of the Weimar Government.

**Study the sources carefully and answer the questions which follow.
You should use your own knowledge where appropriate.**

**Source A** is from "Germany, 1918–1945" by J.A. Cloake.

**Source A**

> Throughout its life the Weimar Republic had few real supporters. It was always associated with the Peace Treaty and its dishonour. It was further disgraced by the French occupation of the Ruhr. Economically, Weimar Germany was saddled with the war debt and reparations. The period of inflation in the early 1920s created insecurity and suffering amongst all classes and most blamed it on the Weimar Government. When the Wall Street Crash triggered the Great Depression, the measures taken by the Weimar Government to cope with the crisis further angered the majority of Germans. Many looked for alternative solutions.

2. How fully does **Source A** show why the Weimar Republic was so unpopular?

    You must use evidence **from the source** and **from your own knowledge** and give reasons for your answer.

5

*Marks*

**Source B** is from "Hitler and the Third Reich" by Richard Harvey.

**Source B**

> The Weimar Republic had a difficult start. By signing the Treaty of Versailles, the Republic, however unfairly, was forever associated with it. It had also been left with a huge national debt and compensation money to pay. As hyperinflation set in, anyone with savings or pensions lost their money and, more importantly, their faith in the Weimar Republic. The American Stock Market crash marked the beginning of the end as Germany was particularly badly hit by the economic crisis which followed. Unable to agree on measures to deal with the Depression, the government lost the support of the people. Many disgruntled Germans began to turn to other political parties.

3. To what extent do **Sources A** and **B** agree about the problems experienced by the Weimar Republic?     4

[END OF CONTEXT IIID]

[END OF QUESTION PAPER]

[BLANK PAGE]

2007 | General

# 1540/402

| NATIONAL QUALIFICATIONS 2007 | FRIDAY, 18 MAY 10.20 AM – 11.50 AM | HISTORY STANDARD GRADE General Level |
|---|---|---|

Answer questions from Unit I **and** Unit II **and** Unit III.

Choose only **one** Context from each Unit and answer Sections A **and** B. The Contexts chosen should be those you have studied.

The Contexts in each Unit are:

    Unit I— Changing Life in Scotland and Britain
        Context A: 1750s–1850s .............................. Pages 2–3
        Context B: 1830s–1930s ............................. Pages 4–5
        Context C: 1880s–Present Day ................... Pages 6–7

    Unit II— International Cooperation and Conflict
        Context A: 1790s–1820s ............................. Pages 8–10
        Context B: 1890s–1920s ............................. Pages 11–13
        Context C: 1930s–1960s ............................. Pages 14–16

    Unit III— People and Power
        Context A: USA 1850–1880 ......................... Pages 17–18
        Context B: India 1917–1947 ........................ Pages 19–20
        Context C: Russia 1914–1941 ..................... Pages 21–22
        Context D: Germany 1918–1939 ................. Pages 23–24

Use the information in the sources, and your own knowledge, to answer the questions.

Number the questions as shown in the question paper.

Some sources have been adapted or translated.

# UNIT I—CHANGING LIFE IN SCOTLAND AND BRITAIN

## CONTEXT A: 1750s–1850s

*SECTION A: KNOWLEDGE AND UNDERSTANDING*

**Study the information in the sources. You must also use your own knowledge in your answers.**

**Source A** is from "The Courier" newspaper describing what happened at Peterloo in 1819.

**Source A**

> At St. Peter's Field in Manchester large crowds began to assemble. Each group, as they came through the streets, kept in military order, with banners and sticks shouldered. One banner was painted with the words "Die like men, and not be sold like slaves". It was twenty minutes to one o'clock before Henry Hunt appeared. He spoke to the crowd appealing for them to be peaceful.

1. Describe what happened at Peterloo in 1819.  **3**

**Source B** was written by William Cobbett in 1828 after he visited a cotton mill.

**Source B**

> In the cotton-spinning work, the child workers are kept in a heat of from eighty to eighty-four degrees. The workers are not allowed to send for water to drink, even in the heat of the factory. In addition, there is the dust which these unfortunate creatures have to inhale. The fact is that healthy men are made old and past work at forty years of age, and children can become deformed.

2. Why was working in a cotton mill harmful to children's health?  **4**

## SECTION B: ENQUIRY SKILLS

The issue for investigating is:

> Conditions in Scotland's growing towns in the nineteenth century were bad for people's health.

**Study the sources carefully and answer the questions which follow.**

**You should use your own knowledge where appropriate.**

In **Source C** Doctor Laurie reports on a visit to a house in Greenock in 1842.

**Source C**

> I found the mother lying on straw on the floor, delirious from fever. The husband had died in the hospital from the same disease. Some of the children were out begging, and the two youngest were crawling on the wet floor. There was a puddle of sewage in the centre of the floor. The children were actually starving and the mother was dying.

3. How useful is **Source C** for investigating conditions in the growing towns of Scotland in the nineteenth century?     **3**

**Source D** is from a report written by a Glasgow doctor after visiting the homes of cotton workers in 1833.

**Source D**

> The following is an example of the families visited. Andrew Bruce, a spinner, has a good room and kitchen on the third floor. There is a wash-house below. He pays a rent of £4 a year. Mrs Bruce has been six years married and is in excellent health. She has always been able to cook, wash, make and mend for her husband and her children. They have fresh meat three or four times a week and sometimes tea and coffee.

4. What evidence in **Source C** agrees with the view that conditions in the growing towns were bad for people's health?

   What evidence in **Source D** does **not** agree with the view that conditions in the growing towns were bad for people's health?     **5**

5. How far do you agree that conditions in the growing towns in nineteenth century Scotland were bad for people's health?

   You must use evidence **from the sources** and **your own knowledge** to come to a conclusion.     **4**

[END OF CONTEXT IA]

**Now turn to the Context you have chosen in Unit II.**

Marks

# UNIT I—CHANGING LIFE IN SCOTLAND AND BRITAIN

## CONTEXT B: 1830s–1930s

### SECTION A: KNOWLEDGE AND UNDERSTANDING

Study the information in the sources. You must also use your own knowledge in your answers.

**Source A** is evidence given by an eleven year old child to the Children's Employment Commission in 1842.

**Source A**

> I open the air-doors for the putters from six in the morning till six at night. Mother wakes me up at five and gives me a piece of cake which is all I get till I return home. There is plenty of water in the pit. The pit I'm in, it's up to my knees. I did go to school before I was taken down the pit and I could read a bit then. I know I shall die young because many people do so in East Houses pits.

1. Why was working in a coal mine harmful to children's health?     **4**

**Source B** is from the "Aberdeen Journal" of November 30th, 1912.

**Source B**

> A sensation was created yesterday afternoon when three Suffragettes with "explosive bombs" were found in the Music Hall, three hours before Mr Lloyd George was to address a great meeting. The protestors were arrested. While Mr Lloyd George was departing in a motor car, a Suffragette threw a brick at the car. Then, just as he reached Glenburnie Park, another Suffragette, with a large stone in her hand, thrust it at the car and crashed it through the window.

2. Describe the militant tactics used by the Suffragettes.     **3**

## SECTION B: ENQUIRY SKILLS

**The issue for investigating is:**

> Conditions in Scotland's growing towns in the nineteenth century were bad for people's health.

**Study the sources carefully and answer the questions which follow.**

**You should use your own knowledge where appropriate.**

**Source C** is from a lecture given in the early 1880s by J.B. Russell, Medical Officer of Health for Glasgow.

**Source C**

> At the present time, 25% of the population of Glasgow live in one-room houses. Those small houses cause Glasgow's high death rate, especially in childhood. One of every five born in a house of one room never sees the end of their first year. Of those who die so young, a third have never been seen in their sickness by a doctor. The bad air in the houses leads to death from lung disease at all ages. As a result of poor conditions, the streets are filled with bandy-legged children.

3. How useful is **Source C** for investigating conditions in the growing towns of Scotland in the nineteenth century? 

    *Marks: 3*

**Source D** is from a report written by a Glasgow doctor after visiting the homes of cotton workers in 1833.

**Source D**

> The following is an example of the families visited. Andrew Bruce, a spinner, has a good room and kitchen on the third floor. There is a wash-house below. He pays a rent of £4 a year. Mrs Bruce has been six years married and is in excellent health. She has always been able to cook, wash, make and mend for her husband and her children. They have fresh meat three or four times a week and sometimes tea and coffee.

4. What evidence in **Source C** agrees with the view that conditions in the growing towns were bad for people's health?

    What evidence in **Source D** does **not** agree with the view that conditions in the growing towns were bad for people's health?

    *Marks: 5*

5. How far do you agree that conditions in the growing towns in nineteenth century Scotland were bad for people's health?

    You must use evidence **from the sources** and **your own knowledge** to come to a conclusion.

    *Marks: 4*

[END OF CONTEXT 1B]

**Now turn to the Context you have chosen in Unit II.**

# UNIT I—CHANGING LIFE IN SCOTLAND AND BRITAIN

## CONTEXT C: 1880s–Present Day

### SECTION A: KNOWLEDGE AND UNDERSTANDING

**Study the information in the sources. You must also use your own knowledge in your answers.**

**Source A** is from "Change in Scotland, 1880 – 1980".

**Source A**

> Throughout the nineteenth century, working people in Scotland had a very hard life. In order to improve their working conditions, many skilled craft unions were formed in the 1880s. Later on, unskilled workers combined into larger trade unions. In 1889 dock workers marched through the streets carrying fish heads to show what they lived on. More people now believed that the poor should be able to join a trade union to fight for a better standard of living. Others hoped it would raise their wages.

1. Why did trade unions grow during the period 1880–1914? **4**

**Source B** is from the "Aberdeen Journal" of November 30th, 1912.

**Source B**

> A sensation was created yesterday afternoon when three Suffragettes with "explosive bombs" were found in the Music Hall, three hours before Mr Lloyd George was to address a great meeting. The protestors were arrested. While Mr Lloyd George was departing in a motor car, a Suffragette threw a brick at the car. Then, just as he reached Glenburnie Park, another Suffragette, with a large stone in her hand, thrust it at the car and crashed it through the window.

2. Describe the militant tactics used by the Suffragettes. **3**

*Marks*

## SECTION B: ENQUIRY SKILLS

**The issue for investigating is:**

> Conditions in Scotland's growing towns and cities from 1880 to 1939 were bad for people's health.

**Study the sources carefully and answer the questions which follow.**

**You should use your own knowledge where appropriate.**

**Source C** is from a lecture given in the early 1880s by J.B. Russell, Medical Officer of Health for Glasgow.

**Source C**

> At the present time, 25%, of the population of Glasgow live in one-room houses. Those small houses cause Glasgow's high death rate, especially in childhood. One of every five born in a house of one room never sees the end of their first year. Of those who die so young, a third have never been seen in their sickness by a doctor. The bad air in the houses leads to death from lung disease at all ages. As a result of poor conditions, the streets are filled with bandy-legged children.

3. How useful is **Source C** for investigating conditions in the growing towns and cities of Scotland in the period 1880–1939? **3**

**Source D** is from "Expansion, Trade and Industry" by C. Culpin.

**Source D**

> By 1939, city life for working people had improved a little. Housing Acts forced Councils to demolish disease-ridden slums. Councillors recognised that health meant fresh air as well, so parks were provided in many towns and cities. Some lucky families were able to escape to a cleaner, healthier environment in the council housing estates which began to be built. However, there were never enough of these new houses.

4. What evidence in **Source C** agrees with the view that conditions in the growing towns and cities were bad for people's health?

   What evidence in **Source D** does **not** agree with the view that conditions in the growing towns and cities were bad for people's health? **5**

5. How far do you agree that conditions in the growing towns and cities in Scotland from 1880 to 1939 were bad for people's health?

   You must use evidence **from the sources** and **your own knowledge** to come to a conclusion. **4**

[END OF CONTEXT IC]

**Now turn to the Context you have chosen in Unit II.**

## UNIT II—INTERNATIONAL COOPERATION AND CONFLICT

### CONTEXT A: 1790s–1820s

*SECTION A: KNOWLEDGE AND UNDERSTANDING*

Study the information in the sources. You must also use your own knowledge in your answers.

**Source A** is from "The British Navy" by Oliver Warner.

**Source A**

> The men of the lower deck, who fired the guns and went aloft and won battles, had every reason for unrest. Many of them were tied to a life they loathed, enduring conditions which were dreadful. Their pay had not increased for nearly 150 years and deductions were made for the chaplain and for the surgeon who often had very little skill.

1. Explain why British sailors did not like life in Nelson's navy. **4**

**Source B** comes from "A History of Modern Europe" by H.L. Peacock.

**Source B**

> By 1827, it was clear that the Great Powers could not remain permanently united on important European matters as had been hoped in 1815. The Congress System had really come to an end although the idea that the great states should attempt to settle affairs by agreement was by no means dead. Many important meetings were held and there was no major European war for forty years after the Congress of Vienna.

2. How important was the Congress System in maintaining peace in Europe after 1815? **3**

## SECTION B: ENQUIRY SKILLS

The following sources are about the effects of the Revolutionary Wars on civilians in Britain.

**Study the sources carefully and answer the questions which follow.**

**You should use your own knowledge where appropriate.**

**Source C** is a cartoon drawn in 1795. It shows the Prime Minister, William Pitt, as a butcher giving a customer some meat as bread is too expensive.

**Source C**

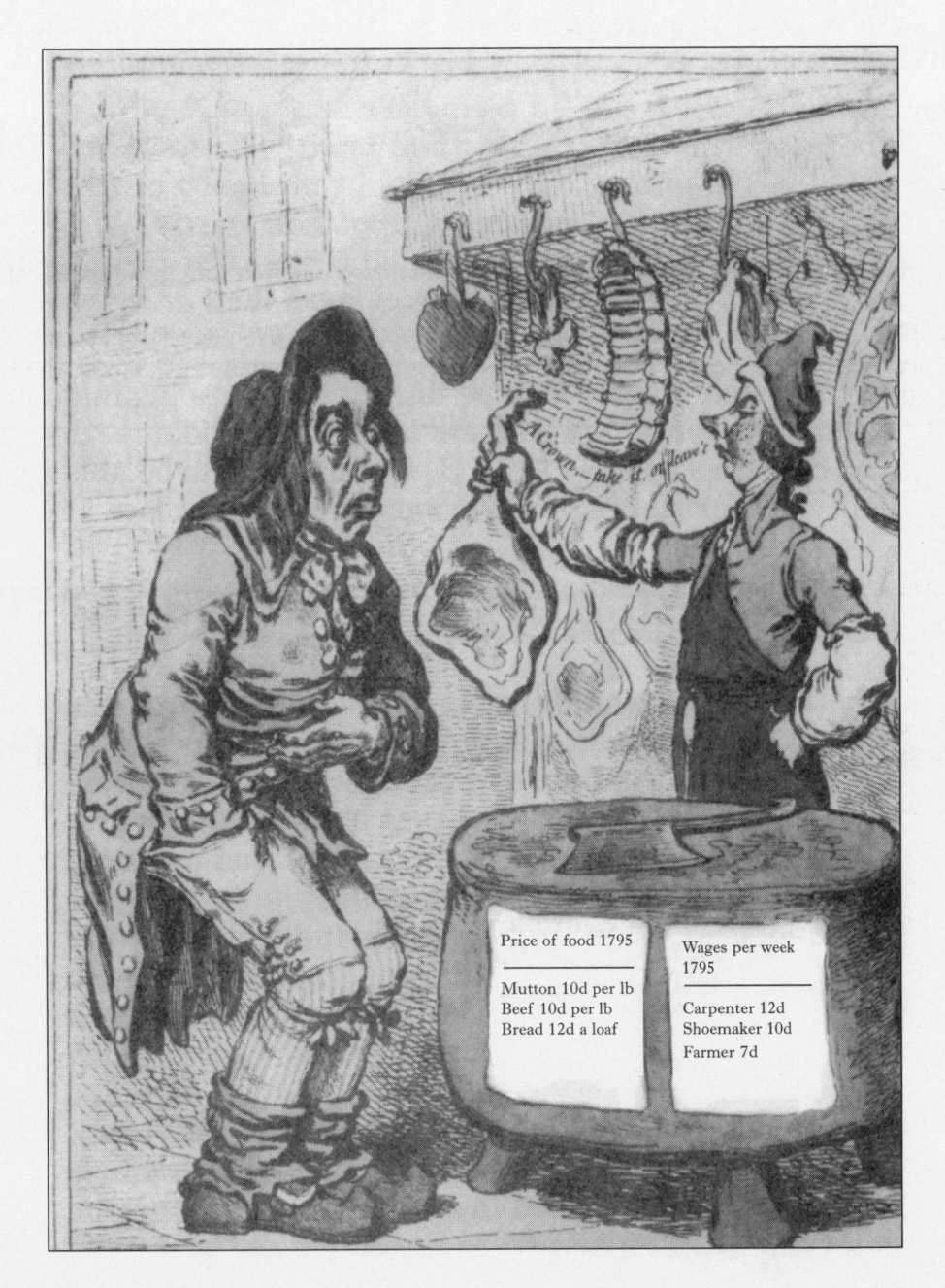

Price of food 1795

Mutton 10d per lb
Beef 10d per lb
Bread 12d a loaf

Wages per week 1795

Carpenter 12d
Shoemaker 10d
Farmer 7d

3. How useful is **Source C** as evidence of the effects of the Revolutionary Wars on people in Britain?

3

[Turn over

Source D describes the effects of the Revolutionary Wars upon British people.

**Source D**

> The Continental System interfered with trade and led to some unemployment but merchants often looked for new markets in South America. Farmers benefited from the drop in the amount of food being imported into Britain. This drop, however, led to increased prices for bread and other foodstuffs. For the workers this was a disaster as wages stayed low.

4. How far do **Sources C** and **D** agree about the effects of the Revolutionary Wars upon people in Britain?

   **4**

**Source E** is part of a message from the French Government to the people of France.

**Source E**

> From this moment on, until our enemies have been driven out of the lands of the French Republic, all the French people are permanently enlisted into the service of the armies. Young men will go and fight. Married men will make arms and transport supplies. Women will make tents and clothes and serve in the hospitals. Children will make old linen into bandages. Old men will teach hatred of Kings.

5. How fully does **Source E** describe the effects of the Revolutionary Wars on the people in France?

   You must use evidence **from the source** and **from your own knowledge** and give reasons for your answer.

   **4**

[END OF CONTEXT IIA]

**Now turn to the Context you have chosen in Unit III.**

## UNIT II—INTERNATIONAL COOPERATION AND CONFLICT

### CONTEXT B: 1890s–1920s

*SECTION A: KNOWLEDGE AND UNDERSTANDING*

Study the information in the sources. You must also use your own knowledge in your answers.

**Source A** is taken from "Forgotten Voices of the Great War".

**Source A**

> By 1915, the trench system stretched for hundreds of miles. In a trench you can just imagine the agony of a fellow standing up to his waist in mud, with just his mess tin to bale the water out. Trench foot was common, owing to mud soaking through your boots. In many cases your toes nearly rotted off. When a fellow got a very high temperature, you could tell he'd probably got trench fever.

1. Explain why many soldiers were unhappy with life in the trenches. **4**

**Source B** was written by historian John Clare.

**Source B**

> The League of Nations aimed to stop wars, encourage disarmament and enforce the Treaty of Versailles. Judged against these aims, the League was quite successful in the 1920s. It stopped border squabbles turning into wars. It solved a dispute between Sweden and Finland over the Aaland Islands in 1922. The League also improved people's lives.

2. How successful was the League of Nations in solving the world's problems in the 1920s? **3**

*[Turn over*

## SECTION B: ENQUIRY SKILLS

The following sources are about the Home Front in Britain during the First World War.

**Study the sources carefully and answer the questions which follow.**

**You should use your own knowledge where appropriate.**

Source C is a poster produced by the British Government in 1917.

**Source C**

[Poster: V.A.D. NURSING MEMBERS, COOKS, KITCHEN-MAIDS, CLERKS, HOUSE-MAIDS, WARD-MAIDS, LAUNDRESSES, MOTOR-DRIVERS, ETC. ARE URGENTLY NEEDED. APPLICATION TO BE MADE TO]

3. How useful is **Source C** as evidence of women's contribution to the war effort during the First World War?  3

Source D describes women's war work during the First World War.

**Source D**

> Many thousands of women became nurses. Some of these women had a chance to work abroad. Others worked in military hospitals and army bases in Britain. The Voluntary Aid Detachment was an organisation set up to provide help for the sick and wounded, in case of enemy invasion. For this work, the VADs were at first unpaid but, from 1915, they were paid £20 a year. Although they had free board and lodgings, they had to buy their uniform out of their earnings.

4. How far do **Sources C** and **D** agree about the work women did during the First World War?  4

Marks

**Source E** is from "Britain and the Great War" by G. Hetherton.

**Source E**

> Desperate attempts were made to grow more food. Nearly everybody started to keep an allotment where they could grow food. The amount of land used for farming increased from eleven million acres in 1914 to fourteen million in 1918. However, many farmers had joined the army, and much of the work on the land was now carried out by the new Women's Land Army.

5. How fully does **Source E** describe the ways the British people managed to get food during the First World War?

   You must use evidence **from the source** and **from your own knowledge** and give reasons for your answer.  **4**

[END OF CONTEXT IIB]

**Now turn to the Context you have chosen in Unit III.**

# UNIT II—INTERNATIONAL COOPERATION AND CONFLICT

## CONTEXT C: 1930s–1960s

### SECTION A: KNOWLEDGE AND UNDERSTANDING

Study the information in the sources. You must also use your own knowledge in your answers.

**Source A** is about Britain after the Second World War.

**Source A**

> The British people finally achieved victory in 1945. Britain came out of the Second World War poorer than in 1939. Fighting the war needed a lot of money. Britain had dug deep into the country's savings. A great deal of the nation's trade had been lost. The two new giants were the USSR and the USA. Britain was proud and victorious but was now no longer as great as it had been.

1. Explain why Britain was less powerful after 1945. **4**

**Source B** describes the work of the United Nations Organisation.

**Source B**

> The UN Charter set out to save the world from the evil of war. Although the United Nations has not always succeeded in preventing conflicts, it has provided a place for discussions. It has sometimes dispatched a peacekeeping force. The achievement of the peacekeeping force in limiting minor wars has been very important. This was achieved in a divided Cyprus. Minor wars are not minor to the people caught up in them.

2. How successful was the United Nations in keeping the world peaceful after the Second World War? **3**

*Marks*

## SECTION B: ENQUIRY SKILLS

The following sources are about the Home Front in Britain during the Second World War.

**Study the sources carefully and answer the questions which follow.**

**You should use your own knowledge where appropriate.**

**Source C** is an official government poster used during the Second World War.

**Source C**

['We could do with thousands more like you..'

JOIN THE WOMEN'S LAND ARMY]

3. How useful is **Source C** as evidence of the role of British women during the Second World War?     3

In **Source D** a member of the Women's Land Army describes her work during the Second World War.

**Source D**

> I had lived in Leeds with my older sister. We both joined the Land Army at the same time and there were many hard days. I remember one bitterly cold day when we were told to lift parsnips. We had to try and kick the parsnips out of the frozen earth. A colleague appeared in an old, long coat which reached from her ears to her ankles. This was not what we had looked forward to when we volunteered.

4. How far do **Sources C** and **D** disagree about the working lives of women during the Second World War?     4

[Turn over

In **Source E** Kathleen Monham writes about her childhood during the Second World War.

**Source E**

> I was a school pupil during the Blitz. At night, people in towns had to be very careful not to show lights. This could let German bombers know where to drop their bombs. For the same reason, cars drove without lights. House windows had to be screened with dark material. Some people were very careless at first. I remember a very familiar sound from the warden: "Put out that light!"

5. How fully does **Source E** describe the effects of air raids during the Blitz?

   You must use evidence **from the source** and **from your own knowledge** and give reasons for your answer.

   **4**

[END OF CONTEXT IIC]

**Now turn to the Context you have chosen in Unit III.**

## UNIT III—PEOPLE AND POWER

### CONTEXT A: USA 1850–1880

*SECTION A: KNOWLEDGE AND UNDERSTANDING*

Study the information in the sources. You must also use your own knowledge in your answers.

**Source A** is about slavery in the Southern states of America.

**Source A**

> By the 1850s, slaves made up about one third of the population in the South, although most farms and plantations employed less than 50 slaves. Some slave owners treated their slaves quite well. But many subjected their slaves to many rules and regulations. Discipline was harsh. Owners often broke up slave families. Slaves had little or no freedom to visit family or friends owned by other slave owners.

1. Explain why some people were opposed to slavery in America. **3**

**Source B** is a description of the Confederate attack on Fort Sumter.

**Source B**

> The President took the view that after a state seceded, federal forts within the Confederacy became the property of the US government. On 12th April 1861, the Confederate commander, General Beauregard, demanded that Major Anderson surrender Fort Sumter in Charleston Harbour. Anderson replied that he would be willing to leave the fort when his supplies were exhausted. Beauregard rejected the offer.

2. Describe what happened at Fort Sumter in April 1861. **3**

[Turn over

*Marks*

## SECTION B: ENQUIRY SKILLS

The following sources are about life in the South during Reconstruction.

**Study the sources carefully and answer the questions which follow.**

**You should use your own knowledge where appropriate.**

In **Source C** Mrs Mary Platt remembers life in the South during the period of Reconstruction after the Civil War.

**Source C**

> Before the war we had good hogs but the war changed all that. Through the terrible days of Reconstruction, many people were unable to feed their livestock. There were no Negroes (African Americans) to work the farm and everything went to ruin. During the four years of war, times were hard enough but this only prepared the way for the suffering afterwards. The carpetbaggers stirred the freed slaves to lawlessness.

3. What was the attitude of Mrs Platt in **Source C** towards life in the South during Reconstruction?

3

**Source D** is from "America, A Narrative History".

**Source D**

> The defeat of the Confederacy changed much of Southern society. However, new Republican state governments in the South were very like the old ones. By introducing the Black Codes, they intended to preserve slavery as nearly as possible. These Codes gave African Americans certain new rights but also restricted their freedom. The homeless were punished with severe fines and could be sold into private service if unable to pay.

4. How fully does **Source D** describe how African Americans were treated in the South during the period of Reconstruction?

   You must use evidence **from the source** and **from your own knowledge** and give reasons for your answer.

4

*[END OF CONTEXT IIIA]*

Marks

UNIT III—PEOPLE AND POWER

CONTEXT B: INDIA 1917–1947

SECTION A: KNOWLEDGE AND UNDERSTANDING

Study the information in the sources. You must also use your own knowledge in your answers.

Source A describes the importance of India to Britain.

Source A

> Britain had many colonies but India was by far the most important. To stress the importance of the colony, the Viceroy of India was paid twice as much as the British Prime Minister. India's huge population of around 300 million bought enormous amounts of British goods. India also supplied Britain with a wide range of cheap foods.

1. Explain why Britain wanted to keep control of India. 3

Source B is from "The British Raj" by Zachary Nunn.

Source B

> In some ways the Raj was a bluff. Some 300 million Indians were ruled by barely 1500 British administrators of the Indian Civil Service. There were about 3000 British Officers in charge of the Indian Army. Many British people thought this was as it should be. They thought that handing over power to the Indian people would bring disaster.

2. Describe in what ways the British controlled India. 3

[Turn over

*Marks*

## SECTION B: ENQUIRY SKILLS

The following sources are about the partition of India and its effects upon Indians.

**Study the sources carefully and answer the questions which follow.**

**You should use your own knowledge where appropriate.**

In **Source C** Muhammad Ali Jinnah gives his views on the partition of India.

**Source C**

> I cannot imagine a united India, containing both Hindus and Muslims. Hindus and Muslims have different religions and social customs. To join two such nations together under a single state, one as a majority and the other as a minority, must lead to a growing discontent. This, in turn, would result in the final destruction of such a united state.

3. What was the attitude of Muhammad Ali Jinnah in **Source C** towards the future of India?

    **3**

**Source D** describes the situation in India at the time of partition.

**Source D**

> The partition of India was not a simple matter and Gandhi was no longer able to influence developments. The partition of India led to millions of people becoming refugees. Muslims fled to Pakistan and Hindus flocked into India. Pakistan was torn into two parts, separated by one thousand miles of Indian territory.

4. How fully does **Source D** describe the problems caused by the partition of India?

    You must use evidence **from the source** and **from your own knowledge** and give reasons for your answer.

    **4**

[*END OF CONTEXT IIIB*]

# UNIT III—PEOPLE AND POWER

## CONTEXT C: RUSSIA 1914–1941

### SECTION A: KNOWLEDGE AND UNDERSTANDING

**Study the information in the sources. You must also use your own knowledge in your answers.**

**Source A** describes Tsar Nicholas II.

**Source A**

> Nicholas II, Tsar of all the Russias, had been the Emperor for many years and was seen as an excellent family man. However, many Russians thought he was weak and too easily controlled by his German wife. They also thought he had too much power. In 1915 Nicholas took personal command of the Russian army but it continued to retreat.

1. Explain why many Russians disliked being ruled by the Tsar.   **3**

In **Source B** historian David Armstrong describes the Bolshevik Revolution of October 1917.

**Source B**

> The Provisional Government knew what the Bolsheviks were planning and had officer cadets and a women's battalion on duty at the Winter Palace. Red Guards took over most of the key points in Petrograd. By the morning of 25 October all railway stations, bridges and government offices were in Bolshevik hands. By the next morning the Winter Palace had been captured without much of a fight.

2. Describe how the Bolsheviks seized power in Petrograd in October 1917.   **3**

[Turn over

Marks

## SECTION B: ENQUIRY SKILLS

The following sources are about Russia in the period of War Communism.

**Study the sources carefully and answer the questions which follow.**

**You should use your own knowledge where appropriate.**

**Source C** is from "The Russian Revolution" by John Quinn.

**Source C**

> By 1921, Russia had been at war for seven years, first against Germany and then against herself. Bad harvests produced one of the worst ever famines. Production dropped: steel making was down by 96% and coal mining down by 90%. The great cities were like ghost towns as workers fled to the countryside in search of food.

3. How fully does **Source C** describe the problems faced by the Russian people in 1921?

    You must use evidence **from the source** and **from your own knowledge** and give reasons for your answer.     4

**Source D** is from the Manifesto of the Kronstadt rebels, issued in 1921.

**Source D**

> We joined the Communist Party to help the workers and peasants. But under War Communism the worker has become the slave of the factory instead of its master. He cannot work where he wants to work or turn down work which is beyond his physical strength. Those who dare to say the truth are put in prison where they suffer torture or are shot.

4. What was the attitude of the authors of **Source D** towards War Communism?     3

[END OF CONTEXT IIIC]

# UNIT III—PEOPLE AND POWER

## CONTEXT D: GERMANY 1918–1939

### SECTION A: KNOWLEDGE AND UNDERSTANDING

**Study the information in the sources. You must also use your own knowledge in your answers.**

**Source A** is from a German newspaper, published in 1919.

**Source A**

> The terms of the peace settlement conducted at Versailles have now been revealed. This treaty has left Germany a torn and tattered country. Germany has been denied the right to have any say in her own future. Large amounts of German territory have been torn off. This peace treaty is unacceptable.

1. Explain why many Germans hated the Treaty of Versailles. **3**

**Source B** is about the Spartacist Revolt of 1919.

**Source B**

> In January 1919 the Spartacists launched an armed uprising in Berlin. They aimed to seize power from Ebert, the leader of the new Provisional Government. Ebert could not rely on the army because it had been broken up after the Armistice was signed. Instead, he used the Freikorps: bands of ex-servicemen who hated socialism in any form. Brutally, the Freikorps crushed the Spartacist revolt.

2. Describe what happened during the Spartacist Revolt. **3**

[Turn over

## SECTION B: ENQUIRY SKILLS

The following sources are about Church opposition to the Nazis.

**Study the sources carefully and answer the questions which follow.**

**You should use your own knowledge where appropriate.**

**Source C** is from "Germany 1918–1945" by Josh Brooman.

**Source C**

> Germany's Protestants belonged to twenty eight church groups. In 1933, under Nazi pressure, they agreed to unite to form a "Reich" Church. Many Protestants broke away and set up their own Confessional Church. This was a clear challenge to Nazi power. As a result, several hundred Confessional Church ministers were arrested and many were put into concentration camps. The Church's youth organisation was also banned.

3. How fully does **Source C** describe the steps taken by the Nazis to control the churches in Germany?

   You must use evidence **from the source** and **from your own knowledge** and give reasons for your answer. **4**

**Source D** is from a statement issued by the Confessional Church in Germany in 1935.

**Source D**

> The Nazis officially deny any intention to interfere in the life of the Confessional Church but in fact they constantly interfere. Several years ago the Nazis banned the Church's youth organisation. We are also alarmed that Christian influence in public life has grown weaker. In addition, the Confessional Church is ashamed that concentration camps still exist.

4. What is the attitude of the Confessional Church in **Source D** towards the Nazi Government? **3**

[END OF CONTEXT IIID]

[END OF QUESTION PAPER]

2007 | Credit

[BLANK PAGE]

# 1540/403

NATIONAL QUALIFICATIONS 2007

FRIDAY, 18 MAY 1.00 PM – 2.45 PM

**HISTORY STANDARD GRADE**
Credit Level

Answer questions from Unit I **and** Unit II **and** Unit III.

Choose only **one** Context from each Unit and answer Sections A **and** B. The Contexts chosen should be those you have studied.

The Contexts in each Unit are:

Unit I— Changing Life in Scotland and Britain
- Context A: 1750s–1850s .............................. Pages 2–3
- Context B: 1830s–1930s .............................. Pages 4–5
- Context C: 1880s–Present Day .................... Pages 6–7

Unit II— International Cooperation and Conflict
- Context A: 1790s–1820s .............................. Pages 8–9
- Context B: 1890s–1920s .............................. Pages 10–11
- Context C: 1930s–1960s .............................. Pages 12–13

Unit III— People and Power
- Context A: USA 1850–1880 ......................... Pages 14–15
- Context B: India 1917–1947 ........................ Pages 16–17
- Context C: Russia 1914–1941 ..................... Pages 18–19
- Context D: Germany 1918–1939 ................. Pages 20–21

Number the questions as shown in the question paper.

Some sources have been adapted or translated.

Marks

# UNIT I—CHANGING LIFE IN SCOTLAND AND BRITAIN

### CONTEXT A: 1750s–1850s

## SECTION A: KNOWLEDGE AND UNDERSTANDING

> The population began a dramatic increase, unprecedented in its continuity and size.

1. Why did the population of Scotland increase between 1750 and 1820?  4

> Some farm houses in the late eighteenth century began to show signs of improvement.

2. Describe housing conditions in the countryside in the late eighteenth century.  4

## SECTION B: ENQUIRY SKILLS

**The issue for investigating is:**

> The Agricultural Revolution between 1750 and 1850 benefited everyone in Scotland.

**Study the sources carefully and answer the questions which follow.**
**You should use your own knowledge where appropriate.**

**Source A** was written by the Rev. Andrew Robertson, minister of Inverkeithing in Fife, in the New Statistical Account, 1845.

**Source A**

> Almost every piece of ground capable of cultivation is under the plough. Much waste land from moss has been reclaimed in the upper part of the parish. There is however no pasture except a small quantity on the steepest hills. There are no longer areas of common land. The lowest rent of land in the parish is £1 and 5 shillings (£1.25); the highest approaches £4. The average rent is nearer the higher figure. The leases are almost, without exception, for nineteen years.

3. How useful is **Source A** for investigating the impact of the Agricultural Revolution in Scotland between 1750 and 1850?  4

*Marks*

**Source B** is by the historian T.C. Smout.

**Source B**

> Many features of the new farming did encourage emigration. The increase in the size of farms was said to lead to smaller populations. In many districts there had been great destruction of cottages and eviction of those people who were not essential to the day to day running of the farm. Small's plough alone halved the number of men needed to cultivate the land. On the other hand, the rise in wages for farm labourers showed that employers did not have it all their own way. The people remaining in the countryside were clearly somewhat better off in terms of their material standard of living.

**Source C** is from "The Case of Day-Labourers in Husbandry", written in 1795 by the Rev. D. Davies.

**Source C**

> The landowner, by uniting several small farms into one, is able to raise the rent considerably. Thus, thousands of farmers who formerly gained a livelihood on those separate farms have been gradually reduced to the class of day-labourers. But day-labourers sometimes cannot find work so they resort to the parish poor fund. It is a fact that thousands of parishes have now half the number of farmers which they had formerly. As the number of farming families has decreased, so the number of poor families has increased.

**Look at Sources A, B and C.**

4. What evidence is there in the sources that the Agricultural Revolution benefited people in Scotland?

   What evidence is there in the sources that the Agricultural Revolution did **not** benefit people in Scotland? **6**

5. How far do you agree that everyone in Scotland benefited from the Agricultural Revolution between 1750 and 1850?

   You must use evidence **from the sources** and **your own knowledge** to reach a **balanced conclusion**. **5**

[*END OF CONTEXT 1A*]

Marks

# UNIT I—CHANGING LIFE IN SCOTLAND AND BRITAIN

### CONTEXT B: 1830s–1930s

*SECTION A: KNOWLEDGE AND UNDERSTANDING*

> The number of Scots continued to grow until the 1920s.

1. Why did the population of Scotland increase between 1830 and the 1920s? — 4

> The houses which farm labourers lived in were often just as bad as those in the cities.

2. Describe housing conditions in the countryside in the late nineteenth century. — 4

*SECTION B: ENQUIRY SKILLS*

**The issue for investigating is:**

> The coming of the railways brought benefits to all people in nineteenth century Scotland.

**Study the sources carefully and answer the questions which follow.**
**You should use your own knowledge where appropriate.**

**Source A** is from the written recollections of the railway engineer who was trying to build the Perth to Inverness Railway in the 1840s.

**Source A**

> I remember a visit to Cullen House to seek approval for the railway across the Seafield Estates on Speyside. Lady Seafield very decidedly told us that she hated railways. "Cheap travel", she said, "brought together such an objectionable variety of people." Lord Seafield was no more enthusiastic, maintaining that the railway would frighten away the grouse from his moors. "Besides", he went on, "what would become of the floaters—the men who have for many years been employed to float timber down the River Spey to the sea. Would a railway replace them?"

3. How useful is **Source A** for investigating attitudes to the building of railways in nineteenth century Scotland? — 4

*Marks*

**Source B** is from "A Regional History of the Railways of Great Britain" by John Thomas and David Turnock.

**Source B**

> The effect of the railway on the North of Scotland is difficult to assess. With the reduction of transport costs, there was much greater competition to supply markets where previously there had been a near monopoly for local manufacturers. Consequently, prices went down. However, many workers found the railways were not so beneficial and their employment became less regular. With the influx of cheaper clothing, the manufacture of shawls and plaids in Kinross went into decline and all the local factories ceased to exist.

**Source C** is from "The Shaping of Nineteenth Century Aberdeenshire" by Sydney Wood.

**Source C**

> The flurry of activity that was an inevitable part of the construction of the railways alarmed the authorities. Navvies had earned a bad reputation and when they reached Inverness they found that the town had sworn in more special constables. The coming of the railways marked the decline of other transport methods. Coaching inns were replaced by new railway hotels which had modern facilities like hot showers. Inverurie lay, in the railway age, close to the heart of a complex network of rail routes and this proved a new stimulus to the industries in the town.

**Look at Sources A, B and C.**

4. What evidence is there in the sources that the coming of the railways benefited people in Scotland?

   What evidence is there in the sources that the coming of the railways did **not** benefit people in Scotland?    **6**

5. How far do you agree that the coming of the railways benefited all people in nineteenth century Scotland?

   You must use evidence **from the sources** and **your own knowledge** to reach a **balanced conclusion**.    **5**

*[END OF CONTEXT IB]*

# UNIT I—CHANGING LIFE IN SCOTLAND AND BRITAIN

### CONTEXT C: 1880s–Present Day

*SECTION A: KNOWLEDGE AND UNDERSTANDING*

> In the 60 years before the outbreak of World War Two, Scotland's population increased three-fold.

1. Why did the population of Scotland increase between 1880 and 1939? **4**

> By the 1930s, rural housing conditions were still basic but better on the whole than in the industrial cities.

2. Describe housing conditions in the countryside in the first half of the twentieth century. **4**

*SECTION B: ENQUIRY SKILLS*

**The issue for investigating is:**

> Technological change was the main reason that shipbuilding declined in Britain in the twentieth century.

**Study the sources carefully and answer the questions which follow.
You should use your own knowledge where appropriate.**

**Source A** is from the recollections of a retired British shipyard manager, written in the late 1980s.

**Source A**

> I've heard many opinions but, in my view, the collapse of the ship building industry in the 1960s was certainly the fault of the trade unions. Their attitude towards progress was really lamentable. The Swedes invented a small, portable hand-welding machine. In Sweden, four machines were worked by one man. The same happened in Germany and France. But in Britain, it was one man to one machine, so it took much longer for work to be done. The fact that the machine was automatic was what British shipyard workers objected to and the trade unions backed them up.

3. How useful is **Source A** for investigating the causes of the decline of British shipbuilding in the twentieth century? **4**

*Marks*

**Source B** is from a history textbook written by historian Faith Geddes in 2002.

**Source B**

> After World War Two, the British government gave fewer subsidies than most foreign governments gave to their shipyards. Relations between management and men in British yards were often far from good. The frequent disputes and stoppages of work often led to late deliveries and setbacks to Britain's reputation as a shipbuilder. Only yards which adopted modern technology survived in Scotland. But even Yarrows, which pioneered glass-fibre hulls, were still forced to lay off men from time to time.

**Source C** describes problems with British shipbuilding in the twentieth century.

**Source C**

> A world slump in shipbuilding after World War Two affected Britain more than its rivals who modernised their yards and introduced the latest technology. On the other hand, British yards were slow to adapt to new technology. Industrial disputes over such factors as pay and conditions often resulted in strike action. Management attempts to introduce more modern, labour-saving devices led to lengthy demarcation disputes. Consequently, in 1985, Britain was producing only 2% of the world's new ships.

**Look at Sources A, B and C.**

4. What evidence is there in the sources that technological change was a reason for the decline in shipbuilding?

   What evidence is there in the sources to suggest that there were **other** reasons for the decline in shipbuilding? **6**

5. How far do you agree that technological change was the main reason that shipbuilding declined in Britain in the twentieth century?

   You must use evidence **from the sources** and **your own knowledge** to reach a **balanced conclusion**. **5**

[*END OF CONTEXT IC*]

Marks

## UNIT II—INTERNATIONAL COOPERATION AND CONFLICT

### CONTEXT A: 1790s–1820s

### SECTION A: KNOWLEDGE AND UNDERSTANDING

> Everywhere the tide of sentiment turned against Napoleon.

**(Note: for this answer you should write a short essay of several paragraphs including an introduction and a conclusion.)**

1. In the Coalition victory over France by 1815, how important were:

   **EITHER**

   (a) the strengths of the Coalitions?  8

   **OR**

   (b) the weaknesses of the French?  8

### SECTION B: ENQUIRY SKILLS

The following sources are about reaction to the events in France in the 1790s.

**Study the sources carefully and answer the questions which follow.
You should use your own knowledge where appropriate.**

**Source A** is from "The Scottish Nation 1700–2000" by T.M. Devine.

**Source A**

> In December 1792, events in France took a dramatic turn. The bloodbath of the French nobility and clergy in the "September Massacres" attracted widespread coverage in the Scottish Press and it did not spare the readers any of the gory details of the grisly executions by guillotine. From this point on, the Revolution was represented as a grave threat to the entire social order. The French proceeded to terrify the ruling classes all over Europe in their Edict of Fraternity, offering military aid to all people seeking liberty from oppression.

2. How fully does **Source A** describe British reaction to events in France up to 1792?

   You must use evidence **from the source** and **your own knowledge** and give reasons for your answer.  5

Marks

**Source B** is from a speech made by the British Prime Minister, William Pitt, in 1793.

**Source B**

> To insist upon the opening of the River Scheldt is an act which the French had no right to do. France has no right to cancel the laws regarding the Scheldt nor any other treaties between the Powers of Europe. England must act. If Holland had not applied to England when Antwerp was taken, the French would have overrun that territory. Unless we wish to stand by and suffer state after state coming under the power of the French, we must declare our firm resolution to oppose French ambition and aggrandisement which intend the destruction of England and of Europe.

3. Discuss the attitude of William Pitt in **Source B** towards France.   3

**Source C** is from "An Illustrated History of Modern Europe".

**Source C**

> After September 1792, the French set up a Republic and the French Revolutionary Army swept into the Austrian Netherlands. This established a French naval power on the Dutch coastline and threatened British control of the North Sea. The French also used Antwerp as a naval base, sending warships down the River Scheldt, ignoring Dutch neutrality and breaking the international Treaty of Utrecht. When all this was added to the French decrees of November, 1792, which promised to help all people wishing to recover their liberty from their own government, war between France and Britain became certain.

4. How far do **Sources B** and **C** agree about the French threat in 1792?   5

[END OF CONTEXT IIA]

# UNIT II—INTERNATIONAL COOPERATION AND CONFLICT

## CONTEXT B: 1890s–1920s

### SECTION A: KNOWLEDGE AND UNDERSTANDING

> The year was 1918 and the Great War was finally over.

**(Note: for this answer you should write a short essay of several paragraphs including an introduction and a conclusion.)**

1. In the Allied victory over Germany by 1918, how important was:

   **EITHER**

   (a) Allied use of new technology?  8

   **OR**

   (b) the collapse of the German home front?  8

### SECTION B: ENQUIRY SKILLS

The following sources are about the causes of the First World War.

**Study the sources carefully and answer the questions which follow. You should use your own knowledge where appropriate.**

**Source A** was said by Serbian nationalist, Dragutin Dimitrevic (called "Apis"), in 1912.

**Source A**

> War between Serbia and Austria is inevitable. If Serbia wants to live in honour, she can only do this by war. This war is determined by our duty to our traditions and our culture. This war results from the duty of our race which will not permit itself to be conquered by the Austrians. This war must bring about the everlasting freedom of Serbia, indeed of all the South Slavs in the Balkans. Our whole race must stand together to halt the attack of these aliens from Austria.

2. Discuss the attitude of Dragutin Dimitrevic in **Source A** towards Austria.  3

*Marks*

**Source B** is from "The Origins of the First World War" by James Joll.

**Source B**

> During the days immediately after the murder of the Archduke, the Austro-Hungarian government discussed what form of action it should take against Serbia. Serbia was disliked as it was accused of encouraging national feelings among the Southern Slavs inside the Austro-Hungarian Empire, and was therefore seen as a direct threat to the existence of the Empire. The assassination of Franz Ferdinand provided an excellent excuse for taking action against Serbia.

3. How far do **Sources A** and **B** agree about tension in the Balkans before World War One?  5

**Source C** was written by historian Tony Allan.

**Source C**

> In 1879 Germany and Austria-Hungary signed a formal alliance and it was joined three years later by Italy creating the Triple Alliance. German foreign policy changed when Kaiser Wilhelm II came to power in 1888. Within months, Russia and France had entered negotiations with one another and, by 1893, they had formally allied. Germany was now faced with the prospect of someday having to fight a war on two fronts. Britain, feeling somewhat isolated, searched for allies and, in 1902, signed a treaty with Japan.

4. How fully does **Source C** describe the system of alliances and understandings in existence by 1914?

    You must use evidence **from the source** and **your own knowledge** and give reasons for your answer.  5

[*END OF CONTEXT IIB*]

## UNIT II—INTERNATIONAL COOPERATION AND CONFLICT

### CONTEXT C: 1930s–1960s

### SECTION A: KNOWLEDGE AND UNDERSTANDING

> The war in Europe ended with the surrender of Germany but continued in Asia and the Pacific until 2 September 1945.

**(Note: for this answer you should write a short essay of several paragraphs including an introduction and a conclusion.)**

1. In the Allied victory over Germany and Japan, how important was:

   **EITHER**

   (a) Allied use of new technology? **8**

   **OR**

   (b) the efforts of civilians on the British home front? **8**

### SECTION B: ENQUIRY SKILLS

The following sources are about the causes of World War Two.

**Study the sources carefully and answer the questions which follow.
You should use your own knowledge where appropriate.**

**Source A** is part of a speech made by Hitler in 1934.

**Source A**

> We need space to make Germany independent. We must restore our great military strength. In the East, Germany must have mastery as far as the Caucasus Mountains. In the West, we will take the French coast. We need Belgium and Holland. Germany must become a colonial power equal to that of Britain. Germany must rule Europe or fall apart as a nation. In the centre, I shall place the steely core of a Greater Germany. Then we will take Austria and the Sudetenland. We will have a block of one hundred million people, without an alien element in it. If all this needs war, then so be it.

2. Discuss the attitude of Hitler in **Source A** towards Germany's place in Europe. **3**

**Source B** is from "World War Two" by C. Bayne Jardine.

**Source B**

> In 1935 compulsory military service was brought back in Germany as it was in other countries. Germany was then able to agree an increase in its naval strength with Britain, and the Luftwaffe was being increased in strength. German industries now began to produce weapons of war. Hitler was prepared to risk a general war as he carried out his policies of territorial expansion. Hitler saw such a war as the price Germany had to pay for the pursuit of a German Empire.

3. How far do **Sources A** and **B** agree about Hitler's plans for Germany?  5

**Source C** is about the German attack on Poland.

**Source C**

> The next phase of Hitler's aggression was the plan to attack Poland, resulting in the start of aggressive war. Poland was attacked on September 1st, 1939. The German attack, code named Operation White (Fall Weiss), started at 04:45 hours when blitzkrieg tactics tore through the Polish forces. By the end of the month, Poland had surrendered to the Germans and the country was occupied.

4. How fully does **Source C** describe the attack on Poland in 1939?

   You must use evidence **from the source** and **your own knowledge** and give reasons for your answer.  5

[END OF CONTEXT IIC]

# UNIT III—PEOPLE AND POWER

## CONTEXT A: USA 1850–1880

### SECTION A: KNOWLEDGE AND UNDERSTANDING

> Slavery was not the only source of tension between the North and the South.

1. How important was slavery as a cause of tension between the North and the South in 1860? **4**

> The new Republican Party announced its main policies at a convention in Chicago on 16 May, 1860.

2. What were the main aims of the Republican Party in 1860? **4**

### SECTION B: ENQUIRY SKILLS

The following sources are about the Native American reaction to Westward expansion.

**Study the sources carefully and answer the questions which follow.**
**You should use your own knowledge where appropriate.**

**Source A**, titled "Emigrants Attacked by Comanches", was drawn for a book published in 1853 by Captain Seth Eastman, a soldier-artist who spent some time in frontier forts.

**Source A**

3. How useful is **Source A** as evidence of the ways in which the Native Americans reacted to Westward expansion? **4**

**Source B** is part of an interview with Black Elk, a Sioux holy man.

**Source B**

> My people had lived in the Black Hills for many years. The white men wanted to have a road up through our country to the place where the yellow metal was. But my people did not want the road. It would scare the bison and make them go away. Also, it would let the other white men come in like a river. And so, when the white soldiers came and built themselves a fort, my people knew that they meant to have their road and take our country and maybe kill us all when they were strong enough.

4. How fully does **Source B** explain the reasons for the 1876 Sioux Revolt?

    You must use evidence **from the source** and **your own knowledge** and give reasons for your answer.

    **4**

[END OF CONTEXT IIIA]

*Marks*

## UNIT III—PEOPLE AND POWER

### CONTEXT B: INDIA 1917–1947

### SECTION A: KNOWLEDGE AND UNDERSTANDING

> The British became increasingly unpopular in India in the twentieth century.

1. How important were economic factors in causing discontent with British rule by the 1930s? **4**

> The Congress Party wanted to change the way India was ruled.

2. What were the main aims of the Congress Party? **4**

### SECTION B: ENQUIRY SKILLS

The following sources are about the reaction of Indians to British policies.

**Study the sources carefully and answer the questions which follow.
You should use your own knowledge where appropriate.**

**Source A** is a photograph showing followers of Gandhi making salt illegally on the beach at Dandi. It appeared in the "Bombay Chronicle" in April 1930.

**Source A**

3. How useful is **Source A** as evidence of Indian reaction to the Salt Tax? **4**

**Source B** is from "The Far East and India" by P. J. Larkin.

**Source B**

> As the Second World War progressed, Britain faced problems in many areas. India was a major area of concern. In 1942 the British government sent Sir Stafford Cripps to India to try to get some agreement with Gandhi but the Indian leader demanded a full and immediate transfer of power to India. With the Japanese threatening Burma and Assam, the British had to refuse. Further terrorism and open revolt followed, and Gandhi was sent back to prison.

4. How fully does **Source B** describe the results of the Cripps Mission of 1942?

   You must use evidence **from the source** and **your own knowledge** and give reasons for your answer.

   **4**

[END OF CONTEXT IIIB]

# UNIT III—PEOPLE AND POWER

## CONTEXT C: RUSSIA 1914–1941

### SECTION A: KNOWLEDGE AND UNDERSTANDING

> By the autumn of 1917 many Russians were losing patience with the Provisional Government.

1. How important was the First World War in causing discontent with the Provisional Government?

   **4**

> The Bolsheviks wanted sudden and drastic changes in Russia.

2. What were the main aims of the Bolsheviks when they came to power in 1917?

   **4**

### SECTION B: ENQUIRY SKILLS

The following sources are about Stalin's policies in the 1930s.

**Study the sources carefully and answer the questions which follow.
You should use your own knowledge where appropriate.**

**Source A** is a Soviet government photograph from the 1930s. The words on the banner are "We demand collectivisation and the wiping out of the Kulaks".

**Source A**

3. How useful is **Source A** as evidence of how Russian peasants felt about Stalin's policy of collectivisation?

   **4**

Source B is from "Russia and the USSR, 1905–1956" by Nigel Kelly.

**Source B**

> The Purges dominated politics in the USSR in the 1930s. Even now, historians argue over the causes. Stalin held show trials in which leading Communists confessed to trying to overthrow the government. Few, if any, of these people were guilty of the crimes to which they confessed. Their confessions often followed months of torture or a false promise that they would not be executed if they confessed. Thousands of other party members were sent to labour camps.

4. How fully does **Source B** describe Stalin's Purges?

    You must use evidence **from the source** and **your own knowledge** and give reasons for your answer.

    **4**

[END OF CONTEXT IIIC]

## UNIT III—PEOPLE AND POWER

### CONTEXT D: GERMANY 1918–1939

*SECTION A: KNOWLEDGE AND UNDERSTANDING*

> As far as most Germans were concerned, the cause of their problems was the Weimar Republic.

1. How important were economic problems in making the Weimar Government unpopular by 1923?  **4**

> By 1933 there was a spectacular increase in the number of Germans who were willing to vote for the Nazis.

2. In what ways did the Nazi party manage to attract many German people by January 1933?  **4**

*SECTION B: ENQUIRY SKILLS*

The following sources are about the Nazis in power.

**Study the sources carefully and answer the questions which follow.
You should use your own knowledge where appropriate.**

**Source A** is a photograph of Nazis enforcing the boycott of Jewish-owned shops in 1933. The poster says "Germans fight back. Buy nothing Jewish."

**Source A**

3. How useful is **Source A** as evidence of the way the Nazis treated Jewish people?  **4**

Source B is from "Hitler's Germany" by Josh Brooman.

**Source B**

> In many ways life in Nazi Germany became more like military life. Many mass rallies took place. The most famous of them were held each year at Nuremberg in one of four specially built arenas outside the town. Just one of these arenas could hold 400,000 people. There they watched military parades and listened to choirs and to speeches. Each event at the rally was staged to perfection. At the 1937 rally, 100,000 men, each exactly 0.75 metres apart, marched past Hitler carrying 32,000 flags and banners.

4. How fully does **Source B** describe the military features of life in Nazi Germany?

    You must use evidence **from the source** and **your own knowledge** and give reasons for your answer.

    **4**

[END OF CONTEXT IIID]

[END OF QUESTION PAPER]

2008 | General

[BLANK PAGE]

**1540/402**

NATIONAL QUALIFICATIONS 2008

MONDAY, 26 MAY 10.20 AM – 11.50 AM

HISTORY STANDARD GRADE General Level

Answer questions from Unit I **and** Unit II **and** Unit III.

Choose only **one** Context from each Unit and answer Sections A **and** B. The Contexts chosen should be those you have studied.

The Contexts in each Unit are:

> Unit I— Changing Life in Scotland and Britain
> > Context A: 1750s–1850s .............................. Pages 2–3
> > Context B: 1830s–1930s .............................. Pages 4–5
> > Context C: 1880s–Present Day .................... Pages 6–7

> Unit II— International Cooperation and Conflict
> > Context A: 1790s–1820s .............................. Pages 8–11
> > Context B: 1890s–1920s .............................. Pages 12–13
> > Context C: 1930s–1960s .............................. Pages 14–15

> Unit III— People and Power
> > Context A: USA 1850–1880 ......................... Pages 16–17
> > Context B: India 1917–1947 ......................... Pages 18–19
> > Context C: Russia 1914–1941 ...................... Pages 20–21
> > Context D: Germany 1918–1939 .................. Pages 22–23

Use the information in the sources, and your own knowledge, to answer the questions.

Number the questions as shown in the question paper.

Some sources have been adapted or translated.

# UNIT I—CHANGING LIFE IN SCOTLAND AND BRITAIN

## CONTEXT A: 1750s–1850s

### SECTION A: KNOWLEDGE AND UNDERSTANDING

**Study the information in the sources. You must also use your own knowledge in your answers.**

**Source A** is about housing in the countryside in the late eighteenth century.

**Source A**

> Many new houses have been built and old houses allowed to go to ruin. Farm houses have been built two stories high with slate roofs. Houses are much cleaner and have better furniture in them. People are better dressed. Instead of mean, dirty houses, built with stones, without cement, houses are now built by good builders using mortar. They are finished on the outside with lime.

1. Describe the improvements made to housing in the countryside between 1750 and 1850. **3**

**Source B** is about changes in the textile industry.

**Source B**

> In 1779 Samuel Crompton developed a spinning machine, Crompton's Mule. The Mule was able to produce a thread that was both soft and strong. This machine could spin 300 threads at once. From about 1790 steam-driven machines were introduced into the mills. A steam-driven mule needed only one operator to control a total of 1,200 spindles at the same time. As a result, by around 1830 large numbers of skilled spinners were no longer needed.

2. How important was new technology in the development of textile mills in Britain? **4**

## SECTION B: ENQUIRY SKILLS

**The issue for investigating is:**

> Improvements in diet and food supply were the main causes of population growth in Scotland between 1750 and 1850.

**Study the sources carefully and answer the questions which follow.**

**You should use your own knowledge where appropriate.**

**Source C** is taken from the Statistical Account of Scotland, 1791–1799, for Perthshire.

**Source C**

> Within the past forty years there has been a great increase in the number of people, especially from the Highlands, who settle in Blairgowrie. The situation of the village is very healthy and it is well supplied with water. The village has plenty of butcher meat and other articles. Food supplies have increased very much within these few years. The inhabitants of Blairgowrie enjoy a reasonable degree of benefits and comforts of society.

3. How useful is **Source C** for investigating the causes of population growth in Scotland between 1750 and 1850? **3**

**Source D** is from a modern textbook.

**Source D**

> The population of Scotland grew rapidly in the 100 years after 1750. There were big improvements in personal hygiene which reduced the spread of disease. With the introduction of cheap soap and better water supplies, more people were able to wash themselves and their clothes. As industry expanded in the towns, there were many more jobs for young workers. Better housing conditions led to less disease.

4. What evidence is there in **Source C** that improved diet and food supply caused population growth in Scotland between 1750 and 1850?

   What evidence is there in **Source D** that other factors caused population growth in Scotland between 1750 and 1850? **5**

5. How far do you agree that improved diet and food supply were the main causes of population growth in Scotland between 1750 and 1850?

   You must use evidence **from the sources** and **your own knowledge** to come to a conclusion. **4**

[END OF CONTEXT IA]

**Now turn to the Context you have chosen in Unit II.**

# UNIT I—CHANGING LIFE IN SCOTLAND AND BRITAIN

## CONTEXT B: 1830s–1930s

### SECTION A: KNOWLEDGE AND UNDERSTANDING

Study the information in the sources. You must also use your own knowledge in your answers.

**Source A** is about housing in the countryside in the late nineteenth century.

**Source A**

> By the late nineteenth century, a great number of minor improvements were made. Following the end of the window tax, small windows became quite common. In some houses the fireplaces had a proper chimney. This helped overcome the problem of smoke. A door was cut on the front wall of the house so the door between the byre and the house was now blocked off. Earthen floors continued in most houses.

1. Describe the improvements which were made to housing in the countryside by the late nineteenth century. **3**

**Source B** is about the railways.

**Source B**

> Railways went on developing after 1850. Steel rails replaced iron from the 1870s. Four tracks were laid on busy main lines. Many more branch lines were opened. The block signalling system which divided the line into sections and only allowed one train in each section at a time, made travelling safer and faster. The design of locomotives made them more powerful and reliable. Britain's railways were at their peak around 1900.

2. How important was new technology in the development of railways in Britain? **4**

## SECTION B: ENQUIRY SKILLS

The issue for investigating is:

> Improvements in diet and food supply were the main causes of population growth in Scotland between 1830–1930.

**Study the sources carefully and answer the questions which follow.**

**You should use your own knowledge where appropriate.**

**Source C** is from the memories of Thomas Jones who grew up in Glasgow around 1900.

**Source C**

> Great changes have taken place since the 1880s. Food is now more varied. Fresh fruit is available all year round. Cattle byres are now beyond the city outskirts and the milk supply is much cleaner. There is less drunkeness. Barefooted women and children were common 50 years ago. No-one ever sees them today.

3. How useful is **Source C** for investigating the causes of population growth in Scotland between 1830 and 1930? **3**

**Source D** is from the New Statistical Account for Dundee.

**Source D**

> There has been an extraordinary increase in the population. The increase is chiefly due to the great expansion of the linen trade which has produced so many jobs in spinning mills. The harbour has been extended and this has brought employment to thousands. Plenty of work has encouraged early marriages which has led to larger families. It has also brought families in from other parts of Scotland and from Ireland.

4. What evidence is there in **Source C** that improved diet and food supply caused population growth in Scotland between 1830 and 1930?

   What evidence is there in **Source D** that other factors caused population growth in Scotland between 1830 and 1930? **5**

5. How far do you agree that improved diet and food supply were the main causes of population growth in Scotland between 1830 and 1930?

   You must use evidence **from the sources** and **your own knowledge** to come to a conclusion. **4**

[END OF CONTEXT IB]

**Now turn to the Context you have chosen in Unit II.**

Marks

UNIT I—CHANGING LIFE IN SCOTLAND AND BRITAIN

CONTEXT C: 1880s–Present Day

SECTION A: KNOWLEDGE AND UNDERSTANDING

Study the information in the sources. You must also use your own knowledge in your answers.

Source A is about housing in the countryside after 1880.

Source A

> The farmhouse in the village of Banavie, near Fort William, was once a two room stone cottage. The second storey of two bedrooms was added in 1889. Other improvements at that time included piped water from a dam on the hill. A flush toilet with a septic tank was also added to the house, something which was not widespread in many rural areas before 1930.

1. Describe the improvements which were made to housing in the countryside after 1880.  3

Source B is about the growth of the motor car industry.

Source B

> The motor car industry was a new industry in 1900. New technology meant that the car industry could use mass production methods. It produced a large number of cars cheaply and quickly. Machinery made the parts to the same quality. Workers specialised in one task only, which they could do quickly and which earned them good wages. In 1914 Britain produced 34,000 cars; by 1930 output had risen to 180,000.

2. How important was new technology in the development of the motor car industry?  4

Marks

## SECTION B: ENQUIRY SKILLS

**The issue for investigating is:**

> Improvements in diet and food supply were the main causes of population increase in Scotland 1900–1970.

**Study the sources carefully and answer the questions which follow.**

**You should use your own knowledge where appropriate.**

**Source C** is from the Third Statistical Account of Scotland for the Parish of Moulin in Perthshire, written in 1962.

**Source C**

> The population of the parish has steadily increased. This is due to a number of factors, including people enjoying a more varied diet. The provision of school meals helps improve the diet. So too does the increasing pre-packing of food. This has given housewives more freedom to work in shops or hotels. Refrigeration provides a greater variety of fresh meat and fish throughout the year.

3. How useful is **Source C** for investigating the causes of population growth in Scotland between 1900 and 1970?   3

**Source D** is from "British Economic and Social History 1850–Present Day" by Philip Sauvain.

**Source D**

> There were many reasons why the population grew in the twentieth century. The infant mortality rate fell. The removal of slums and building of better homes was another factor. Much higher standards of cleanliness also helped. People were eating better, more nourishing food, such as fruit and vegetables. Improvements in medicine meant people lived longer.

4. What evidence is there in **Source C** that improved diet and food supply caused population growth in Scotland between 1900–1970?

    What evidence is there in **Source D** that other factors caused population growth in Scotland between 1900 and 1970?   5

5. How far do you agree that improved diet and food supply were the main causes of population growth in Scotland 1900–1970?

    You must use evidence **from the sources** and **your own knowledge** to come to a conclusion.   4

[END OF CONTEXT IC]

**Now turn to the Context you have chosen in Unit II.**

Marks

## UNIT II—INTERNATIONAL COOPERATION AND CONFLICT

### CONTEXT A: 1790s–1820s

*SECTION A: KNOWLEDGE AND UNDERSTANDING*

**Study the information in the sources. You must also use your own knowledge in your answers.**

**Source A** is about the causes of war between Britain and France.

**Source A**

> The French Government decided to spread word of the revolution. However, the fact they were prepared to use force was a worry for other countries. They called on the lower classes everywhere to join in the revolution. The British Government was frightened that some of the British lower classes might listen to them and rebel. This increased the hostility between the French and British Government. In 1793 war broke out.

1. How important was the fear of revolution in causing war with France?     **3**

**Source B** is about the Congress of Vienna.

**Source B**

> Although the Vienna Settlement had great faults, some of its decisions showed much wisdom. The British representative decided that France should not be unfairly treated for the faults of Napoleon. Therefore he left France with no grievances. The Great Powers managed to establish a balance of power between themselves. They attempted to settle European problems by meeting together regularly.

2. Explain why the Congress of Vienna maintained peace in Europe after 1815.     **4**

[Turn over for Section B on *Page ten*

## SECTION B: ENQUIRY SKILLS

The following sources are about methods of naval warfare.

**Study the sources carefully and answer the questions which follow.**

**You should use your own knowledge where appropriate.**

**Source C** was written by a crew member on one of Nelson's ships during the Battle of Trafalgar, 1805.

**Source C**

> We were now unable to manoeuvre the ship since our yards, sails and masts were disabled. In this condition we lay by the side of the enemy firing away, and now and then we received fire from them. Often during the battle we could not see for the smoke, whether we were firing at an enemy or friend. However, our sailors fired at the enemy so fast that some went into the water.

3. How useful is **Source C** for investigating naval battle tactics in the early nineteenth century?

3

Source D is a painting of the Battle of Trafalgar, 1805.

Source D

4. How far do **Sources C** and **D** agree about the methods of naval warfare during the Napoleonic Wars? **4**

5. How fully do **Sources C** and **D** describe the methods of fighting at sea during the Napoleonic Wars?

   You must use evidence **from the sources** and **from your own knowledge** and give reasons for your answer. **4**

[END OF CONTEXT IIA]

**Now turn to the Context you have chosen in Unit III.**

# UNIT II—INTERNATIONAL COOPERATION AND CONFLICT

### CONTEXT B: 1890s–1920s

*SECTION A: KNOWLEDGE AND UNDERSTANDING*

Study the information in the sources. You must also use your own knowledge in your answers.

**Source A** is about the causes of the First World War.

**Source A**

> Britain had not needed friends in Europe but she felt threatened by the system of alliances. By 1900 Europe was divided into two separate alliances. France's humiliating defeat by the Germans in 1871 led to her desire for revenge. In 1904, Britain and France signed the Entente Cordiale. Three years later, Britain also reached agreement with Russia. In 1914 war broke out.

1. How important was the Alliance System in causing tension in Europe before the First World War? **3**

**Source B** is about the effects of the Treaty of Versailles.

**Source B**

> In 1920 Keynes published a book criticising the Treaty of Versailles. He said that the Treaty would eventually prove disastrous. He was very critical of the economic terms of the Treaty. The reparations, he said, could never work. Keynes argued that the Treaty would cripple Germany. A poor Germany would mean a poor Europe. Many Britons growing up during the next twenty years agreed that the Treaty of Versailles was not worth defending.

2. Explain why many people criticised the Treaty of Versailles. **4**

## SECTION B: ENQUIRY SKILLS

The following sources are about the use of new technology during the First World War.

**Study the sources carefully and answer the questions which follow.**

**You should use your own knowledge where appropriate.**

**Source C** is taken from the diary kept by George Coppard who fought in the First World War, 1914–1918.

**Source C**

> The Vickers machine gun proved to be successful, being highly efficient, reliable, compact and reasonably light. The tripod was the heaviest component, weighing about 50 pounds; the gun itself weighed 28 pounds without water. In good condition the rate of fire was 600 bullets a minute. The use of front and rear sights increased the accuracy of the weapon. Machine guns killed thousands of men.

3. How useful is **Source C** for investigating the use of machine guns during the First World War? *(3)*

**Source D** is a diagram of a machine gun taken from a history text book.

**Source D**

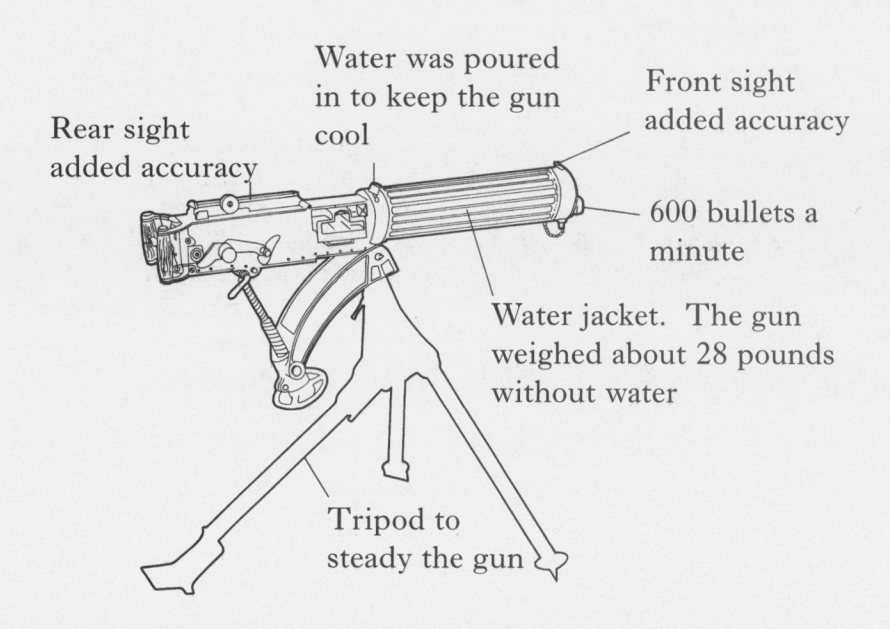

*Diagram labels:*
- Rear sight added accuracy
- Water was poured in to keep the gun cool
- Front sight added accuracy
- 600 bullets a minute
- Water jacket. The gun weighed about 28 pounds without water
- Tripod to steady the gun

4. How far do **Sources C** and **D** agree about the Vickers machine gun? *(4)*

5. How fully do **Sources C** and **D** describe the new technology used on the Western Front during the First World War?

   You must use evidence **from the sources** and **from your own knowledge** and give reasons for your answer. *(4)*

[END OF CONTEXT IIB]

**Now turn to the Context you have chosen in Unit III.**

## UNIT II—INTERNATIONAL COOPERATION AND CONFLICT

CONTEXT C: 1930s–1960s

*SECTION A: KNOWLEDGE AND UNDERSTANDING*

**Study the information in the sources. You must also use your own knowledge in your answers.**

**Source A** is about the causes of the Second World War.

**Source A**

> On September 1 1939, Germany invaded Poland. By that time both France and Britain had decided that they could not give into Hitler any more. They had both told Poland that they would support her if she was attacked by Germany. Hitler thought he could get away with force as Britain and France wanted to avoid a war. However, when Hitler invaded Poland, Britain and France sent Germany an ultimatum. War began on 3rd September.

1. How important was Hitler's attack on Poland in causing the Second World War?  **3**

**Source B** is about the effects of building the Berlin Wall in 1961.

**Source B**

> To stop the huge numbers of young, talented and educated Berliners leaving for the West, the East German government built a concrete wall. It divided the city of Berlin into two parts. Any East Berliner who tried to escape over the wall was shot. The Americans were furious. President Kennedy tried to persuade the Soviet Union to pull down the wall, but he failed. The wall stayed up and the killings continued. Each escape attempt and each killing raised tension between East and West.

2. Explain why the building of the Berlin Wall caused a crisis in 1961.  **4**

*Marks*

## SECTION B: ENQUIRY SKILLS

The following sources are about the effects of new technology used during the Second World War.

**Study the sources carefully and answer the questions which follow.**

**You should use your own knowledge where appropriate.**

In **Source C** a Hiroshima survivor describes what happened shortly after the first atomic bomb was dropped on Hiroshima on 6 August 1945.

**Source C**

> Suddenly a glaring pinkish light appeared in the sky, followed by a huge tremor. Almost immediately, a wave of heat and wind swept away everything in its path. Many were killed instantly, others were lying on the ground screaming in agony from the intolerable pain of their burns. Everything standing upright in the way of the blast–walls, housing, factories and other buildings–was completely destroyed.

3. How useful is **Source C** for investigating the effects of the atomic bomb dropped on Japan in 1945? ... 3

**Source D** is a diagram showing the damage caused to Hiroshima by the atomic bomb.

**Source D**

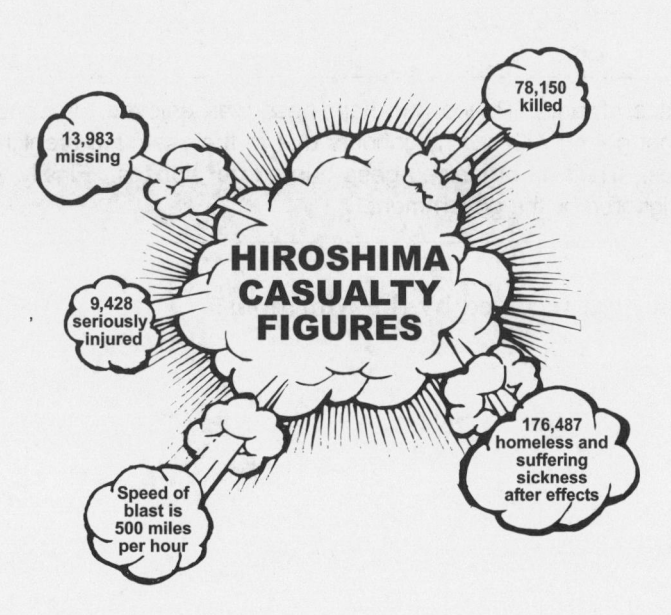

[Diagram: HIROSHIMA CASUALTY FIGURES — 78,150 killed; 13,983 missing; 9,428 seriously injured; 176,487 homeless and suffering sickness after effects; Speed of blast is 500 miles per hour]

4. How far do **Sources C** and **D** agree about the effects of the atomic bomb? ... 4

5. How fully do **Sources C** and **D** describe the effects of new technology in the Second World War?

    You must use evidence **from the sources** and **from your own knowledge** and give reasons for your answer. ... 4

[END OF CONTEXT IIC]

**Now turn to the Context you have chosen in Unit III.**

## UNIT III—PEOPLE AND POWER

### CONTEXT A: USA 1850–1880

*SECTION A: KNOWLEDGE AND UNDERSTANDING*

Study the information in the sources. You must also use your own knowledge in your answers.

**Source A** is about the problems Westward expansion caused Native Americans.

**Source A**

> The Native American tribes were not especially troubled by the first pioneers. Soon, however, the white settlers poured west in ever increasing numbers. Hunters virtually wiped out the buffalo. Buffalo Bill killed 4,280 buffalo in eighteen months. This helped destroy the traditional Native American way of life. Tribes were moved onto reservations where they were treated badly by white traders.

1. Explain the problems affecting Native Americans as a result of Westward expansion. **3**

**Source B** was written by Joseph Smith, a Mormon leader, describing how Mormons were treated.

**Source B**

> We made purchases of land. Peace and happiness was enjoyed throughout our neighbourhood. However, we did not get on with our neighbours due to their sabbath breaking and gambling. They began to ridicule us. Then an organised gang burned our houses. Finally, they drove us from our homes. This was ignored by the government.

2. Describe the treatment received by the Mormons. **3**

## SECTION B: ENQUIRY SKILLS

The following sources are about Abraham Lincoln's election as President.

**Study the sources carefully and answer the questions which follow.**

**You should use your own knowledge where appropriate.**

**Source C** describes Southerners' views about the election of President Lincoln.

**Source C**

> During the 1860 election, the Republican Party candidate, Abraham Lincoln, won every Northern state. Only a handful of Southerners voted for Lincoln. For many Southerners, Lincoln's election was the final straw. They said that the North had elected a president who believed slavery was a terrible injustice. This would lead to slavery's extinction. This seemed a threat and offended Southern honour.

3. What was the attitude of the Southerners, in **Source C**, towards the election of Lincoln? **3**

**Source D** is about the election of 1860.

**Source D**

> In 1860, the leaders of the Republican Party asked Abraham Lincoln to run for president. Most people in the North voted for Lincoln. However, he had little support in the South. He did not insist on ending slavery in the South, but he would not let it spread to new territories. However, plantation owners in the South were terrified that slavery would die out. This would ruin their plantations and make them poor. Lincoln won the election in November 1860.

4. How far do **Sources C** and **D** agree about the election of Lincoln? **4**

[END OF CONTEXT IIIA]

*Marks*

## UNIT III—PEOPLE AND POWER

### CONTEXT B: INDIA 1917–1947

*SECTION A: KNOWLEDGE AND UNDERSTANDING*

**Study the information in the sources. You must also use your own knowledge in your answers.**

**Source A** is about how Britain benefited from ruling India.

**Source A**

> Britain took control of India in the 18th century. India became the "Jewel in the Crown" of the British Empire. The British army in India was paid for by Indians and was used in other parts of Asia and Africa. The army provided many important jobs for Britons. India was a valuable trading partner for Britain as India bought a lot of cloth from Lancashire.

1. Explain why Britain benefited from ruling India.     **3**

**Source B** is about the way Untouchables were treated in India.

**Source B**

> Caste not only determines a person's job, but how others treat them. The Untouchables are outside the caste system. Untouchables have to do jobs no-one else will do such as toilet cleaning. They have to use separate entrances to buildings. They must drink from separate wells.

2. Describe how many Indians treated the Untouchables.     **3**

## SECTION B: ENQUIRY SKILLS

The following sources are about the appeal of Ghandi.

**Study the sources carefully and answer the questions which follow.**
**You should use your own knowledge where appropriate.**

**Source C** was said by the English judge who sent Ghandi to jail in 1922.

**Source C**

> I know that you are different from any other person I have tried. It would be impossible to ignore the fact that to millions of your countrymen you are a great patriot and a great leader. Even those who hold different views from you look up to you as a man of high and saintly ideals. I do not forget you have done much to prevent violence.

3. What was the attitude of the English judge, in **Source C**, towards Ghandi? 3

**Source D** is part of a speech by Nehru who worked closely with Ghandi.

**Source D**

> Ghandi got on so well with the masses of the Indian people. This meant that older leaders were pulled towards him. The fact that stood out about Ghandi was how he attracted people of different kinds. He thereby became a link between different groups from the poorest peasant, to rich businessmen. I have come across no-one like him in my life.

4. How far do **Source C** and **D** agree about Ghandi's appeal? 4

[END OF CONTEXT IIIB]

Marks

### UNIT III—PEOPLE AND POWER

CONTEXT C: RUSSIA 1914–1941

*SECTION A: KNOWLEDGE AND UNDERSTANDING*

**Study the information in the sources. You must also use your own knowledge in your answers.**

**Source A** is about the difficulties faced by the Provisional Government.

**Source A**

> The Provisional Government in 1917 wanted to build a democratic Russia. By July 1917, the crowds on the streets had freedom. There was a shortage of food because the railways could not bring enough to the cities. Many Russian soldiers had decided to desert. In the factories there were many strikes.

1. Explain why the Provisional Government faced difficulties in 1917.    3

**Source B** is about how Stalin treated the Kulaks.

**Source B**

> Since the death of Lenin, Stalin had been building up his control of the Communist party. In the winter of 1929 he began the policy of combining farms known as collectivisation. Many wealthier peasants or Kulaks resented this. Stalin's soldiers shot peasants who were resisting collectivisation. Poor peasants were encouraged to denounce these wealthier peasants as Kulaks. Any Kulak could be sent to prison.

2. Describe the ways in which Stalin treated the Kulaks.    3

## SECTION B: ENQUIRY SKILLS

The following sources are about the appeal of Lenin.

**Study the sources carefully and answer the questions which follow.**

**You should use your own knowledge where appropriate.**

**Source C** is from the memoirs of a Russian, Ivan Sukhanov, who knew Lenin.

**Source C**

> Lenin could rightfully claim he created the Communist party. Several times when our hold on power was threatened he took bold action to save it. Lenin did this by signing an unpopular peace treaty in 1918. He also introduced the New Economic Policy in 1921. Lenin made Russian Communism a world force. He never boasted about his great achievements but I, like thousands, mourned his death.

3. What is the attitude of Sukhanov, in **Source C**, towards Lenin?   3

**Source D** is from "Hammer and Sickle" by Tony Howarth.

**Source D**

> When Lenin died in 1924, the Communist party that he had created had grown to half a million members. Thousands of sad Russians queued for hours in the biting cold of Moscow to see his body. They wanted to see the man who had made Communism a world force. He was the man who brought in the New Economic Policy. The Party changed the name of Petrograd to Leningrad as an honour to him.

4. How far do **Sources C** and **D** agree about Lenin?   4

[END OF CONTEXT IIIC]

## UNIT III—PEOPLE AND POWER

### CONTEXT D: GERMANY 1918–1939

*SECTION A: KNOWLEDGE AND UNDERSTANDING*

**Study the information in the sources. You must also use your own knowledge in your answers.**

**Source A** describes the problems of hyperinflation faced by Germany in 1923.

**Source A**

> In Germany, 1923 was the year of hyperinflation. Old people with pensions suffered because, as prices rose, their income stayed the same. People with money in the bank found their savings lost their value. Workers were paid twice a day so they could spend their wages on food before prices went up again. Others did well out of the economic difficulties. Those who had borrowed money previously, found it very easy to repay their debts.

1. Explain why hyperinflation caused hardship for German people.     **3**

**Source B** is from "Hitler's Domestic Policy" by Andrew Boxer.

**Source B**

> In 1933 the Nazi Government introduced a number of restrictions on Jews. In April, laws were passed forcing Jews out of the Civil Service and legal professions. President Hindenburg insisted this should not apply to Jews who had fought in the war and Hitler agreed. Later, in April, a law banned Jewish doctors from working for the state. Increasing numbers of Jews now tried to leave Germany.

2. Describe the ways Hitler treated the Jews before 1939.     **3**

*Marks*

## SECTION B: ENQUIRY SKILLS

The following sources are about the appeal of Adolf Hitler to the German people.

**Study the sources carefully and answer the questions which follow.**
**You should use your own knowledge where appropriate.**

**Source C** is from Kurt Ludecke's book "I Knew Hitler", published in 1938.

**Source C**

> When Hitler stepped onto the platform, there was not a sound to be heard. Then he began to speak, quietly at first. Before long, however, his voice had risen to a hoarse shriek that gave an extraordinary effect. He was holding the masses, and me with them, under a hypnotic spell. I don't know how to describe the emotions that swept over me as I heard this man. When he spoke of the disgrace of Versailles, I felt ready to spring on any enemy.

3. What is the attitude of the author, in **Source C**, towards Hitler's appeal as a speaker? **3**

**Source D** describes Hitler speaking at a Nazi rally.

**Source D**

> When Hitler moved onto the stage, 100,000 people became silent. Hitler started his speech very quietly. People had to strain to hear him. By the end, however, he was yelling at the crowd and the crowd yelled back. Hitler spoke of how awful the Treaty of Versailles was and of the need to tear it up. The crowd were hypnotised by Hitler. When he finished, the audience rose and cheered and cheered.

4. To what extent do **Sources C** and **D** agree about Hitler as a speaker? **4**

[END OF CONTEXT IIID]

[END OF QUESTION PAPER]

[BLANK PAGE]

2008 | Credit

# 1540/403

NATIONAL
QUALIFICATIONS
2008

MONDAY, 26 MAY
1.00 PM – 2.45 PM

HISTORY
STANDARD GRADE
Credit Level

Answer questions from Unit I **and** Unit II **and** Unit III.

Choose only **one** Context from each Unit and answer Sections A **and** B. The Contexts chosen should be those you have studied.

The Contexts in each Unit are:

Unit I— Changing Life in Scotland and Britain
   Context A: 1750s–1850s .............................. Pages 2–3
   Context B: 1830s–1930s ............................. Pages 4–5
   Context C: 1880s–Present Day .................... Pages 6–7

Unit II— International Cooperation and Conflict
   Context A: 1790s–1820s ............................. Pages 8–9
   Context B: 1890s–1920s ............................. Pages 10–11
   Context C: 1930s–1960s ............................. Pages 12–13

Unit III— People and Power
   Context A: USA 1850–1880 ........................ Pages 14–15
   Context B: India 1917–1947 ....................... Pages 16–17
   Context C: Russia 1914–1941 .................... Pages 18–19
   Context D: Germany 1918–1939 ................. Pages 20–21

Number the questions as shown in the question paper.

Some sources have been adapted or translated.

# UNIT I—CHANGING LIFE IN SCOTLAND AND BRITAIN

### CONTEXT A: 1750s–1850s

## SECTION A: KNOWLEDGE AND UNDERSTANDING

> Population movements had a great impact on the lives of many people.

**(Note: for this answer you should write a short essay of several paragraphs including an introduction and a conclusion.)**

1. Explain the impact upon people's lives of:

   **EITHER**

   (a) The Highland Clearances       8

   **OR**

   (b) Scottish emigration overseas.   8

## SECTION B: ENQUIRY SKILLS

**The issue for investigating is:**

> There was little support for the militant Radicals, 1815–1830.

**Study the sources carefully and answer the questions which follow.**
**You should use your own knowledge where appropriate.**

**Source A** is a description of the Peterloo Massacre written by a leading Reform Radical, Samuel Bamford, in 1819.

**Source A**

> The Reform campaign planned an assembly in Manchester. We decided that the meeting had to be as peaceful as possible. The crowd gathered in an orderly fashion. Many were singing hymns. The magistrates, however, ordered the Cavalry to arrest Orator Hunt. Yet the Cavalry could not, with all their weight of men and horse, break through that mass of human beings. They used their sabres to hack through naked hands and defenceless heads. By the end of 1820 most of our campaign leaders were in jail.

2. How useful is **Source A** for investigating the actions of the Reform Radicals in the early nineteenth century?       4

**Source B** is from the Glasgow Courier newspaper describing incidents in the Greenock area following the earlier battle of Bonnymuir in April 1820.

**Source B**

> The Radicals want Parliamentary reform. These rebellious Radicals of Glasgow alarmed the authorities. A whole company of loyal volunteers took five of the rebels to Greenock Jail. On the march to Greenock a small crowd of men and boys met the troops. This crowd increased considerably as they marched. When the prisoners were taken inside the jail a number of men attacked the guards with a volley of stones. Several of the company were injured. On their return the mob attacked. Soldiers fired into the mob killing nine. In the evening the mob attacked the jail and released the Radicals.

**Source C** is from "The Scottish Nation 1700–2000" by T. M. Devine, published in 1999.

**Source C**

> At one level the 1820 campaign was another failure for the Radical cause. The call to arms attracted only a handful of Radicals, mainly in a few weaving areas. It was a protest by a dying craft rather than a working class rebellion. However, the government could not guarantee control of many areas in the west of Scotland. Reports of large numbers of armed men drilling openly worried the authorities. They were saved because the Army continued to be loyal. The propertied classes strongly supported the authorities.

**Look at Sources A, B and C.**

3. What evidence is there in the sources to support the view that there was little support for the militant Radicals, 1815–1830?

   What evidence is there in the sources that there was support for the militant Radicals, 1815–1830? **6**

4. How far do you agree that there was little support for the militant Radicals, 1815–1830?

   You must use evidence **from the sources** and **your own knowledge** to reach a **balanced conclusion**. **5**

[END OF CONTEXT IA]

# UNIT I—CHANGING LIFE IN SCOTLAND AND BRITAIN

## CONTEXT B: 1830s–1930s

### SECTION A: KNOWLEDGE AND UNDERSTANDING

> Population movements had a great impact on the lives of many people.

**(Note: for this answer you should write a short essay of several paragraphs including an introduction and a conclusion.)**

1. Explain the impact upon people's lives of:

   **EITHER**

   (a) Irish immigration into Scotland. **8**

   **OR**

   (b) Scottish emigration overseas. **8**

### SECTION B: ENQUIRY SKILLS

The issue for investigating is:

> Suffragette militancy helped the cause of votes for women.

Study the sources carefully and answer the questions which follow.
You should use your own knowledge where appropriate.

**Source A** was written by Sylvia Pankhurst in her autobiography recalling her involvement in the W.S.P.U.

**Source A**

> I was deeply unhappy with this new policy of militancy. In my opinion we would lose public sympathy. Fire raising reduced support whilst increasing opposition. On the other hand, the heroism of the militants, and the Government's poor handling of them, largely balanced out any harm that their violence had done. Masses of people felt that, against a Government so stubborn, women had no choice but to use violence. Men had done this in the past when struggling for the vote.

2. How useful is **Source A** for investigating the impact of Suffragette militancy upon their cause? **4**

**Source B** is by Mrs Millicent Fawcett, leader of the Suffragists.

**Source B**

> I detest militancy and so do the majority of Suffragists. None of the great triumphs of the women's movement have been won by physical force. However, the stupid mistakes of the politicians have caused some women to turn to violence. I don't like it but such self-sacrifice has moved people who would otherwise sit still and do nothing. I am told that the reporters who actually see what takes place in the streets are impressed; but they are not allowed to report things as they happened. Nothing is reported except what can be turned into ridicule.

**Source C** is from "A Century of Women. The History of Women in Britain and the United States" by Sheila Rowbottom, published in 1997.

**Source C**

> Militancy as a tactic had contradicting effects. The bravery of the Suffragettes won them admiration. They had support not only from women but from men of all classes. Dockers formed part of Mrs Pankhurst's bodyguard when she spoke in Glasgow in 1914. Some men formed a movement to support the Suffragettes. However, militancy provoked considerable ridicule and hostility. A letter to the "Daily Express" in June 1914 called for shaving the heads of every militant Suffragette.

**Look at Sources A, B and C.**

3. What evidence is there in the sources to support the view that Suffragette militancy helped their cause?

   What evidence is there in the sources to support the view that Suffragette militancy harmed their cause? **6**

4. How far do you agree that Suffragette militancy helped the cause of votes for women?

   You must use evidence **from the sources** and **your own knowledge** to reach a **balanced conclusion**. **5**

[*END OF CONTEXT IB*]

# UNIT I—CHANGING LIFE IN SCOTLAND AND BRITAIN

## CONTEXT C: 1880s–Present Day

### SECTION A: KNOWLEDGE AND UNDERSTANDING

> Population movements had a great impact on the lives of many people.

**(Note: for this answer you should write a short essay of several paragraphs including an introduction and a conclusion.)**

1. Explain the impact upon people's lives of:

   **EITHER**

   (a) Immigration into Scotland    **8**

   **OR**

   (b) Scottish emigration overseas.    **8**

### SECTION B: ENQUIRY SKILLS

The issue for investigating is:

> Suffragette militancy helped the cause of votes for women.

**Study the sources carefully and answer the questions which follow.**
**You should use your own knowledge where appropriate.**

**Source A** was written by Sylvia Pankhurst in her autobiography recalling her involvement in the W.S.P.U.

**Source A**

> I was deeply unhappy with this new policy of militancy. In my opinion we would lose public sympathy. Fire raising reduced support whilst increasing opposition. On the other hand, the heroism of the militants, and the Government's poor handling of them, largely balanced out any harm that their violence had done. Masses of people felt that, against a Government so stubborn, women had no choice but to use violence. Men had done this in the past when struggling for the vote.

2. How useful is **Source A** for investigating the impact of Suffragette militancy upon their cause?    **4**

**Source B** is by Mrs Millicent Fawcett, leader of the Suffragists.

**Source B**

> I detest militancy and so do the majority of Suffragists. None of the great triumphs of the women's movement have been won by physical force. However, the stupid mistakes of the politicians have caused some women to turn to violence. I don't like it but such self-sacrifice has moved people who would otherwise sit still and do nothing. I am told that the reporters who actually see what takes place in the streets are impressed; but they are not allowed to report things as they happened. Nothing is reported except what can be turned into ridicule.

**Source C** is from "A Century of Women. The History of Women in Britain and the United States" by Sheila Rowbottom, published in 1997.

**Source C**

> Militancy as a tactic had contradicting effects. The bravery of the Suffragettes won them admiration. They had support not only from women but from men of all classes. Dockers formed part of Mrs Pankhurst's bodyguard when she spoke in Glasgow in 1914. Some men formed a movement to support the Suffragettes. However, militancy provoked considerable ridicule and hostility. A letter to the "Daily Express" in June 1914 called for shaving the heads of every militant Suffragette.

**Look at Sources A, B and C.**

3. What evidence is there in the sources to support the view that Suffragette militancy helped their cause?

   What evidence is there in the sources to support the view that Suffragette militancy harmed their cause? **6**

4. How far do you agree that Suffragette militancy helped the cause of votes for women?

   You must use evidence **from the sources** and **your own knowledge** to reach a **balanced conclusion**. **5**

[*END OF CONTEXT IC*]

# UNIT II—INTERNATIONAL COOPERATION AND CONFLICT

## CONTEXT A: 1790s–1820s

### SECTION A: KNOWLEDGE AND UNDERSTANDING

> In November 1792, the French Government called upon the lower classes to revolt when they issued the Edict of Fraternity.

1. Describe the events after the Edict of Fraternity that led to the outbreak of war in 1793. **4**

> The Great Powers met together in Congresses to consider questions which might threaten the Peace of Europe.

2. How successful was the Congress System in dealing with the problems Europe faced after 1815? **4**

### SECTION B: ENQUIRY SKILLS

The following sources are about the effects of war on Britain.

**Study the sources carefully and answer the questions which follow.
You should use your own knowledge where appropriate.**

**Source A** is a British cartoon about the Continental System, produced in 1807. The caption for the cartoon is "The Giant Commerce Overwhelming Napoleon's Blockade".

**Source A**

3. How useful is **Source A** as evidence of the effects of the Continental System on Britain? **4**

**Source B** is taken from "Britain 1714–1851" by Denis Richards and Anthony Quick.

**Source B**

> Napoleon decided to concentrate on the defeat of Britain. All lands controlled by France were forbidden to import British goods. Britain retaliated. In 1807 Britain gained control of the Danish fleet and kept the Baltic Sea open to shipping. The "Continental System" failed to break Britain's will to resist. She increased her trade across the oceans to America and India. Even Napoleon's army was supplied with 50,000 overcoats and 200,000 pairs of boots from Britain.

4. To what extent do **Sources A** and **B** agree about the effects of Napoleon's blockade of Britain? **4**

5. How fully do **Sources A** and **B** describe the effects of the Napoleonic Wars on British civilians?

    You must use evidence **from the sources** and **your own knowledge** and give reasons for your answer. **5**

*[END OF CONTEXT IIA]*

Marks

# UNIT II—INTERNATIONAL COOPERATION AND CONFLICT

## CONTEXT B: 1890s–1920s

### SECTION A: KNOWLEDGE AND UNDERSTANDING

> By 1914 the European situation was so unstable that any incident could start a war.

1. Describe the events after the assassinations at Sarajevo which led to the outbreak of the First World War by August 1914. **4**

> From the outset, the League of Nations faced many difficulties in its role of maintaining peace.

2. How successful was the League of Nations in dealing with the problems it faced after 1919? **4**

### SECTION B: ENQUIRY SKILLS

The following sources are about the effects of war on Britain during the First World War.

**Study the sources carefully and answer the questions which follow.**
**You should use your own knowledge where appropriate.**

**Source A** is a photograph taken in London on the 8th September 1915 after a Zeppelin air raid.

**Source A**

3. How useful is **Source A** as evidence of the effects of German air raids in Britain during the First World War? **4**

*Marks*

**Source B** is taken from "The First World War" by Hew Strachan.

**Source B**

> On the 8th September 1915, a Zeppelin commanded by Heinrich Mathy killed twenty two people and caused £500,000 worth of damage to Aldersgate in London. Several shops were badly damaged. Massive fires started in warehouses north of St. Paul's. The Zeppelins scored direct hits on two packed buses. In addition, many houses were destroyed, windows were broken and roofs blown off. The power of the bomb was illustrated by the large crater that one bomb made in the road.

4. To what extent do **Sources A** and **B** agree about the effects of German air raids during the First World War? **4**

5. How fully do **Sources A** and **B** describe the effects of the war on British civilians?

    You must use evidence **from the sources** and **your own knowledge** and give reasons for your answer. **5**

[*END OF CONTEXT IIB*]

*Marks*

# UNIT II—INTERNATIONAL COOPERATION AND CONFLICT

CONTEXT C: 1930s–1960s

## SECTION A: KNOWLEDGE AND UNDERSTANDING

> Munich failed to bring about the peace in Europe that people hoped for.

1. Describe the events after the Munich Agreement which led to the outbreak of the Second World War in September 1939.

   **4**

> Many feared that the United Nations Organisation would have no more success than the League of Nations in the 1920s and 1930s.

2. How successful was the United Nations Organisation in dealing with the problems it faced after 1945?

   **4**

## SECTION B: ENQUIRY SKILLS

The following sources are about the effects of war on Britain during the Second World War.

**Study the sources carefully and answer the questions which follow.**
**You should use your own knowledge where appropriate.**

**Source A** is a photograph taken on 14th March 1941, the morning after the first night of the bombing of Clydebank.

**Source A**

3. How useful is **Source A** as evidence of the effects of German air raids on Britain during the Second World War?

   **4**

**Source B** is an eyewitness account of the effects of a German bombing raid.

**Source B**

> We heard afterwards that many had been killed in the raid. When I got near to the butcher's shop I could see that the big house and tenement blocks close by had been bombed. I was told that there had been many killed. It was a night I shall never forget. There was not a shop with their windows left intact. We were running on a carpet of broken glass and debris and I could feel it crunching under my feet. The searchlights were scanning the skies. No. 12 was burning, but there were no fire brigades to put out the fires. Not that it mattered as there was no water, the mains supply being ruptured.

4. To what extent do **Sources A** and **B** agree about the effects of German air raids on Britain during the Second World War? **4**

5. How fully do **Sources A** and **B** describe the effects of war on British civilians?

    You must use evidence **from the sources** and **your own knowledge** and give reasons for your answer. **5**

[*END OF CONTEXT IIC*]

Marks

UNIT III—PEOPLE AND POWER

CONTEXT A: USA 1850–1880

SECTION A: KNOWLEDGE AND UNDERSTANDING

> On Southern plantations before 1860 many slaves were cruelly treated and lived in great unhappiness.

1. Describe the lack of rights for slaves on Southern plantations before 1860. **4**

> In 1858 gold was discovered in the Black Hills and a new gold rush began.

2. How important was the discovery of gold in causing tension between the Native Americans and the white settlers? **4**

SECTION B: ENQUIRY SKILLS

The following sources are about the treatment of black Americans during Reconstruction.

**Study the sources carefully and answer the questions which follow.
You should use your own knowledge where appropriate.**

**Source A** is an eyewitness report to the US Government in 1872.

**Source A**

> The Klansmen said that I had committed a great wrong; I had kept a Sunday school which was forbidden. Many school houses were burned down. Hostility was shown to the school teachers like me who taught in schools for Blacks. Two school board directors were warned by the Ku Klux Klan to leave the Board and one of them did. The Ku Klux Klan went at night and gave these warnings. I asked them while they were whipping me what I had done. They said I wanted to make these blacks equal to the white men; that this was a white man's country.

3. Discuss the attitude of the Ku Klux Klan to black Americans according to the author of **Source A**. **4**

Source B is from "Civil Rights in the USA, 1863–1980".

Source B

> The violence that the Ku Klux Klan committed was directed not only at black people but anyone who furthered their cause. Teachers became key figures so they were frequently intimidated by the Klan. These attacks usually took place at night and were carried out by Klansmen leaving behind a burning cross. Dressed in white robes and hoods they beat, mutilated and murdered. Black Americans were reluctant to resist as they wanted to be seen as peaceful and law-abiding.

4. To what extent do **Sources A** and **B** agree about the treatment of black Americans during Reconstruction? **4**

[END OF CONTEXT IIIA]

UNIT III—PEOPLE AND POWER

CONTEXT B: INDIA 1917–1947

SECTION A: KNOWLEDGE AND UNDERSTANDING

> After fighting in the First World War, Indians hoped to have a greater say in running their own affairs.

1. Describe the lack of rights for Indian people during British rule. **4**

> Through the 1920s, little progress towards independence was made, and Congress under Ghandi began a campaign of civil disobedience.

2. How important were Ghandi's non-violent actions in putting pressure on Britain to grant India more freedom? **4**

SECTION B: ENQUIRY SKILLS

The following sources relate to the events in Calcutta immediately after Direct Action Day on 16th August 1946.

**Study the sources carefully and answer the questions which follow.
You should use your own knowledge where appropriate.**

**Source A** describes the situation in Calcutta immediately after Direct Action Day in August 1946.

**Source A**

> Fearing trouble, Brigadier MacKinlay confined his troops to their barracks, pending orders. A marked feeling of panic especially among Hindu traders in North Calcutta had been a feature of the situation. The troops were called out of their barracks and found fires burning, homes and shops sacked. Dead bodies were everywhere. A train, the 36 Down Parcel express, was stopped and looted and the crew butchered. Calcutta was beginning to look like a battlefield. The Sikhs charged through the Muslim area killing indiscriminately. They showed no mercy. Lines of refugees lined the streets and Howrah railway station became a seething mass of people desperate to get out.

3. Discuss the attitude of the author of **Source A** towards the events that followed Direct Action Day. **4**

Marks

**Source B** is from the book "Liberty or Death" by John French and describes events in Calcutta immediately after Direct Action Day.

**Source B**

> That night, small gangs set out with knives and short swords, and, the next morning, hundreds of corpses were lying in the gutters. Troops were called out. One general claimed that parts of Calcutta on Saturday morning were as bad as anything he saw when he was a soldier on the Somme. At the end of three days killing, the official report stated that 4,000 people had been killed and 3,000 injured. India's mass migration was beginning. Terrified groups of people left in search of safer areas.

4. To what extent do **Sources A** and **B** agree about events in Calcutta immediately after Direct Action Day?   4

*[END OF CONTEXT IIIB]*

## UNIT III—PEOPLE AND POWER

### CONTEXT C: RUSSIA 1914–1941

*SECTION A: KNOWLEDGE AND UNDERSTANDING*

> Short of revolution, there was no way in which the Russian people could influence the Tsar's Government.

1. Describe the limited rights of the Russian people under the Tsar before 1917. **4**

> In October 1917 the Bolsheviks seized control of Petrograd.

2. How important were the weaknesses of the Provisional Government in explaining the success of the Bolshevik Revolution in October 1917? **4**

*SECTION B: ENQUIRY SKILLS*

The following sources are about the purges of Joseph Stalin in the 1930s.

**Study the sources carefully and answer the questions which follow.
You should use your own knowledge where appropriate.**

**Source A** is part of the memoirs of a survivor of Stalin's political prisons in Russia.

**Source A**

> The Secret Police had been ordered to purge more innocent men as counter revolutionaries. Without any warning, the prison guards forced everyone out of their cells in the camp. They read out an enormous list of names. I was relieved that my name was not read out. There was a terrible confusion in the square. These men were given two hours to prepare. Some ran frantically to gather up things. Others sadly tried to say farewell to old comrades. Whole columns of prisoners slowly marched out with their knapsacks. I am upset to say they were executed but glad that I survived.

3. Discuss the attitude of the author of **Source A** to his experiences in one of Stalin's prison camps. **4**

**Source B** is from "Kings of the Kremlin" by Sol Shulman.

**Source B**

> After the murder of Kirov in 1934, over 40,000 were arrested in Leningrad alone. Almost a million were arrested across the country. The country was almost a huge concentration camp. Tens of thousands of Party members were killed. All of the 1917 Central Committee was soon to be disposed of. Forty thousand high ranking military officers were also executed by the Secret Police. Stalin sent many others of his fellow citizens to prisons. Millions were also sent to Labour camps. Nineteen million were rounded up in these purges. At least seven million of them were executed.

4. To what extent do **Sources A** and **B** agree on the methods used in Stalin's Purges?     **4**

[END OF CONTEXT IIIC]

Marks

UNIT III—PEOPLE AND POWER

CONTEXT D: GERMANY 1918–1939

SECTION A: KNOWLEDGE AND UNDERSTANDING

> The Weimar constitution tried very hard to protect people's rights.

1. Describe the rights which Germans were given in the Weimar Republic. 4

> With the failure of the Munich Putsch of 1923, most people believed that Hitler and the Nazis were finished.

2. How important was the Munich Putsch in causing Hitler and the Nazis to lose support in the 1920s? 4

SECTION B: ENQUIRY SKILLS

The following sources are about the Night of the Long Knives.

**Study the sources carefully and answer the questions which follow.
You should use your own knowledge where appropriate.**

**Source A** is from an account by a National Socialist of the reactions of Germans to the Night of the Long Knives.

**Source A**

> Hitler's courage in taking decisive action has made him a hero in the eyes of many Germans. He has won strong approval and sympathy for the steps he took. People think his action is proof that he wants order and decency in Germany. Reports from different parts of the country are unanimous that people are expressing satisfaction that Hitler has acted so decisively against the serious threat posed by Rohm and the SA to Germany and her people.

3. Discuss the attitude of Germans to the Night of the Long Knives as shown by the author of **Source A**. 4

Marks

**Source B** is from "Hitler's Domestic Policy" by Andrew Boxer.

**Source B**

> On the morning of 30th June 1934, Rohm and other SA leaders were arrested and eventually shot. Hitler's personal popularity soared as a result of the Night of the Long Knives, as this event became known. Most Germans disliked the corruption and arrogance of the SA and welcomed the decisive action against it. President Hindenburg's telegram to Hitler seemed to sum up the relief felt by most Germans: "By your determined action and gallant personal intervention, you have saved the German nation from serious danger. For this, I express to you my most grateful thanks and that of the German people."

4. To what extent do **Sources A** and **B** agree about the attitude of Germans to the Night of the Long Knives?  4

[END OF CONTEXT IIID]

[END OF QUESTION PAPER]

[BLANK PAGE]

[BLANK PAGE]

[BLANK PAGE]

# Acknowledgements

Leckie & Leckie is grateful to the copyright holders, as credited, for permission to use their material:
Wendy Doran & Richard Dargie for extracts reproduced from Change in Scotland 1830–1930 (2007 General p 6);
Philip Sauvain for an extract from British Economic and Social History (2006 Credit p 7);
The Mirror Group for an extract from 'The new country life' by Richard Fenton, taken from The Sunday Mail History of Scotland (2006 General p 4);
Express Newspapers for an article taken from the Daily Express, 1909 (2006 General p 5);
The illustration 'And now let's learn to live together' from The Daily Mirror © Mirrorpix (2006 General p 16);
Extract from Black People of America by B. Rees & M .Sherwood. Reprinted by permission of Harcourt Education (2006 General p 19);
Anova Books for an extract from Nehru's autobiography in 1941 (2006 General p 20);
Extract from Germany 1918–1939 by John Kerr. Reprinted by permission of Harcourt Education (2006 General p 24);
Extract from America: A Native History 4th edition by George Brown Tindall & David E Shi. Copyright © 1996, 1992, 1988, 1984 by W.W. Norton & Company Inc. Used by permission of W.W. Norton & Company, Inc (2006 Credit p 14 and 2007 General p 18);
Scott Ferris Associates for an extract from 'The Last Days of the Raj' by T Royle (2006 Credit pp 16 & 17);
The National Portrait Gallery for the cartoon The British Butcher © National Portrait Gallery, London (2007 General p 9);
Robert Hale for an extract from 'Traditional Life in Shetland' by James R. Nicolson (2008 General p 4);
Luath Press Ltd for an extract from 'Reportage Scotland' by Louise Yeoman (2008 Credit p 3);

The following companies/individuals have very generously given permission to reproduce their copyright material free of charge:

Hodder and Stoughton for extracts from Scotland and Britain, 1830-1980 by Chalmers and Cheyne (2006 General p 5);
Extracts from The Oxford Companion to Scottish History by Lynch, Michael (2001). By permission of Oxford University Press (2006 General p 2);
Pearson Education for extracts from The Penguin History of the United States by Hugh Brogan (2006 General p 19);
Photograph courtesy of the Imperial War Museum, London (2005 Credit p 19);
The Penguin Group for two extracts adapted from The Scottish Nation 1700-2000 by T. M. Devine (2006 General p 4 and 2008 Credit p 3);
Adam & Charles Black for an extract from Memorials of His Time by Henry Cockburn (2006 General p 3);
HarperCollins Publishers for an extract from A History of the Scottish People by T. C. Smout (2006 General p 3);
Pearson Education for an extract from Changing Lives by Sydney Wood (2006 General p 6);
Hodder & Stoughton for an extract from British Social and Economic History by Ben Walsh (2006 General p 6);
Extract from Trafalgar, the Nelson Touch by David Howarth, published by Weidenfeld and Nicolson, a division of the Orion Publishing Group (2006 General p 8);
Pearson Education for an illustration from An Illustrated History of Modern Europe 1789-1945 (2006 General p 9);
Extract adapted from David Evans, Teach Yourself First World War (Hodder Arnold, 2004), (c) 2004 David Evans, reproduced by permission of Hodder & Stoughton (2006 General p 11);
HarperCollins Publishers for an extract from Making History, World History from 1914 to the Present Day by C. Culpin (2006 General p 11)
Cambridge University Press for an extract from Modern World History by T McAleavy, P Grey, R Little (2006 General p 13);
Chambers Harrap Publishers Ltd for an extract from Conflict and Cooperation 1930–1960 by Richard Dargie & Wendy Doran (2006 General p 15);
Two extracts from Our World Today (Oxford University Press 1985) by permission of the publisher (2006 General p 17);
Pearson Education for an extract from The American West 1840-95 by Rosemary Rees (2006 General p 18);
The Penguin Group for an extract adapted from Empire 2003 by Professor Niall Ferguson (2006 General p 20);
Hodder & Stoughton for an extract from Reaction and Revolution by Michael Lynch (2006 General p 22);
Cambridge University Press for an extract from Germany 1918–1945 by P. Grey & R. Little (2006 General p 24);
Pearson Education for an extract from Germany 1918–1945 by J. Brooman (2006 General p 25);
Hodder & Stoughton for an extract from Germany 1918–1945 by Greg Lacey & Keith Shepherd (2006 General p 25);
Scottish Record Office for an extract from Report to Highland Destitution Commission HD61 and The Scots in Canada (2006 Credit p 3) © Crown copyright (2006 Credit p 2 and p 3);
Birlinn Ltd for an extract from Lowland Perceptions of the Highlands and the Clearances during the famine years 1845-1855 by Krisztina Fenyo (2006 Credit p 4);
Strathclyde Regional Council Archives for an extract from Support Pack on Changing Life (2006 Credit p 5);
Pearson Education for a cartoon from Modern Europe by D. Richards (2006 Credit p 8);
The Imperial War Museum for two posters (2006 Credit pp 10 & 12);
Hodder & Stoughton for an extract from Cooperation & Conflict 1890–1930 by J. Harkness, H. McMillan & D. Moore (2006 Credit p 11);

Folens Publishers for an extract from Era of the Second World War by Carole Browne (2006 Credit p 13);
Hodder & Stoughton for an extract from People & Power: Russia by David Armstrong (2006 Credit p 18);
HarperCollins Publishers for an extract from Russia in Revolution by John L Taylor (2006 Credit p 19);
Oxford University Press for an extract from Germany 1918-45 by John Cloake (2006 Credit p 20);
Nelson Thornes for an extract from Hitler & the Third Reich by R Harvey (2006 Credit p 21).
Aberdeen Journals for two extracts from The Aberdeen Journal, 1912 (2007 General p 6);
DC Thomson & Co for an article from The Courier (2007 General p 2);
HarperCollins Publishers for an extract from Expansion, Trade and Industry by C Culpin (2006 Credit p 7 and 2007 General p 2);
Random House for an extract from Forgotten Voices of the Great War by Max Arthur (2007 General p 11);
Pearson Education for an extract from The World Re-made: The Results of the First World War by Josh Boorman (2007 General p 2);
Imperial War Museum for a poster produced by the British Government in 1917 (2007 General p 12);
Random House for two extracts from How We Lived Then by Longmate (2007 General p 12 and 2007 General p 15);
Pearson Education for an extract from Germany 1918-45 by Josh Brooman (2007 General p 23);
The Penguin Group for an extract from The Scottish Nation 1700-2000 by T M Devine (2007 Credit p 8);
Pearson Education for an extract from An Illustrated History of Modern Europe by Richards and Hunt (2007 Credit p 9);
Pearson Education for two extracts from The Origins of the First World War by James Joll (2007 Credit pp 10-11);
www.historylearningsite.co.uk for an extract (2007 Credit p 13);
Nicollet County Historical Society for the painting Emigrants Attacked by Comanches by Captain Seth Eastman (2007 Credit paper p 14);
Pearson Education for an extract from Hitler's Germany by Josh Brooman (2007 Credit p 21);
Osprey Publishing for an extract from 'Trafalgar 1805: Nelson's Crowning Victory' by Gregory Fremont-Barnes (2008 General p 10);
Pearson Education fro an extract from 'Britain and Europe: 1848-1890' (2008 General p 12);
Chambers Harrap Publishers Ltd for an extract from "Conflict and Cooperation 1930–1960" by Richard Dargie & Wendy Doran (2008 General p 14);
Pearson Education for an extract from 'Britain and the World, the 20th Century' by Tony & Steve Lancaster (2008 General p 15);
Pearson Education for an extract from 'The American West 1840-1895' by R.A. Rees & S.J. Styles (2008 General p 16);
Cambridge University Press for an extract from 'Russia and the USSR 1905-1991' by Philip Ingram, 1997 (2008 General p 20);
Random House Group for an extract from 'A History of Britain Vol 3' by Simon Schama, published by BBC Worldwide (2008 Credit p 2);
Pearson Education for an extract from 'The Suffragette Movement' By Sylvia Pankhurst (2008 Credit p 4);
The Penguin Group for an extract from 'A Century of Women - The History of Women in Britain and the United States' by Sheila Rowbotham (2008 Credit p 5 and p 7);
Oxford University Press for a picture from 'A Portrait of Europe 1789-1914: Machines and Liberty' by Martin Roberts (2008 Credit p 8);
Jonathan Cape Publishing for an extract from 'The Proudest Day: India's Long Road to Independence' by Anthony Read and David Fisher (2008 Credit p 16);
The Penguin Group for an extract from 'Gulag: A History' by Anne Applebaum (2008 Credit p 18).

# Pocket answer section for SQA General and Credit History 2006–2008

© 2008 Scottish Qualifications Authority/Leckie & Leckie, All Rights Reserved
Published by Leckie & Leckie Ltd, 3rd Floor, 4 Queen Street, Edinburgh EH2 1JE
tel: 0131 220 6831, fax: 0131 225 9987, enquiries@leckieandleckie.co.uk, www.leckieandleckie.co.uk

## Marking at General Level

Marks should be awarded to the candidate for:
carrying out the correct process
using relevant presented evidence
using relevant recall.

### Section A (Knowledge and Understanding)

All answers to items in Section A of the paper **must** make use of at least one piece of relevant recall to obtain full marks.

A *selection* of possible recall is given in the Marking Instructions. The marker will use professional judgement to determine the relevance of other possible recall.

The use of duly selected, presented evidence is permitted. Only where a candidate has **done nothing at all** with presented evidence should it then be regarded as simply copying.

### Section B (Enquiry Skills)

In Section B (Enquiry Skills) any item which requires the use of relevant recall is clearly indicated and full marks can only be awarded to those items when such recall is used.

At General Level, in an ES1 item it is not enough to state that a source is useful as it is a "primary source" or that it was "written at the time (of the investigation)". In order to attract a mark the candidate must relate this statement directly to the source.

Examples:

This source is useful as it is written at the time (of the investigation).  = 0 marks

This source is reliable as it was written by a man living then (at the time).  = 0 marks

This source is valuable as it was written during the period under investigation.  = 0 marks

In a K3 question a candidate should be credited for either explaining the importance of the factors in the presented evidence and/or by assessing the relative importance of relevant, recalled evidence.

It is now acceptable (and worthy of a mark) if a candidate evaluates a source and correctly identifies its use as:

"written at the time of the investigation/issue/topic under discussion"

"written during the time period under investigation"

"written by someone who was actually there at the time."

At General Level the correct demonstration of process or application of judgement where required **must be automatically rewarded** *if reinforced* with relevant and appropriate evidence:

Examples:

This source is useful as it was written during a period of great changes in farming in the late 18th century.  = 2 marks

This source is useful as it comes from an official government report.  = 2 marks

I agree that machinery improved coal mining as it increased productivity.  = 2 marks

Sources C and D agree that the Germans felt angry at the Treaty of Versailles.  = 2 marks

In all ES1 (source evaluation responses) the **ideal**, developed response concerning the contemporaneity of the source is given. It is sufficient however, for 1 mark, **at General Level**, for a student to respond that a source is useful as "it is a primary source, written at the time".

In an ES2 question 1 mark is given for a simple comparison and 2 marks for a developed point. Examples are given in the Marking Instructions.

In an ES4 item asking the candidate to put a source into its historical context, full marks cannot be awarded unless relevant recall is given.

In order to obtain **full** marks, an item which requires the suggestion of a conclusion (ES6 item: ie Q.5 in Unit 1) must use presented evidence **and** recalled evidence. Any response based on either presented evidence **only** or recalled evidence **only** may attract a maximum of 2 marks, even if the process is correct.

(A response giving three points of recall and one piece of presented evidence  = 4 marks

A response giving three points of presented evidence and one piece of recall  = 4 marks)

The abbreviations K1 – K3, and E1 – E6 used above indicate the particular sub skills of the extended EGRC to which an individual question relates:

K1: description; K2: explanation; K3: importance;
ES1: evaluation; ES2: comparison; ES3: point of view; ES4: set in context; ES5: select evidence; ES6: present conclusion.

In an ES5 item (selection of evidence) listing or copying of relevant evidence from the presented source(s) is allowed and should be fully credited. Recall or personal judgement cannot be credited in this item.

## Marking at General Level (cont.)

### INTRODUCTION
**Knowledge and Understanding**
Answers are given as bullet points. Candidates must always respond in full sentences, addressing the correct process and actually responding to the item: either describing, explaining or assessing importance (preferably with reference to other important factors).

In the 8 mark, extended writing exercise the candidate should structure the response appropriately with an introduction, six points of relevant, supporting evidence and a conclusion which clearly addresses the specific requirements of the item.

**Enquiry Skills**
**Evaluation of evidence**: normally, only 1 mark will be allocated for each type of evaluation offered: contemporaneity; authorship; content; purpose etc.
**Comparing Sources**: 1 mark is allocated for a simple comparison; 2 marks for a developed comparison. Examples of both types are given.
**Assessing attitude**: 1 mark is allocated for each assessment or explanation.
**Putting a source in context**: full marks can only be awarded if recall is used.
**Selecting evidence to address an issue**: this is the only area where a candidate can supply bullet points or list evidence.
**Providing a conclusion**: full marks cannot be awarded unless the candidate uses presented evidence + recall + balance in their response.

## Marking at Credit Level

Marks should be awarded to the candidate for:
carrying out the correct process
using relevant recalled evidence
using relevant presented evidence (in Section B, Enquiry Skills, only)

In Section B any item which requires the use of relevant recall is clearly indicated and full marks can only be awarded to these items when such recall is used.

### Section A (Knowledge and Understanding)
All questions are based on recalled evidence. A *selection* of possible recall is given in the Marking Instructions. The marker will use professional judgement to determine the relevance of other possible recall.

In a K3 answer (assessing the importance) the candidate should be credited for either explaining the importance of the presented factor and/or by assessing the relative importance of relevant recalled evidence. In both cases a judgement should be offered.

### Section B (Enquiry Skills)
NB: At Credit Level, process in itself is not rewarded.

In an ES1 item in Unit I it is not enough to say that a source is useful because it deals with the issue/investigation under discussion. The evaluation must make specific reference to the actual source/s as in all ES1 type items.

Examples:
This source is useful as it was written during a period of great changes in farming in the late 18th century = 1 mark
This source is useful as it was written by a reputable historian who will have studied the relevant primary sources = 1 mark
This source is useful as it was written at the time (of the investigation) = 0 marks
This source is reliable as it was written by a man living then (at the time) = 0 marks
This source is valuable as it was written during the period under investigation = 0 marks

In Unit I, in an ES1 item, if a candidate makes references to the usefulness of the content of each of the two sources a maximum of 2 marks can be awarded.

If a candidate makes an accurate evaluation which relates to both sources 2 marks can be awarded.

Examples:
These sources are useful as they are both eye witness accounts = 2 marks
These sources are useful as they were written at both ends of the time period we are studying and allow us to compare changes from 1830–1930 = 2 marks

In all other ES1 questions, in Units II and III, only 1 mark can be awarded for an accurate evaluation of content.

In an ES2 question 1 mark is given for a simple comparison and 2 marks for a developed point. Examples are given in the Marking Instructions.

In an ES4 item, which asks the candidate to put a source into its historical context, full marks cannot be awarded unless relevant recall is given.

In an ES5 item (Question 4 of Unit I) listing or copying of relevant evidence from the presented sources **is allowed** and should be **fully credited**.

Recall or personal judgement *cannot* be credited at all.

If evidence is selected on only one side of the given issue, the maximum obtainable is 3 marks.

In an ES6 item (Question 5 of Unit I) the candidate must:

use presented evidence

show relevant recall

show some balance of answer

If any of the above three requirements is not met, the maximum obtainable is 2 marks.

(NB: There is no need for a balanced conclusion as such but the answer must show balance.)

The 8 mark, extended response (in Unit I in the 2002 examination) must be correctly structured as an **essay: ie correctly addressing the detailed requirements of the item, in paragraphs, with an introduction and an appropriate conclusion. Marks will be deducted for any failure to satisfy these requirements**.

The abbreviations K1 – K3, and E1 – E6 used above indicate the particular sub skills of the extended EGRC to which an individual question relates:

K1: description; K2: explanation; K3: importance;
ES1: evaluation; ES2: comparison; ES3: point of view; ES4: set in context; ES5: select evidence; ES6: present conclusion.

## INTRODUCTION

**Knowledge and Understanding**
Answers are given as bullet points. Candidates must always respond in full sentences, addressing the correct process and actually responding to the item: either describing, explaining or assessing importance (preferably with reference to other important factors).

In the 8 mark, extended writing exercise the candidate should structure the response appropriately with an introduction, six points of relevant, supporting evidence and a conclusion which clearly addresses the specific requirements of the item.

**Enquiry Skills**
**Evaluation of evidence**: normally, only 1 mark will be allocated for each type of evaluation offered: contemporaneity; authorship; content; purpose etc.
**Comparing Sources**: 1 mark is allocated for a simple comparison; 2 marks for a developed comparison. Examples of both types are given.
**Assessing attitude**: 1 mark is allocated for each assessment or explanation.
**Putting a source in context**: full marks can only be awarded if recall is used.
**Selecting evidence to address an issue**: this is the only area where a candidate can supply bullet points or list evidence.
**Providing a conclusion**: full marks cannot be awarded unless the candidate uses presented evidence + recall + balance in their response.

# History General Level 2006

**UNIT I – Context A: 1750s – 1850s**

### Section A

1. The candidate describes new methods of farming the land using **presented evidence** such as:
   - use of iron ploughs
   - seed-sowing machines
   - use of threshing-mills.
   
   and **recalled evidence** such as:
   - Small's two-horse plough
   - new crop rotations
   - (Bell's) reaping machine
   - (Jethro Tull's) seed drill
   - (Andrew Meikle's) threshing machine
   - use of steam power to drive threshing mills
   - enclosing fields
   - introduction of chemical fertiliser.

2. The candidate assesses the importance of improved food supply in causing population growth using **presented evidence** such as:
   - ending of famines and many deaths
   - better farming improved food supply
   - fewer died from starvation
   - people ate better (and mortality rates dropped).
   
   and **recalled evidence** such as:
   - crop yields increased
   - variety of food stuffs improved/better diets
   - mothers' fertility improved
   - infant mortality dropped.
   
   and other **possible factors** such as:
   - earlier marriages (due to less need for long apprenticeships)
   - lack of contraception
   - improved standard of living
   - slowly improving hygiene
   - Jenner's vaccination against smallpox
   - slowly improving medical knowledge
   - immigration from Ireland.

### Section B

3. The candidate evaluates the usefulness of **Source C** using evidence such as:
   - contemporaneity: a primary source written at/near the time
   - authorship: eyewitness/first hand knowledge
   - content: detail on the Radical War/use of troops
   - accuracy: matches candidates own knowledge – eg …
   - purpose: written in an autobiography/a memoir – to give information on events in his lifetime
   - limitation: only one viewpoint/hostile to government action.

# History General Level 2006 (cont.)

4. The candidate selects evidence from **Source C** that government use of force was wrong such as:
   - country was suffering from distress/unemployment
   - (only) a few radicals demanded change
   - situation was exaggerated
   - government over-reacted (called it a revolution/civil war)
   - weavers were unemployed and unhappy.

   The candidate selects evidence from **Source D** that government use of force was correct such as:
   - a Glasgow Radical committee was possibly planning a revolution
   - 300 angry Radicals clashed with government troops
   - a party of Radicals tried to march to Carron to get guns.

5. The candidate comes to a conclusion on the issue using presented evidence as outlined above and from **recalled evidence** such as:
   for the issue:
   - Radicals had genuine grievances – government should have listened to them eg provided employment/poor relief
   - Radicals were often handloom weavers out of work because of industrial changes
   - Radicals were protesting for better conditions
   - Radicals had hoped that the end of war with France would mean changes/more democracy/revolution was unlikely in Britain
   - Peterloo was a peaceful meeting where 11 were killed, 400 injured by government troops
   - use of agents provocateurs to exaggerate situations
   - Bonnymuir march was brutally crushed: arrests and executions followed.
   
   BUT
   - government feared a revolution like that in France
   - there were rumours that the Radical army was going to attack Edinburgh banks
   - government had no proper policing control
   - physical force radicals did exist, eg United Scotsman

## UNIT I – Context B: 1830s – 1930s

### Section A

1. The candidate describes new methods of farming the land using **presented evidence** such as:
   - the use of underground drainage
   - the level surfaces of fields led to further crop improvements such as potatoes
   - it was easier to manage the different kinds of livestock
   - the quick adoption of new equipment
   - the back-up services of farming toolmakers
   - fields were levelled (and easier to farm)
   - further crop improvements such as potatoes
   - field design/shape was better/all fields became enclosed.
   
   and **recalled evidence** such as:
   - improved ploughs
   - improved reaping machines
   - steam powered threshing machinery
   - McCormack's binder
   - tractors/lorries (gradually replacing horses)
   - increased use of chemical fertiliser/nitrates
   - growth of specialised market garden/dairy/livestock
   - 4-field crop rotation
   - selective breeding of animals

2. The candidate assesses the importance of an improved food supply using **presented evidence** such as:
   - the revolution in agriculture helped to feed urban population
   - increase in food production helped population growth
   - urban working class could eat grain, milk, potatoes and meat from Scottish farms
   - people ate healthier/better.
   
   and **recalled evidence** such as:
   - detail on agricultural revolution/enclosure movement/better farming methods
   - quality and variety of food stuffs/better diets for all
   - fertility of mothers increased
   - infant mortality dropped
   - contributory factors of railways towards improved food supply.
   
   and **other possible factors** such as:
   - earlier marriages
   - lack of effective contraception
   - improved standard of living
   - improvements in hygiene/soap and public water supplies
   - vaccinations
   - improvement in clothing
   - improving medical knowledge
   - migration from Ireland and areas of Europe

### Section B

3. The candidate evaluates **Source C** using evidence such as:
   - contemporaneity: a primary source written at the time (of militant Suffragette activity)
   - authorship: an eyewitness account/newspaper journalist
   - content: details support for government actions
   - accuracy: similar to other evidence, eg …/biased against Suffragettes
   - purpose: urging government to take firm action
   - limitation: only view of one newspaper/anti-Suffragette

4. The candidate selects evidence from **Source C** such as:
   - militant Suffragettes had gone too far
   - agrees militant Suffragettes need to be stopped/time for dealing gently had ended
   - approves of those responsible for the trouble being arrested
   - supports the government's use of force against the WSPU.
   
   The candidate selects evidence from **Source D** such as:
   - people were shocked at the cruelty of the government
   - government accused of brutality to the hunger strikers
   - many admired the bravery of those being force fed
   - led to some men taking the Suffragettes more seriously

5. The candidate comes to a conclusion on the issue using **presented evidence** as outlined above and **recalled evidence** such as:
   **for the issue**
   - women were breaking the law
   - government couldn't release women from jail to commit more crimes
   - had to show they would not give in to people who broke the law
   - had to force feed hunger strikers as it didn't want any martyrs
   - didn't want to encourage other groups to break the law to try and get what they wanted
   - highlighted how foolish and irresponsible women were being/too silly to be trusted with the vote
   - government had other urgent priorities to deal with.

   **against the issue**
   - women were treated like common criminals and sent to jail
   - forceful actions gained the militant Suffragettes a lot of publicity
   - forceful actions gained a great deal of public sympathy
   - caused the government great embarrassment
   - made some women even more determined to get the vote
   - risked serious/permanent injury to prisoners being force fed
   - government was accused of torture/doctors refused to carry out force feeding
   - drove women to more violent actions, eg firebomb attacks on property
   - Scottish examples of violence/arson.

## UNIT I – Context C: 1880s – Present Day

1. The candidate describes the changes which made it easier for women to work after 1945, using **presented evidence** such as:
   - new household gadgets made housework easier/quicker
   - men helped more with housework (letting women go out to work)
   - changes in industry created more jobs for women
   - the growth of part-time work suited some women.

   and **recalled evidence** such as:
   - attitudes changed towards women working due to their efforts during the Second World War
   - birth control made it easier for women to plan a family and still have a career
   - better child care facilities
   - better education/qualifications opened up a wider range of jobs to women
   - growth of service/new light industries provided jobs for women
   - new laws passed to protect women's rights at work, eg Equal Pay Act; Sex Discrimination Act
   - the work of the Equal Opportunities Commission
   - the role played by trade unions
   - decline of old, male-dominated heavy industries.

2. The candidate assesses the importance of a better diet in Scotland's population increasing after 1880 using **presented evidence** such as:
   - cleaner water eradicated serious diseases such as cholera/typhoid fever
   - more spent on fresh fruit which was good for people's health
   - a good diet builds up resistance to disease
   - a better diet reduces the risk of heart disease and cancer

   and **recalled evidence** such as:
   - free school meals/milk provided for poor children
   - infant mortality rate fell
   - improvements in working conditions
   - better housing helped stop the spread of disease
   - immigrants coming to Scotland (from Ireland, Italy, Asia, Poland, England etc)
   - medical improvements reduced death rate: X-rays; vaccinations, antibiotics
   - better qualified doctors and nurses
   - people more aware of importance of personal hygiene
   - NHS provided free medical care
   - improved public health: better sanitation.

**Section B**

3. The candidate evaluates **Source C** using evidence such as:
   - contemporaneity: primary source written at the time (of militant Suffragette activity)
   - authorship: an eyewitness account/a newspaper journalist
   - content: details support for government actions
   - accuracy: similar to other evidence, eg …/biased against Suffragettes
   - purpose: urging government to take firm action
   - limitation: only view of one newspaper/anti-Suffragette.

4. The candidate selects evidence from **Source C** such as:
   - militant Suffragettes had gone too far
   - agrees militant Suffragettes need to be stopped/time for dealing gently had ended
   - approves of those responsible for the trouble being arrested
   - supports the government's use of force against the WSPU.

   The candidate selects evidence from **Source D** such as:
   - people were shocked at the cruelty of the government
   - government accused of brutality to the hunger strikers
   - many admired the bravery of those being force fed
   - led to some men taking the Suffragettes more seriously
   - support for the Liberal government declined.

# History General Level 2006 (cont.)

5. The candidate comes to a conclusion on the issue using **presented evidence** as outlined above and **recalled evidence** such as:
   **for the issue**:
   - women were breaking the law
   - government couldn't release women from jail to commit more crimes
   - had to show they would not give in to people who broke the law
   - had to force feed hunger strikers as it didn't want any martyrs
   - didn't want to encourage other groups to break the law to try and get what they wanted
   - highlighted how foolish and irresponsible women were being/too silly to be trusted with the vote
   - government had other urgent priorities to deal with.
   **against the issue**:
   - women were treated like common criminals and sent to jail
   - forceful actions gained the militant Suffragettes a lot of publicity
   - forceful actions gained a great deal of public sympathy
   - caused the government great embarrassment
   - made some women even more determined to get the vote
   - risked serious/permanent injury to prisoners being force fed
   - government was accused of torture/doctors refused to carry out force feeding
   - drove women to more violent actions, eg firebomb attacks on property
   - Scottish examples of violence/arson.

## UNIT II – Context A: 1790s – 1820s

### Section A

1. The candidate describes the strengths of the Fourth Coalition using **presented evidence** such as:
   - fewer allied losses at Leipzig
   - Fourth Coalition able to field a larger army
   - larger number of nations/states in the Coalition.
   and **recalled evidence** such as:
   - Coalition armies were better trained
   - Coalition had good leadership
   - Napoleon's Russian Campaign had failed
   - French army weakened (by 300,000) after retreat from Moscow
   - French were weakened by years of war.

2. The candidate assesses the importance of poor diet as a cause of complaint using **presented evidence** such as:
   - meat was old
   - biscuits were infested with maggots
   - water was dirty/full of weevils
   - the wine was unpleasant/like bullock's blood and sawdust.

and **recalled evidence** such as:
   - complaints about very young boys being employed in the navy
   - punishments were severe: flogging; keel-hauling; hanging
   - dangers of ship life: falling from rigging
   - rats spread disease
   - accommodation was poor
   - pay was poor
   - many sailors were press-ganged
   - shore leave was limited
   - scurvy often occurred
   - the sick were poorly attended to.

### Section B

3. The candidate evaluates the completeness of **Source C** using presented evidence such as:
   - events in Spain had affected other countries
   - Spanish revolt started a tide of protest against established governments/influenced Naples and Piedmont
   - events in Spain could have led to uprisings throughout Italy
   - events in Spain threatened France and Germany.
   and **recalled evidence** such as:
   - the influence of Metternich
   - alarm at rising tide of protest against established governments
   - Congress powers wanted to save Europe from widespread destruction
   - desire to preserve the balance of power.

4. The candidate establishes the opinion of the author such as:
   - critical of the Congress System
   - thinks the powers are divided
   - thinks countries are pulling against each other
   - thinks Congress System will destroy itself/collapse over Greek independence
   - thinks larger powers will win at the expense of smaller powers.

5. The candidate compares **Source D** and **Source E** using **presented evidence** such as:
   Sources agree that the Congress powers were divided:
   - **Source D** says/shows: divisions among powers
   - **Source E** says: Russia was acting (with others) against Austria.
   Sources agree that the Greek revolt would lead to the collapse of the Congress System:
   - **Source D** shows: countries pulling against each other over Greece
   - **Source E** says: Greek revolt marked the end of the Congress System.
   Sources agree that Russia sided with Britain and France against Austria:
   - **Source D** shows: Russia teamed with France and Britain against Austria
   - **Source E** says: Russia was acting with Britain and France in opposition to Austria.
   Only **Source E** says that Canning was against the Congress System.

## UNIT II – Context B: 1890s – 1920s

### Section A

1. The candidate describes the arms race prior to the First World War using **presented evidence** such as:
   - naval arms race was between Britain and Germany
   - Britain had constructed 29 Dreadnoughts to Germany's 17
   - Britain had many more Destroyers than Germany
   - Britain had many more submarines than Germany.
   
   and **recalled evidence** such as:
   - naval bases built in Britain and Germany
   - Kiel Canal widened (to aid the Baltic fleet)
   - on land Germany was involved in an arms race with France and Russia
   - all nations were building bigger armies
   - army reforms (eg Haldane's)
   - the Triple Alliance/Triple Entente spent huge sums on armaments
   - Anglo-French Naval Convention
   - detail on Dreadnought making other ships obsolete
   - detail(s) on the Naval Race.

2. The candidate assesses the importance of aircraft during the First World War using **presented evidence** such as:
   - used to protect troops in trenches
   - used for reconnaissance, ascertain enemy actions
   - used to photograph enemy lines
   - fighter planes built (to shoot down enemy planes)
   - creation of RAF implies importance of air technology.
   
   and **recalled evidence** such as:
   - planes were used to bomb opposition trenches
   - planes were used to strafe enemy trenches
   - aircraft design improved and planes became more effective
   - new air technology slowed down the German Spring Offensive
   - both sides also used airships during the war.
   
   and also:
   - use of tanks to break stalemate on the WF
   - use of poison gas, chlorine, phosgene, mustard
   - artillery was developed to become more deadly
   - machine guns/Lewis guns were developed
   - flame throwers were used.

### Section B

3. The candidate assesses the attitude of the author of **Source C** towards the problems faced by the League of Nations using evidence such as:
   - League faces many difficulties/may not achieve peace
   - the woman (representing League of Nations) is in real danger
   - sharks/problems are menacing League of Nations
   - the real dangers to the League are dictators and economic problems
   - disarmament is the next step (to world peace)
   - peace will only be achieved one step at a time
   - League hesitant/acting very slowly/cautiously.

4. The candidate assesses agreement between **Sources C** and **D** using **presented evidence** such as:
   
   Sources agree that disarmament would be the next step:
   - **Source C** shows: League stepping towards disarmament
   - **Source D** says: the next step forward would be disarmament.
   
   Sources agree that economic conditions were difficult:
   - **Source C** shows: (a shark with the words) 'economic crisis'
   - **Source D** says: in such conditions of economic depression.
   
   Sources agree that dictators were a concern:
   - **Source C** shows: a shark with the word 'dictators' on its body
   - **Source D** says: a further problem was the rise of dictators in Europe, (such as Mussolini in Italy).
   
   Sources agree that there are fears for the future of the League:
   - **Source C** shows: dangers looming up
   - **Source D** says: countries less likely to work together/problems existed eg rise of dictators.
   
   Only **Source D** says dictators who seized power by force were not likely to work with others to prevent war/for the peaceful ideals of the League.

5. The candidate evaluates the completeness of **Source E** using **presented evidence** such as:
   - refugees were helped
   - Nansen Passports helped 500,000 POWs in Russia get home
   - League worked in poorer countries to improve health
   - the number of cases of leprosy was reduced.
   
   and **recalled evidence** such as:
   - solved some territorial disputes, eg in 1920 between Sweden and Finland, Aaland Islands
   - had some success against the slave trade/Slavery Convention of 1926
   - reduced the trade in drugs/campaigned against drug trafficking
   - the ILO encouraged many countries to improve working conditions for ordinary workers
   - League successfully organised a rescue plan for the Austrian economy
   - no major wars fought
   - intervened successfully in Bulgaria–Greece dispute/Iraq–Turkey dispute/Poland–Lithuania and, with limited success, in Corfu dispute.

# History General Level 2006 (cont.)

**UNIT II – Context C: 1930s – 1960s**

**Section A**

1. The candidate describes the growth of German armed forces using **presented evidence** such as:
   - number of aircraft went up from 0 to over 4000
   - number of big warships rose from 0 to 4
   - number of submarines went up from 0 to 54.
   
   and **recalled evidence** such as:
   - conscription introduced in 1935
   - the army became much bigger
   - the army got new weapons, eg new types of tank
   - army went back into the Rhineland in 1936
   - the air-force was tested in the Spanish Civil War
   - boys got military training in the Hitler Youth
   - between 1933 and 1935 propaganda encouraged young men to join the military.

2. The candidate assesses the importance of the Cuban Missile crisis in causing tension using **presented evidence** such as:
   - the US found Soviet missile bases in Cuba
   - President Kennedy thought the Soviet Union was about to attack the USA
   - Kennedy was under pressure to bomb Cuba.
   
   and **recalled evidence** such as:
   - Cuba is very close to the United States
   - missiles from Cuba could hit every American city
   - President Kennedy ordered a naval blockade of Cuba
   - Kennedy sent soldiers to Florida
   - the USA disliked the Communist Cuban government
   - serious risk of nuclear war.
   
   and also:
   - the building of the Berlin Wall
   - the U2 spy-plane incident
   - both sides well prepared for nuclear war
   - Russia's concerns over US policy.

**Section B**

3. The candidate evaluates the attitude of the cartoon using **presented evidence** such as:
   - it has a very positive view of the United Nations' role
   - it sees the most important members (the USA, the Soviet Union and Britain) as now being firm friends
   - it sees the United Nations as being responsible for preserving/guarding peace
   - it sees the United Nations as a way of preventing further war/slaughter
   - it sees the UN as a way of encouraging people to live together.

4. The candidate compares **Sources C** and **D** using **presented evidence** such as:
   Sources agree that the UN would promote good relations among countries:
   - **Source C** shows: American, British and Russian soldiers with their arms round each other
   - **Source D** says: UN would develop friendly relations among nations/live together in peace/live as good neighbours.
   
   Sources agree that the UN should prevent the horrors of another war:
   - **Source C** shows: the graves and helmets of many dead soldiers
   - **Source D** says: save generations from the scourge of war.
   
   Sources agree that the UN could make the world a safer place:
   - **Source C** says: let's learn to live together
   - **Source D** says: UN will settle disputes peacefully.
   
   Only **Source D**: talks about practising tolerance
   Only **Source D**: talks about the UN improving living standards.
   
   Sources disagree about who is responsible for maintaining peace:
   - **Source C** shows: (only) US, UK and USSR in charge
   - **Source D** says: we (all members states) are determined to prevent war/develop friendly relations.

5. The candidate assesses the completeness of **Source E** using **presented evidence** such as:
   - the world has become a more dangerous place since 1945
   - the UN has been unable to stop many wars
   - the UN has been unable to stop the spread of nuclear weapons
   - the UN is badly run
   - the UN wastes money.
   
   and **recalled evidence** such as:
   - unable to stop human rights abuses in some states
   - accusations of corruption
   - problems with peacekeeping in the Belgian Congo/Middle East
   - difficulties in Korea, 1950-53
   - not all members were wholehearted supporters of the UN
   - unable to deal with environmental issues
   - UN resolutions defied by countries like Israel
   - delay in admitting Communist China.

# UNIT III – Context A: USA 1850 – 1880

## Section A

1. The candidate describes the results of Lincoln's election as President using **presented evidence** such as:
   - seven Southern states seceded from the Union
   - the Confederate States was established
   - eleven states joined the Confederation.
   
   and recalled evidence such as:
   - South was alarmed at the Republican victory
   - South feared Lincoln would abolish slavery
   - South Carolina seceded first
   - Mississippi, Florida, Alabama, Georgia, Louisiana, and Texas followed
   - Lincoln tried to placate the South/reassure them on slavery issue
   - Lincoln tried to preserve the Union
   - Lincoln warned against Southern seizure of forts/arsenals
   - Fort Sumter fell to the South
   - Lincoln outlawed the Southern states
   - Lincoln called for a militia force of 75,000
   - Civil War broke out
   - South elected (Jefferson) Davis as President of the Confederacy.

2. The candidate explains the reasons why the Mormons were disliked using **presented evidence** such as:
   - people were irritated by the Mormons' hard work and carefulness
   - fears were increased by rumours of a Mormon secret society called the Danites
   - non-Mormons were disgusted by Mormon men having more than one wife at the same time
   - there were fears of a Mormon population which would outnumber non-Mormons.
   
   and **recalled evidence** such as:
   - resentment that Mormons believed they were the "chosen people of God" and regarded others as second-class
   - different beliefs and way of life caused prejudice/distrust
   - dislike of Mormon attempts to convert others
   - people were jealous of Mormon success/prosperity in farming/business
   - failure of Mormon bank led to resentment: thousands of ordinary Americans had invested and lost money
   - Mormons suspected of wanting to abolish slavery
   - they suspected the Mormons of being friendly with the Indians
   - fears about Mormon power: Mormon private army numbered 2000 in 1842
   - alarmed when Joseph Smith announced intention to run as President/feared Mormon laws would be imposed on everyone.

## Section B

3. The candidate evaluates the attitude of the author using **presented evidence** such as:
   - praises the Bureau: positive about its work (holistic)
   - commends heroic work in providing homes and food
   - praises success in establishing schools despite opposition
   - claims health facilities improved by setting up hospitals
   - felt ex-slaves protected when Bureau supervised contracts
   - acknowledged Bureau created resentment from KKK when officials took plantation owners to court
   - respects Bureau's stance against the KKK
   - respects Bureau officials for taking plantation owners to court.

4. The candidate compares **Sources C** and **D** using **presented evidence** such as:
   
   Sources agree that the Bureau distributed food to freedmen:
   - **Source C** says: the Freedmen's Bureau did heroic work in providing food for former slaves
   - **Source D** says: food was given to the poorest Blacks.
   
   Sources agree that the Bureau set up schools for ex-slaves:
   - **Source C** says: it succeeded in establishing 4,000 schools
   - **Source D** says: it…operated over 4,000 primary schools.
   
   Sources agree that the Bureau provided health care for ex-slaves:
   - **Source C** says: it also improved health facilities by setting up 100 hospitals
   - **Source D** says: it opened 100 hospitals.
   
   Sources agree that the Bureau supported ex-slaves looking for work:
   - **Source C** says: the Freedmen's Bureau also protected ex-slaves by supervising the terms under which they were hired
   - **Source D** says: Congress set up the Freedmen's Bureau to help Blacks get employment.
   
   Sources agree that the work of the Bureau was unpopular in the South/with the Ku Klux Klan:
   - **Source C** says: its officials were resented by the Ku Klux Klan
   - Source D says: it alarmed Southern Whites in organisations like the Ku Klux Klan.
   
   Only **Source C** mentions Bureau provided homes.
   Only **Source D** mentions food provided to Whites also.
   Only **Source D** mentions Bureau helped with civil rights.
   Only **Source D** mentions the Freedmen's Bank was opened.

## History General Level 2006 (cont.)

### UNIT III Context B: 1917 – 1947

#### Section A

1. The candidate describes the reactions to the Amritsar massacre using **presented evidence** such as:
   - many saw it as harsh
   - it produced martyrs for the Indian nationalist cause
   - nationalist grievances grew strongly
   - it created a crisis of confidence in Britain
   - British ruthless determination to defend Empire seemed to have vanished.
   
   and **recalled evidence** such as:
   - led to the deaths of 379 and many were wounded
   - other areas saw violence in reaction
   - inquiry/Hunter Report into the events weakened the authorities' policies
   - General Dyer was quickly invalided out of Army
   - British government lost the goodwill of many Indians to the policy of gradual change
   - far fewer Indians believed that the British were wise rulers who deserved to be in charge/British seen now as brutal and racialist
   - Indians began to protest on a bigger scale and with more success: did not want concessions after such brutality
   - Congress no longer wanted to share power with the British: they wanted the British to leave India
   - Gandhi and the Congress Party led these protests/became the main leader of Indian nationalism
   - later unrests over the Simon Commission.

2. The candidate explains why Gandhi's campaign attracted support using **presented evidence** such as:
   - people were attracted to the non-violence aspect of Gandhi's campaign
   - saw it as a way out of our difficulties of campaigning against the British
   - saw it as a good/open and effective method of action
   - campaigners became convinced by/ashamed for doubting Gandhi.
   
   and **recalled evidence** such as:
   - little chances of violence succeeding against British military force
   - Gandhi's peaceful/passive resistance tactics had been effective in Bilhar
   - fasting aspect of Satyagraha also used effectively
   - Hartal campaigners were effective
   - Gandhi encouraged many Indians to join for only a few pence a year/even the weak could take part
   - Gandhi did meet with the authorities and this gave him status
   - British could deal sensitively with his peaceful campaigns.

#### Section B

3. The candidate evaluates the attitude to Indian independence using **evidence** such as:
   - overall view is to agree to Indian independence
   - thinks in general that the British are not wanted and should get out
   - thinks there is growing opposition to British rule
   - thinks that the Congress Party and Gandhi were struggling hard for Indian Independence
   - thinks that Indians should be rewarded for supporting the war effort
   - recognises Britain's military weaknesses and inability to stop independence.

4. The candidate assesses disagreement between **Sources C** and **D** about the need for Indian independence using **presented evidence** such as:
   
   Sources disagree on the need for independence:
   - **Source C** says: the only thing to do is to get out/grant independence
   - **Source D** says: India should never be given up/be independent.
   
   Sources disagree on the benefits of British rule:
   - **Source C** says: we have not given a great deal to the Indian people
   - **Source D** says: the British had built roads and railways/improved medicine/education.
   
   Sources disagree on Britain's strength/ability to keep control of India:
   - **Source C** says: we do not have the military force
   - **Source D** says: British Empire still had the power to control across all continents.
   - Only **Source C** shows strength of desire for independence in India.
   - Only **Source C** shows that India deserved independence because of its contribution in the war.
   - Only **Source D** shows the benefits/wealth Britain got from India – ie do not give it up.
   - Only **Source D** shows the importance of India in the Empire – the Jewel in the Crown.

## UNIT III – Context C: Russia 1914 – 1941

### Section A

1. The candidate describes the results of the February Revolution using **presented evidence** such as:
   - the Duma leaders were forced to take charge of the country
   - Alexander Kerensky became Minister of Justice
   - Soviet gained some direct say in running of the country
   - Provisional Government and Petrograd Soviet formed a 'Dual Government'
   - no one to run the country/provide leadership.
   
   and from **recalled evidence** such as:
   - the Tsar abdicated
   - Russia was no longer an autocracy
   - Russia became a republic
   - 300 years of Romanov rule was ended
   - the war continued
   - Provisional Government passed some important reforms, eg 8 hour day, end of censorship
   - Lenin able to return to Petrograd
   - political prisoners freed
   - Provisional Government arranged to hold elections for a constituent assembly
   - economic problems remained, eg. food shortages, peasants' demand for land
   - Russia was no longer ruled by the Tsar.

2. The candidate explains why the Whites lost the Civil War using **presented evidence** such as:
   - Reds had clear sense of purpose
   - the Whites were not a united force
   - White morale was never high
   - Whites did not have common cause
   - Whites lacked effective leadership
   - Reds had very effective leadership.
   
   and from **recalled evidence** such as:
   - White leaders were lazy, brutal and corrupt
   - White armies were scattered
   - Whites held mainly agricultural areas/little industry
   - Whites caused suffering to peasants and alienated them
   - after 1919 Whites lost the support of the Allies and thus war materials
   - foreign intervention led to growing support for the Reds
   - Reds strengths/resources.

### Section B

3. The candidate evaluates the attitude of Stalin using **presented evidence** such as:
   - he is hostile towards the Kulaks
   - he thinks there is a need to carry out an offensive against the Kulaks
   - he wants to break their resistance
   - he wishes to eliminate them as a class
   - he believes that the Kulaks are the enemies of collectivisation/is opposed to them being allowed to join collective farms.

4. The candidate compares **Sources C** and **D** using **presented evidence** such as:
   
   Sources agree that the Kulaks did not support collectivisation:
   - **Source C** says: break their resistance to collectivisation
   - **Source D** says: the Kulaks were resisting the collective farm movement.
   
   Sources agree that Kulaks were against the peasants and their desire for collectivisation:
   - **Source C** says: Kulaks are against the peasants who are putting collectivisation into practice
   - **Source D** says: Kulaks began to wage a campaign of terror against those who supported and worked for collectivisation.
   
   Sources agree that the Kulaks were the enemy of the collective movement:
   - **Source C** says: they are sworn enemies of the collective farm movement
   - **Source D** says: they tried to destabilise the soviet/socialist economy/began to wage a campaign of terror/sabotaged the grain trade.
   
   Sources agree that the Kulaks must be got rid of:
   - **Source C** says: eliminate them as a class.
   - **Source D** says: the liquidation of the Kulaks as a class became a top priority.
   
   Only **Source D** accuses Kulaks of being selfish, opposing collectivisation, so as to retain their positions.

## UNIT III – Context D: Germany 1918– 1939

### Section A

1. The candidate describes the results of the Beer Hall Putsch using **presented evidence** such as:
   - the Putsch failed
   - Hitler was put on trial
   - Hitler's trial gave him much publicity/made him well-known
   - Hitler was found guilty
   - Hitler received a short prison sentence.
   
   and from **recalled evidence** such as:
   - 16 Nazis killed/some police killed
   - Hitler ran off but was arrested
   - Judge at the trial was sympathetic/Hitler given 5 years in Landsberg castle
   - during his 9 months in prison Hitler wrote "Mein Kampf"
   - government banned Nazi Party and its newspapers (lasted till 1925)
   - Hitler decided to use legal/democratic methods to win power
   - the trial allowed Nazi ideas to be publicised.

2. The candidate explains why Hitler was able to defeat his opponents using **presented evidence** such as:
   - he acted swiftly/without warning
   - he had SA leaders arrested/shot
   - he used violence/had Roehm shot
   - he was ruthless.
   
   and **recalled evidence** such as:
   - opposition was not united
   - they used the Gestapo/SS
   - there was a lack of support for SA
   - there was no resistance from the SA

## History General Level 2006 (cont.)

2.
- SA were taken at dead of night
- SA leaders were all together at a meeting called by Hitler/easy target
- there was backing from group of generals who wanted SA disciplined
- there was army support for the event: weapons, vehicles supplied
- Roehm had enemies within the Nazi movement (esp Goering and Himmler)
- they arrested many political opponents
- they used the concentration camps
- Hitler's popularity
- use of propaganda
- Enabling Act gave him unlimited power
- used law to ban other political parties/trade unions declared illegal
- sacked judges and civil servants he did not trust
- control of mass media
- once Hitler became Führer he had total legal power/it was more difficult to stand up to him.

### Section B

3. The author evaluates the attitude of the author using **evidence** such as:
   - did not support the Nazis/opposed the Nazis
   - avoided saluting the Nazi flag
   - disliked Nazi parades/processions
   - loathed the Brown shirts (as thugs)
   - disgusted at himself for giving the Nazi salute.

4. The candidate compares **Sources C** and **D** using **presented evidence** such as:
   Sources agree that there was resistance to the Nazis/Nazi practices:
   - **Source C** says: I managed to avoid saluting the Nazi flag
   - **Source D** says: some people refused to give the Heil Hitler salute.
   Sources agree that not all Germans were enthusiastic about Nazi parades:
   - **Source C** says: you could steer clear of parades/I turned my back on it
   - **Source D** says: parades were treated with indifference.
   Sources agree that ordinary Germans pretended to support the Nazis:
   - **Source C** says: he had to give the Nazi salute
   - **Source D** says: people supported Nazis as their job might depend on it.
   Sources agree that ordinary Germans were unhappy with the SA pressure:
   - **Source C** says: I could have spat at myself (for giving in to the SA)
   - **Source D** says: ordinary Germans resented aspects like SA.
   Sources agree the SA were brutes:
   - **Source C** says: they are thugs
   - **Source D** says: they use strong-arm tactics.
   Only **Source D** says people refused to join the Nazi party.
   Only **Source D** mentions widespread grumbling against Nazis.

## History Credit Level 2006

### UNIT I – Context A: 1750s – 1850s

### Section A

1. The candidate describes the problems with high rise accommodation using **evidence** such as:
   - overcrowding
   - sanitation problems/sewage disposal
   - hygiene difficulties/spread of disease
   - difficulties with water supply
   - buildings often poorly constructed/maintained.

2. The candidate explains the ways in which new technology affected the textile industry in the late 18th century using **evidence** such as:
   - machines, eg Arkwright's water frame/Crompton's mule speeded up spinning
   - power looms increased production of weaving
   - machines needed water power and factories were built on rivers
   - machines caused unemployment among hand spinners/weavers
   - spinning mills brought new demands of labour
   - machines brought dangers/accidents/dust
   - decline of domestic system
   - textile industry took off/employed thousands.

### Section B

3. The candidate makes a balanced evaluation of **Source A** using **evidence** such as:
   - contemporaneity: primary source written at the time of emigration from Highlands and Islands
   - authorship: eyewitness of emigration/contemporary, involved observer
   - content: detail on causes of emigration, eg accuracy: factual account, matching demonstrated candidate knowledge, eg...
   purpose: to reveal reasons for poverty/causes of emigration in the Highlands
   - limitation: one-sided view/landlord's opinion.

4. The candidate selects and organises evidence for the issue using **evidence** such as:
   **Source A**
   - no longer profitable to collect kelp in the Islands
   - poverty was common/money was very hard to come by
   - farming was difficult in the Highlands and Islands
   - emigrants did well in their new country.
   **Source B**
   - some saw emigration as an adventure.
   **Source C**
   - journeys were good
   - emigrants could build new houses/barns
   - emigrants had hopes of a new life/better farming.
   The candidate selects and organises evidence against the issue using evidence such as:
   **Source A**
   - crofters were removed and replaced with sheep.

4. **Source B**
   - their houses had been swept away
   - the people were driven out of their land
   - they were forced to go to the wilds of Canada
   - some died of hunger/smallpox while going across the ocean.
   - almost everyone was crying/forced to leave
   - the authorities/Bailiffs/Constables made sure they boarded the ship
   - it was a loathsome experience.

   **Source C**
   - Canada was a wild country
   - creating a farm was hard/difficult work
   - starting a new life was difficult with no oxen/limited livestock.

5. The candidate offers a balanced conclusion on the issue using **presented evidence** such as that given in answer 4 and **recalled evidence** such as:
   for the issue:
   - overpopulation put a drain on resources in the Highlands
   - crofting life in Scotland was hard
   - kelp prices fell everywhere when Napoleonic wars ended
   - prices of cattle dropped
   - potato famine caused additional problems in the Highlands
   - many Highlanders were living on Poor Relief
   - there was plenty of land available abroad
   - Scots rose to high positions in Canada, Australia and America
   - many Scots went in a spirit of entrepreneurship
   - many Scots had a family living abroad.

   against the issue:
   - sheep farming required space and few people
   - many crofters had their houses burned down
   - new regulations put a stop to hunting of game
   - migrant ships lacked proper regulations
   - further detail on hardships of ship voyages
   - many Scots missed clan/family/friends
   - many Scots missed their homeland/culture
   - some landlords forced tenants to emigrate
   - many Scots had to work abroad in a form of slavery.

## UNIT I – Context B: 1830s – 1930s

### Section A

1. The candidate describes the living problems of tenements using **evidence** such as:
   - over crowding/lack of privacy
   - sanitation problems/sewage disposal
   - hygiene difficulties/spread of diseases
   - difficulties with water supplies
   - buildings often poorly built/maintained
   - demand often outstripped supply
   - differing levels of quality/relative to rents.

2. The candidate explains the ways in which new technology affected the coal industry before 1930s using **evidence** such as:
   - still largely pick and shovel in most Scottish coalmines
   - wagonways used in underground coal movement
   - steam and electrical power to raise wire rope cages
   - steam and electrical power for drainage pumps
   - safety lamp/lighting
   - ventilation fans
   - metal or concrete pit props
   - electrical coal cutting/conveyor belts.

### Section B

3. The candidate makes a balanced evaluation of **Source A** using **evidence** such as:
   - contemporaneity: primary source written at the time of Highland emigration
   - authorship: eyewitness of emigration
   - content: details on poor conditions in Highland homes, eg...
   - accuracy: supports some Scottish views on Highland life, such as…
   - purpose: to report to a Lowland readership/wants to see them leave
   - limitation: one sided Lowland view
   - recall of other differing views/other reasons for emigration from the Highlands

4. The candidate selects and organises evidence for the issue using **evidence** such as:
   **Source A**
   - they should escape the extraordinary and disgusting filth
   - they would gain by being encouraged to emigrate
   - they would gain clean water/clean air
   - they would get away from dirt, smoke/homes they share with animals.

   **Source B**
   - some men saw emigration as an adventure.

   **Source C**
   - many Scots emigrated because of the better living prospects
   - they had family to welcome them/many other Scots there
   - Scottish emigrants were welcomed by Canadians
   - they stayed on at school till they were fourteen
   - none of them regretted leaving Uist.

   The candidate selects and organises evidence against the issue using **evidence** such as:
   **Source A**
   - no wish to emigrate as they appear quite contented
   - it would be forced as they must be 'instructed'.

   **Source B**
   - their houses had been swept away
   - the people were driven out of their land
   - they were forced to go to the wilds of Canada
   - some died of hunger/smallpox while going across the ocean
   - almost everyone was crying/forced to leave
   - the authorities/Bailiffs/Constables made sure they boarded the ship
   - it was a loathsome experience.

   **Source C**
   - some emigrants had difficulty settling down

## History Credit Level 2006 (cont.)

5. The candidate offers a balanced conclusion to the issue using **presented evidence** such as that given in answer 4 and **recalled evidence** such as:
   for the issue:
   - overpopulation put a drain on Highland/ Scottish resources
   - effects of the kelp crisis after the Napoleonic wars
   - selling prices for cattle impacted on prospects
   - crofting life was hard even after 1886 reforms
   - potato famine in Highlands and Islands in 1840s
   - poor relief system in the 1840s
   - there was plenty of land available abroad
   - there was work available abroad
   - Scottish successes in Canada/Australia/USA
   - voluntary emigration from the Highlands continued
   - seasonal and temporary migration opportunities in other places abroad.
   
   against the issue:
   - sheep farming/grouse moors/deer management/sporting estates required space and less people
   - the brutality of the evictions/burning out of tenants
   - migrant ships lacked proper regulations
   - sense of clan loss/culture breakdown/attacks on Gaelic
   - life overseas was not always successful.

### UNIT I – Context C: 1880s – Present Day

#### Section A

1. The candidate describes the problems faced by people living in high-rise flats, using **evidence** such as:
   - lifts were small/often didn't work
   - many people suffered from loneliness/a sense of isolation
   - some blocks let in wind and rain/bits fell off
   - windows and doors jammed
   - thin walls meant flats could be noisy
   - long dark narrow corridors were unpleasant and scary
   - suffered from vandalism
   - nowhere for children to play/nothing for children to do
   - some couldn't afford to use the underfloor heating
   - flats were damp
   - some residents became ill/suffered from lung disease
   - some residents became depressed
   - lack of shops or other facilities for residents
   - no community spirit
   - too many stairs for elderly/very young.

2. The candidate explains in what ways the everyday lives of Scottish people were changed by motor transport using **evidence** such as:
   - increased personal freedom to travel where and whenever people want to go
   - has made travel faster and easier
   - opened up holiday opportunities
   - boosted tourism
   - brings remote areas more in touch
   - goods can be delivered to people's doors
   - lorries transport goods to shops more cheaply/helps reduce cost of living
   - supplied fresher food
   - motorways, bridges and tunnels have reduced travelling time and distances
   - easier to commute to work
   - provides many jobs, eg building cars, constructing roads, working in garages
   - by-passes and ring roads have reduced bottlenecks in towns
   - children can go to school by bus
   - doctors can visit patients in the countryside.
   
   BUT
   - demolition of houses to make way for roads/motorways
   - traffic congestion/jams
   - road accidents
   - decline of town centres due to out of town stores
   - noise pollution caused by motor vehicles
   - dangerous for pedestrians to cross busy roads
   - parking problems
   - pollution from exhaust fumes
   - brought about closure of local shops which causes difficulties for non car owners
   - some communities are divided by busy roads
   - expense of maintaining a car is a problem for some
   - discourages people from taking exercise/encourages people to be lazy
   - decline in public transport means non car owners suffer.

#### Section B

3. The candidate makes a balanced evaluation of **Source A** using **evidence** such as:
   - contemporaneity: primary source written at the time of emigration from Scotland/a 'memoir' written after the events it describes
   - authorship: eyewitness of emigration/first hand experience of emigration
   - content: gives details of why his family/emigrants settled so well in Canada
   - accuracy: factual account/similar to other evidence such as …
   - purpose: to inform people what life in Canada was like for Scottish emigrants/encourage other Scots to consider emigration
   - limitation: only one person's/family's experience; only shows benefits of emigration.

4. The candidate selects and organises evidence for the issue using evidence such as:
   **Source A**
   - better living prospects in Canada
   - had family in Canada to welcome them/many other Scots there
   - Scottish emigrants were warmly welcomed by Canadians
   - all children stayed on at school till they were fourteen
   - none of them regretted leaving Uist.

   **Source B**
   - to escape the poverty and hardship in Britain
   - promise of greater freedom and wealth overseas.

   **Source C**
   - to escape the terrible living conditions in Britain
   - low wages made life a struggle
   - opportunities for a better future in Canada, Australia, etc
   - cheap farmland available overseas
   - improvement in ships made journey better.

   The candidate selects and organises evidence against the issue using **evidence** such as:
   **Source A**
   - some emigrants had difficulty settling in Canada.

   **Source B**
   - emigrants left a good life in Britain/left comfortable homes and good friends
   - overseas they faced great hardship/hostile land and crowded cities
   - many emigrants returned home
   - they wasted money and time emigrating.

   **Source C**
   - emigrants suffered hardship crossing the oceans.

5. The candidate offers a balanced conclusion to the issue using **presented evidence** such as that given in answer 4 and **recalled evidence** such as:
   for the issue:
   - agriculture changes meant farm workers found it hard to find work
   - slumps in industry led to high unemployment
   - decline in the fishing industry
   - harsh working conditions in factories
   - details of the terrible living conditions
   - Highlanders continued to be pushed off the land
   - in Highlands there wasn't enough good farm land for crofters/faced great hardships
   - many Scots did very well abroad
   - better standard of living/higher wages, better housing
   - lots of employment opportunities, especially for skilled workers
   - Scots rose to high positions in America, Australia and Canada
   - examples of Scots who did well, eg Andrew Carnegie
   - some emigrants made their fortune, eg by finding gold
   - less class prejudice abroad/everyone treated more equally.

   against the issue
   - many Scots missed their family and friends back home
   - Scots missed their homeland/culture
   - Highlanders forced off the land to make way for hunting estates
   - some emigrants weren't made welcome
   - many emigrants were unprepared for the conditions they found overseas
   - some faced great hardship abroad
   - many emigrants got low wages and struggled to survive
   - strange diseases killed emigrants.

## UNIT II – Context A: 1790s – 1820s

### Section A

1. The candidate discusses the importance of the death of King Louis XVI as a cause of war using evidence such as:
   - execution of Louis XVI (on 21.1.1793) horrified many in Britain
   - British authorities feared for monarchy in Britain and elsewhere in Europe
   - the execution made war more likely.

   and also
   - reign of terror was too extreme and this also led to growing opposition
   - fear of unrest spreading to Britain was also a factor
   - Edict of Fraternity alarmed many
   - French conquest of the Austrian Netherlands alarmed many
   - French violation of Dutch neutrality contributed
   - opening of the River Scheldt alarmed Britain
   - French actions threatened British naval supremacy
   - French denunciation of European treaties was a factor
   - French resentment that Pitt refused to recognise the Republic increased tension
   - French actions upset the European balance of power.

2. The candidate describes how the Vienna Settlement finally affected France using **evidence** such as:
   - Louis XVIII to be restored to the throne
   - French frontiers cut back to those of 1790
   - France was to suffer an army of occupation for 3-5 years
   - France to pay an indemnity of 700 million francs
   - France was to lose sections of Belgian territory (to the Netherlands)
   - settlement of N Italy produces a barrier against France
   - Prussia takes over Rhine provinces as a barrier
   - Russia, Austria, Prussia and Britain agree to maintain an alliance against further French aggression
   - Russia, Austria, Prussia and Britain agree to meet at intervals in congresses to consider questions of European peace.

# History Credit Level 2006 (cont.)

## Section B

3. The candidate makes a balanced evaluation of **Source A** using **evidence** such as:
   - contemporaneity: primary source produced at the time of the Revolutionary Wars
   - authorship: contemporary cartoonist with first hand experience
   - content: shows Britain expected to suffer as a result of the Continental System/example of French propaganda
   - accuracy: example of French propaganda
   - purpose: to justify the Continental System/boost French morale
   - limitation: French view/exaggerated/only shows one possible effect of war.

4. The candidate discusses the attitude of the authors using evidence such as:
   - anger at government policies
   - hatred of the poverty caused by the government
   - displeasure at the government destroying commerce/industry
   - hatred of government taxation methods/levels
   - dislike of government recruitment methods.

5. The candidate compares **Sources B** and **C** using **evidence** such as:
   Sources agree that the war caused suffering:
   - **Source B** says: we are suffering from poverty/a barbarous war
   - **Source C** says: war has caused distress/starvation.
   Sources agree that taxation increased:
   - **Source B** says: excessive taxes
   - **Source C** says: income tax introduced.
   Sources agree that the wars lasted a long time:
   - **Source B** says: endless war
   - **Source C** says: a lengthy war.
   Sources agree that young people are recruited into the military forces:
   - **Source B** says: war swallows up the youth
   - **Source C** says: war needs vast amounts of young manpower.
   Only **Source C** mentions the effects on food prices.
   Only **Source C** mentions the effect on wages.

## UNIT II – Context B: 1890s – 1920s

### Section A

1. The candidate assesses the importance of the assassinations at Sarajevo using **evidence** such as:
   - assassinations in Bosnia blamed on Serbian Black Hand
   - AH used assassinations as an excuse to hand ultimatum to Serbia
   - Serbia did not accept all the points of the ultimatum
   - AH declared war on Serbia
   - provided spark that set off chain of events that led to World War I.

1. and also
   - AH wanted an excuse to crush Serbia
   - Russia mobilised in support of Serbia
   - AH/Russian rivalry in the Balkans
   - alliance system comes into play/Triple Alliance vs Triple Entente
   - arms race in Europe
   - naval race between Britain and Germany
   - economic rivalry
   - imperial rivalry.

2. The candidate describes the military terms imposed on Germany in 1919 using **evidence** such as:
   - German army was reduced to 100,000 men
   - no conscription permitted
   - no tanks
   - no heavy machine guns/artillery
   - the Rhineland was demilitarised
   - army of occupation inside Germany
   - German navy was only allowed 6 smaller battleships
   - German navy was forbidden submarines
   - no air force permitted
   - no airships permitted.

### Section B

3. The candidate makes a balanced evaluation of **Source A** using **evidence** such as:
   - contemporaneity: primary source from the time of the First World War
   - authorship: produced by the British government
   - content: shows a soldier asking if Britain is worth fighting for/encouraging men to join up
   - purpose: to persuade civilians to enlist
   - accuracy: agrees with other evidence, eg: …
   - limitation: only one of the many examples of government propaganda/idealised scene.

4. The candidate discusses the attitude of the author as shown in **Source B** using **evidence** such as:
   - dislike of food shortages/very negative view/upset at suffering people faced
   - resentment at continually being hungry
   - antipathy to dandelion tops/turnip greens
   - bitterness towards the monotony of the diet/custard
   - anger at seeing the mother go hungry
   - despair at the continuation of the food shortage.

5. The candidate evaluates the area of agreement between **Sources B** and **C** using **evidence** such as:
   Sources agree that it was an extremely difficult time:
   - **Source B** says: it was a terrible time, terrible
   - **Source C** says: the food situation is unbearable.
   Sources agree that food was short in supply:
   - **Source B** says: had to eat what food was available – dandelions, potatoes
   - **Source C** says: the potato supply has been insufficient/food situation is unbearable.
   Sources agree that people were going hungry:
   - **Source B** says: we were starving
   - **Source C** says: undernourishment is spreading.

5. Sources agree that meat was in short supply:
   - **Source B** says: we never saw a piece of meat for ages
   - **Source C** says: labourers had little meat.
   
   Sources agree that both sides were exhausted by the war:
   - **Source B** says: if it had gone on for many more months I don't know what would have happened to us.
   - **Source C** says: how long can it go on/our strength is spent.
   
   Sources agree that people had to survive on bread:
   - **Source B** says: and we ate it with bread
   - **Source C** says: labourers lived on dry bread.
   
   Sources disagree about the availability of potatoes:
   - **Source B** says: and cook them with potatoes (implies potatoes are readily available)
   - **Source C** says: potato supply has been insufficient.
   
   Only **Source B**: mentions that a mother did not eat to provide for her children
   Only **Source C**: mentions that food was rationed

## UNIT II – Context C: 1930s – 1960s

### Section A

1. The candidate assesses the importance of the Czech crisis in causing international tension using **evidence** such as:
   - importance of Sudeten defences to the Czech state
   - importance of Sudeten industry to the Czech economy
   - meetings between Chamberlain and Hitler
   - details of the Munich Agreement
   - Munich gave Hitler confidence and prestige
   - Munich made some people in Britain turn against appeasement.
   
   and other possible **evidence** such as:
   - German rearmament
   - the remilitarisation of the Rhineland
   - the Spanish Civil War
   - the Anschluss with Austria
   - the German takeover of Czechoslovakia, March 1939
   - the German attack on Poland, September 1939
   - Hitler began to pressurise Poland

2. The candidate describes Britain's decline using **evidence** such as:
   - size of British war debt/poor state of the British economy
   - Britain relied on US economic aid (the Marshall Plan)
   - Britain forced to withdraw from Suez in 1956
   - Britain no longer able to match armed forces of the USA or the Soviet Union
   - break up of the British Empire
   - need to establish new relationship with the Communist countries.

### Section B

3. The candidate makes a balanced evaluation of **Source A** using **evidence** such as:
   - contemporaneity: a primary source from the Second World War
   - authorship: produced by the British government
   - content: warning people to carry their gas masks
   - accuracy: consistent with other evidence, such as …
   - purpose: to keep people vigilant/encourage people to carry gas masks
   - limitation: does not mention other measures like black-outs or shelters.

4. The candidate discusses the attitude of **Source B** using **evidence** such as:
   - fairly positive view of the food supply situation
   - relief that food never ran out
   - content that it was fairly distributed
   - happy that some things were plentiful
   - reasonably happy that her diet was healthy
   - unhappy at lack of variety of food.

5. The candidate compares **Sources B** and **C** using **evidence** such as:
   
   Sources agree there was not enough food:
   - **Source B** says: food was scarce in Britain
   - **Source C** says: food shortages in Germany.
   
   Sources agree there was rationing in both countries:
   - **Source B** says: many things were rationed in Britain
   - **Source C** says: lots of items were rationed in Germany.
   
   Sources agree that you had to save to obtain some things in both countries:
   - **Source B** says: that you had to collect coupons to get a new dress or curtains in Britain
   - **Source C** says: that household goods and clothes were only available on a points system in Germany.
   
   Sources agree that efforts were made in both countries to share food properly:
   - **Source B** says: that a lot was done to distribute food fairly in Britain
   - **Source C** says: that food was shared fairly in Germany.
   
   Sources agree that it wasn't only food that was rationed:
   - **Source B** says: need coupons for dress/curtains
   - **Source C** says: household goods/clothes were only available on a points system.
   
   Only **Source B** refers to some foods being plentiful (in Britain).
   Only **Source B** names rationed food stuffs.
   Only **Source C** refers to price controls stopping inflation.

# History Credit Level 2006 (cont.)

UNIT III – Context A: USA 1850 – 1880

## Section A

1. (a) The candidate explains why conflict developed in America as a result of White attitudes towards Black slaves before 1860 using **evidence** such as:
    - conflict between North/South attitudes was a major cause of Civil War
    - by 1800 slavery ceased in N. states but firmly established in economy of the South
    - by 1860 4 million Black slaves on S. plantations; few in the North
    - slavery profitable in the South as cheap labour
    - Northerners resentful/feared spread into new territories
    - Abolitionists saw slavery as unjust (although few Northerners believed in equality)
    - Southerners uneasy at the threat of abolition affecting their lifestyles
    - Southerners uneasy at the threat of abolition reducing value of slaves
    - many Southern slave owners adopted cruel practices
    - some slave owners looked after their slaves well
    - many Southern slave owners justified use of slaves
    - many Southern slave owners were criticised by Northern abolitionists
    - revelation of slave cruelty (Uncle Tom's Cabin) alarmed many
    - some slaves adopted non-violent opposition
    - some slave uprisings/led to murder of many slaves
    - Underground Railway helped slaves to escape
    - runaway slaves hunted down/punished if caught
    - Lincoln's determination to stop the spread of slavery alarmed South.

    (b) The candidate explains why conflict developed in America as a result of White attitudes towards Native Americans after 1865 using **evidence** such as:
    - White Americans and Native Americans brought into conflict over use of the prairies
    - Native Americans wanted freedom to roam/hunt; White Americans wanted to farm
    - issue of the buffalo brought further conflict/Native Americans fought the Whites
    - Native Americans believed that Great Spirit had created land for their care
    - White Americans had a "property attitude" towards land
    - Manifest Destiny: belief in being able to settle land from Atlantic to Pacific
    - government encouraged White settlers/railway companies to move West
    - Peace Commission set up to remove obstacles to travelling West

1. (b)
    - many Americans favoured setting up reservations
    - Native Americans objected to reservation life/accommodation
    - White Americans wanted to develop the way west – railroads/confident of future
    - Native Americans saw numbers dwindle/alarm at possible extinction
    - Native Americans felt invaded and attacked wagon train homesteads
    - many Whites saw Native Americans as savages
    - White/Indian tensions led to atrocities/massacres/wars
    - Native Americans blamed Whites for introducing new diseases
    - White Agents of Federal Government were often not sympathetic
    - Native Americans often felt betrayed by their treatment/breach of promises
    - White Americans gained from Homestead Act of 1862
    - grants to gold mining companies further alarmed Native Americans
    - humanitarians wanted Native Americans treated with respect.

## Section B

2. The candidate assesses the completeness of **Source A** using **presented evidence** such as:
    - laws imposed severe restrictions on freedmen
    - it seemed that slavery was being maintained
    - prohibited right of freedmen to vote
    - freed slaves could only testify in court when it involved their own race
    - were obliged to sign a Labour Contract every year
    - could be punished if the contracts were broken.
   
   and **recalled evidence** such as:
    - freedmen prevented from carrying guns/using weapons
    - restrictions imposed on renting/owning land (in some states)
    - marriages recognised between freed slaves but not between freed slave and White
    - types of jobs limited to farming/domestic service
    - requirement for a licence to work at other jobs
    - the right to strike or leave employment denied
    - freedmen could not become government officials
    - detail(s) on punishments inflicted on freed slaves.

3. The candidate compares **Sources A** and **B** using **presented evidence** such as:
   Sources agree that Black Codes were restrictive:
    - **Source A** says: laws imposed severe restrictions
    - **Source B** says: Black Codes limited opportunities.
   
   Sources agree that the Black Codes restored slavery:
    - **Source A** says: many thought slavery was on the way back
    - **Source B** says: freedmen not much better off/believed laws were re-establishing slavery.

3. Sources agree that freedmen could not testify against Whites:
   - **Source A** says: freed slaves could testify only when their own race was involved
   - **Source B** says: freedmen were kept from giving evidence against Whites.

   Sources agree that freedmen were obliged to sign contracts:
   - **Source A** says: were obliged to sign a Labour Contract every year
   - **Source B** says: had to sign an annual binding agreement with their employer.

   Sources agree that freedmen could be punished for breach of contracts:
   - **Source A** says: punishments if the contracts were broken
   - **Source B** says: strict penalties if the terms were breached.

## UNIT III – Context B: India 1917 – 1947

### Section A

1. (a) The candidate explains the economic effects of British rule on India using **evidence** such as:
   - British control allowed economic "exploitation" to exist
   - natural resources exploited eg raw cotton
   - iron and steel industry was developed – but largely for British benefit
   - little other industry was developed
   - finished products were sold back to India, eg cotton goods
   - many Indians worked as house servants
   - salt tax imposed, caused hardship among the poor
   - British businessmen in positions of power
   - British interests were in charge of the railways
   - railways enabled speedy famine relief/supplied employment
   - roads and railways ran where the British wanted them/strategic ones
   - "Cotton roads," in Bombay and the Central Provinces designed to have access to the ports
   - imposition of taxation on Indians.

   (b) The candidate explains the political and social effects on India using **evidence** such as:
   - use of the English language (good and bad effects)
   - British maintenance of law and order/uniform system of justice
   - British policy of repression, imprisonment of Gandhi and Nehru
   - pampered existence of many British
   - British 'snobbery' towards the Indians
   - British ignored/critical of Indian culture
   - King of Britain was "Emperor of India"
   - Civil Service/government was in British control

1. (b)
   - very few Indians were in positions of responsibility in Civil Service
   - educational opportunities for Indians were limited
   - British and Indian army regiments were usually kept apart
   - Indian troops fought in WW1, WW2
   - British remained separate: clubs, manners, dress
   - British in charge of law and order.

### Section B

2. The candidate assesses the completeness of **Source A** using presented **evidence** such as:
   - widespread devastation/rioting
   - hundreds of people lying dead on the roadside
   - many fires burning
   - shops were looted
   - houses were burned down
   - "civilised" people (who knew the victim) were willing to use violence.

   and from **recalled evidence** such as:
   - called by Muslim League leader, Muhammad Ali Jinnah
   - won wide support from Muslims
   - started in Calcutta
   - Hindu and Muslim communities fought each other
   - four days of violence/ten days in Calcutta
   - some villages completely wiped out
   - large number of refugees
   - British army was stretched to limits to control violence
   - Gandhi attempted to end the violence
   - Indian army used to restore order.

3. The candidate assesses the agreement between **Sources A and B** using **presented evidence** such as:

   Sources agree that Direct Action/riots began in August (1946):
   - **Source A** says: that night of 15-16th August
   - **Source B** says: scenes took place in August.

   Sources agree that many people were killed:
   - **Source A** says: hundreds of people lying dead on the roadside
   - **Source B** says: many were killed/the streets were piled high with corpses.

   Sources agree that buildings/houses were on fire:
   - **Source A** says: still the fire burned all over the place, many houses were burned
   - **Source B** says: houses were burnt/a pall of smoke from burning houses hung over the city.

   Sources agree that many shops were looted:
   - **Source A** says: many shops were being looted
   - **Source B** says: shops were looted.

   Sources agree that rioters even attacked the old:
   - **Source A** says: an old washerman was beaten up
   - **Source B** says: rioters slaughtered the old.

   Sources agree that death figures are uncertain/imprecise:
   - **Source A** says: hundreds of people were lying dead
   - **Source B** says: it will never be known how many were killed.

   Only **Source B** says rioters targeted anyone/the young without restraint.

# History Credit Level 2006 (cont.)

UNIT III – Context C: Russia 1914 – 1941

## Section A

1. (a) The candidate fully explains the effects of Lenin's New Economic Policy using **evidence** such as:
   - kept government control of large industries
   - allowed private enterprise in small business
   - introduced worker bonuses/gave incentives to work
   - encouraged foreign investment
   - led to increased industrial production: steel; coal; iron
   - ended requisitioning of grain
   - led to more food being grown/reduced starvation
   - introduced fairer system of taxation in the countryside
   - made the Kulaks more numerous and richer
   - reduced discontent in Russia
   - made some Communists angry
   - restored stability to the currency (the rouble).

   (b) The candidate fully explains the effects of Stalin's Five Year Plans using **evidence** such as:
   - USSR was turned into a modern industrial state
   - production rose in electricity supply (through dams/hydro-electric schemes)
   - industrial production increased
   - dramatic increases in production of coal, oil and steel
   - new cities grew up
   - improvement in transport/communications (eg Moscow Underground)
   - introduction of new farm machinery/tractors
   - unemployment dropped
   - some improvement in education
   - some improvement in medical facilities
   - human suffering was terrible (strict discipline/use of secret police/slave labour)
   - labour camps were established
   - some disappointing results through inefficiency, waste, duplication of effort
   - wages fell
   - targets had to be met
   - Russia sold grain to pay for essential materials.

## Section B

2. The candidate assesses the completeness of **Source A** using **presented evidence** such as:
   - the army was in retreat
   - the situation did not improve when the Tsar took command
   - the soldiers were discontented
   - growing discontent in cities
   - less food grown/food was scarce in cities
   - prices were rising
   - people could not keep warm.

2. and **recalled evidence** such as:
   - the Tsar was seen as weak
   - the Tsar had no military knowledge or experience
   - the Tsarina had too much power
   - the Tsarina was seen as a German spy
   - Rasputin had too much influence/was murdered
   - frequent strikes
   - the army lacked modern equipment
   - injured soldiers got little medical help
   - the peasants were demanding more land
   - transport problems
   - discontent/protest encouraged Revolutionaries.

3. The candidate compares **Sources A** and **B** using **evidence** such as:
   Sources agree that soldiers were unhappy:
   - **Source A** says: that the soldiers' anger grew
   - **Source B** says: that unrest was growing in the army.
   
   Sources agree that many peasants were in the army:
   - **Source A** says: many young men had been conscripted into the army
   - **Source B** mentions: the mobilisation of so many peasants.
   
   Sources agree that there was not enough food in the cities:
   - **Source A** says: that food was short
   - **Source B** says: that there was a shortage of food.
   
   Sources agree that people suffered from the cold:
   - **Source A** says: that people found it hard to stay warm
   - **Source B** mentions: shortages of clothing and fuel.
   
   Sources agree that farms were not producing enough food:
   - **Source A** says: the peasants were growing less food
   - **Source B** says: that farms were lying derelict.
   
   Source agree that the problems had the potential for trouble:
   - **Source A** says: discontent arose
   - **Source B** says: trouble was brewing.
   
   Sources agree that there was discontent with the Tsar's rule:
   - **Source A** says: in cities, discontent rose
   - **Source B** says: Russia was not a contented country.

# UNIT III – Context D: Germany 1918 – 1939

## Section A

1. (a) The candidate explains the way in which Nazi policies affected young people in Germany using **evidence** such as:
   - young were encouraged to join Nazi youth groups from an early age
   - Pimpfen (6-10) Deutsch Jungfolk (10-14) Hitler Youth (14-18)
   - alternatives, eg Church youth groups, discouraged
   - Jewish children persecuted
   - girls and boys in separate groups
   - girls joined Jungmadel Bund (10-14) Bund Deutscher Madel (14-21)
   - 60% of all youth belonged by 1935
   - boys trained for war (military activities/sport/camping)
   - girls trained for motherhood (Kinder, Kirche, Kuche)
   - girls expected to wear appropriate dress
   - youth had to respect/obey/show loyalty to the Führer
   - pressures to conform could be threatening
   - indoctrination at school/emphasis on German history/biology
   - academic standards dropped; emphasis on sport/female subjects; less time for homework
   - some opposition groups: Edelweiss Pirates; Navajos; Swing movement
   - children used as informants
   - children taught to be anti-Semitic.

   (b) The candidate explains the way in which Nazi policies affected the Jews using **evidence** such as:
   - from 1933 Hitler used his power to persecute: Anti-Semitism was official policy
   - anti-Jewish propaganda: blamed for World War One/ Communism/economic ruin/contaminating "Master Race"
   - anti-Semitic education: pupils taught to be hostile to Jews; teachers humiliated Jewish children
   - from 1933 anti-Jewish laws/boycott of Jewish shops/doctors/lawyers/lecturers – dismissed
   - law for the Restoration of the Professional Civil Service banned Jews from government jobs
   - 1935 Jews forbidden to join the army
   - restrictions on opportunities for employment/education
   - civil liberties restricted: anti-Jewish signs displayed in shops/restaurants/cafes
   - 1935 Nuremberg Law for protection of German blood and honour: ban on marriage between Jews and non-Jews
   - sexual relations between Jews and non-Jews outside marriage – criminal/prison offence
   - 1935 National Law of Citizenship meant Jews lost citizenship – no vote/rights
   - 1938 government contracts only for Aryan firms
   - 1938 Only Aryan doctors were allowed to treat Aryan patients
   - 1938 All Jews had to take new first names – Israel and Sarah – adding to signatures
   - 1938 Kristallnacht and massive anti-Semitic campaign: Jewish homes/shops/synagogues destroyed; 100 killed/2000 arrested/sent to camps
   - 1933-39: way paved for Holocaust

## Section B

2. The candidate evaluates the completeness of **Source A** using **presented evidence** such as:
   - Weimar Republic blamed for war debt/Reparations
   - Weimar Republic associated with dishonourable Treaty of Versailles
   - Weimar Republic disgraced by French occupation of the Ruhr 1923
   - insecurity and suffering during period of inflation blamed on Weimar
   - measures taken by Weimar government to cope with the Depression, which followed the Wall St Crash, angered the majority of Germans.

   and **recalled evidence** such as:
   - Weimar government associated with Germany losing World War One
   - Conservatives and nationalists believed Weimar politicians were the "November Criminals"/stab in the back myth
   - left wing politicians felt betrayed by Weimar
   - proportional representation seemed to produce weak governments/disillusionment with democracy
   - appeared unable to stop violent outbreaks; breakdown of public order
   - Ruhr crisis – giving in to foreign powers
   - effects of hyperinflation in 1923
   - effects of 1929 Depression: unemployment rises
   - desire for strong government/dictatorship.

3. The candidate compares the views expressed in **Sources A** and **B** using **presented evidence** such as:
   Sources agree that Weimar's reputation suffered from signing the peace treaty:
   - **Source A** says: Weimar Republic was associated with the Versailles Treaty and its dishonour
   - **Source B** says: by signing the Treaty of Versailles the Republic was forever associated with it.

   Sources agree that the Republic inherited post war economic problems:
   - **Source A** says: economically Weimar was saddled with the war debts and reparations
   - **Source B** says: had been left with huge national debt and reparations from the war.

   Sources agree that Weimar was held responsible for inflation/hyperinflation:
   - **Source A** says: period of inflation was blamed on the Weimar government
   - **Source B** says: as hyperinflation set in, faith in Weimar was lost.

   Sources agree that failure to deal with the Depression affected Weimar:
   - **Source A** says: measures taken by the Weimar government to cope with the economic crisis alienated the majority of Germans
   - **Source B** says: unable to agree on measures to deal with the crisis, the government lost the support of the people.

   Sources agree that people began to turn away from the Republic:
   - **Source A** says: many looked for alternative solutions
   - **Source B** says: began to turn to other political parties.

   Only **Source A** mentions that Weimar had been disgraced by the Ruhr occupation in 1923.

# History General Level 2007

## Section A

### Unit I – Context A: 1750s – 1850s

1. The candidate describes what happened at Peterloo using **presented evidence** such as:
   - large numbers of people gathered for the meeting
   - the crowd marched in an orderly manner
   - people carried banners/sticks
   - Henry Hunt spoke to the crowd/appealed for them to be peaceful
   
   and **recalled evidence** such as:
   - bands led men, women and children from different areas
   - other speakers made more threatening speeches
   - magistrates claimed they read the Riot Act
   - the cavalry surrounded the platform
   - Hunt was seized
   - the cavalry charged/tried to disperse the crowd
   - eleven people were killed and hundreds wounded
   - estimates of crowd size vary from 30,000 – 153,000
   - generally thought to be around 50,000 – 80,000.

2. The candidate explains why it was harmful to children's health to work in cotton mills using **presented evidence** such as:
   - working in very hot temperatures is bad for health
   - not allowed to get a drink of water in hot conditions
   - air is full of harmful dust particles
   - children can become deformed
   
   and **recalled evidence** such as:
   - had to work very long hours
   - grew very tired
   - machines not fenced/accidents were frequent
   - strict discipline
   - badly treated/often beaten by overseers.

## Section B

3. The candidate evaluates Source C using evidence such as:
   - contemporaneity:
     a primary source written at the time (when towns were expanding rapidly)
   - authorship:
     eyewitness account; first hand experience of visiting patients
   - content:
     details of the living conditions of people in towns, e.g....
   - accuracy:
     matches candidate's own presented evidence, eg ...
   - purpose:
     to inform/draw attention to the terrible conditions people lived in
   - limitation:
     based on experience of one doctor/only applies to conditions in one town.

4. The candidate identifies evidence of agreement with the issue in Source C such as:
   - mother ill with fever
   - father had died of fever
   - sewage puddle on the floor would spread disease
   - children were starving.
   
   The candidate identifies evidence of disagreement with the issue in Source D such as:
   - family had a good two-roomed house
   - a wash house in the building/good washing facilities
   - mother was in excellent health
   - enjoyed a good diet/had meat several times a week.

5. The candidate comes to a conclusion on the issue using **presented evidence** as outlined above and recalled evidence such as:
   
   **For the issue**
   - serious overcrowding meant disease spread quickly
   - slum housing/no control over building of housing was bad for health
   - polluted water supply caused disease
   - poor sanitation/lack of drains, sewers, spread disease
   - bad air caused chest/breathing problems
   - sewage attracted vermin, e.g: flies, rats, which spread disease
   - regular epidemics of fatal diseases, eg cholera
   - streets seldom cleaned/dunghills next to houses spread disease
   - narrow streets meant little daylight and bad health
   - terrible working conditions in factories caused illness
   
   **Against the issue**
   - provided people with jobs/better wages to live off
   - tenements provided accommodation for many people
   - some tenement blocks were well looked after/provided good conditions
   - richer people lived in better/bigger houses, eg New Town of Edinburgh
   - new housing planned and built in towns and cities improved conditions
   - better medical facilities in towns.

## Unit I – Context B: 1830s – 1930s

### Section A

1. The candidate explains why working in a coal mine was harmful to children's health using **presented evidence** such as:
   - working long hours is bad for health
   - not getting much food to eat
   - working in wet conditions
   - possibility of dying young

   and **recalled evidence** such as:
   - details of health hazards from jobs done: trappers, putters etc
   - starting work at a very young age
   - often having to eat while working
   - dangers to life from: flooding; gas; cave-ins
   - deprivation of daylight/vitamin D
   - harsh discipline/being beaten
   - breathing in of coal dust/getting "black spit".

2. The candidate describes the militant tactics of Suffragettes using **presented evidence** such as:
   - planted bombs (or tried to)
   - disrupted meetings of/targeted politicians (Lloyd George)
   - threw stones/bricks
   - smashed car windows

   and **recalled evidence** such as:
   - disturbed the peace
   - resisted arrest
   - smashed windows of government buildings
   - threw stones through the windows of the Prime Minister's house
   - went on hunger strike
   - 1910 'Rush' on the House of Commons
   - arson attacks
   - slashing paintings
   - destruction of property/valuable items
   - acid poured on sports pitches/golf courses
   - sports pavilions/grandstands were attacked
   - letterboxes set on fire
   - Emily Wilding Davison's death on Derby Day.

### Section B

3. The candidate evaluates Source C using evidence such as:
   - contemporaneity:
     primary source written at the time (when Scotland's towns were growing)
   - authorship:
     eyewitness: a medical expert; first-hand experience of health and housing in Glasgow
   - content:
     details on size of houses; disease; death rate, e.g....
   - accuracy:
     matches candidate's own presented evidence, e.g....
   - purpose:
     to inform about effects of bad housing
   - limitation:
     one person's opinion/interpretation; refers to just one Scottish town at one particular time.

4. The candidate selects evidence of agreement with the issue from Source C such as:
   - small houses/overcrowding caused high death rate
   - children are especially vulnerable
   - 1 in 5 children born in one-room house dies before 1 year old
   - bad air causes lung disease
   - poor conditions cause bandy legs

   The candidate selects evidence of disagreement with the issue from Source D such as:
   - family had a good two-roomed house
   - a wash house in the building/good washing facilities
   - mother was in excellent health
   - enjoyed a good diet/had meat several times a week.

5. The candidate comes to a conclusion using **presented evidence** such as that given above and **recalled evidence** such as:

   **For the issue**
   - children contracted rickets
   - drinking water was often contaminated
   - bad conditions contributed to diseases such as cholera, typhus
   - shops sold contaminated food
   - sewerage was poor
   - no planning regulations until 1860 caused poor living conditions
   - street rubbish attracted vermin which spread disease
   - toilets were non existent or shared privies and thus unhealthy
   - factories provided poor working conditions and this caused illness
   - damp conditions caused health problems

   **Against the issue**
   - urban middle class had better homes which reduced illnesses
   - growth of suburbs provided good housing which reduced illnesses
   - railways brought better diets
   - gas/electricity was gradually introduced and improved health
   - Public Health Acts improved the situation
   - MOHs insisted on improved sanitation
   - 1875 Artisans Dwelling Act helped to remove slums
   - Municipal Reform Acts improved streets/water supply

# History General Level 2007 (cont.)

## Unit I – Context C: 1880s – Present Day

### Section A

1. The candidate explains why trade unions grew from 1880 – 1914 using **presented evidence** such as:
   - to improve working conditions
   - to represent/incorporate skilled craftsmen
   - to protect unskilled workers
   - to improve standards of living
   - to increase wages
   
   and **recalled evidence** such as:
   - to get shorter hours
   - to get longer holidays
   - unions got better organised
   - many more unions were formed
   - Scottish and English unions joined forces
   - women joined unions
   - women formed their own unions
   - industrial action increased
   - unions became involved in politics
   - National Union of Miners, Transport Workers and Railwaymen formed
   - Triple Industrial Alliance in 1914 encouraged growth
   - were successful in getting better conditions for workers.

2. The candidate describes the militant tactics of Suffragettes using **presented evidence** such as:
   - planted bombs (or tried to)
   - disrupted meetings of/targeted politicians (Lloyd George)
   - threw stones/bricks
   - smashed car windows
   
   and **recalled evidence** such as:
   - disturbed the peace
   - resisted arrest
   - smashed windows of government buildings
   - threw stones through the windows of the Prime Minister's house
   - went on hunger strike
   - 1910 'Rush' on the House of Commons
   - arson attacks
   - slashing paintings
   - destruction of property/valuable items
   - acid poured on sports pitches/golf courses
   - sports pavilions/grandstands were attacked
   - letterboxes set on fire
   - Emily Wilding Davison's death on Derby Day.

### Section B

3. The candidate evaluates Source C using evidence such as:
   - contemporaneity:
     primary source written at the time (when Scotland's towns were growing)
   - authorship:
     eyewitness: a medical expert; first-hand experience of health and housing in Glasgow
   - content:
     details on size of houses; disease; death rate
   - accuracy:
     matches candidate's own presented evidence, eg …
   - purpose:
     to inform about effects of bad housing
   - limitation:
     one person's opinion/interpretation; refers to just one Scottish town at one particular time.

4. The candidate selects evidence of agreement with the issue from Source C such as:
   - small houses/overcrowding caused high death rate
   - children are especially vulnerable
   - 1 in 5 children born in one-room house dies before 1 year old
   - bad air causes lung disease
   - poor conditions cause bandy legs
   
   The candidate selects evidence of disagreement with the issue from Source D such as:
   - by 1939 city life had improved a little
   - Housing Acts forced authorities to demolish slums
   - city parks provided fresh air
   - council housing estates provided cleaner, healthier environment.

5. The candidate comes to a conclusion using **presented evidence** as above and from **recalled evidence** such as:
   
   **For the issue**
   - detail of life in a single end/tenement
   - drinking water was often contaminated
   - bad conditions contributed to diseases such as cholera, typhus
   - shops sold contaminated food
   - sewerage was poor
   - lack of daylight caused rickets
   - weak/poorly enforced planning regulations caused poor living conditions
   - houses were cheaply built
   - street rubbish attracted vermin
   - toilets were non-existent or shared privies
   - factories provided poor working conditions
   - lack of free medical care
   - some council estates built on poor land/next to gas works
   - problem families put into some areas
   - damp conditions caused health problems

## 5. (continued)

**Against the issue**
- urban middle class had better homes (suburbs)
- growth of suburbs provided good housing
- gas/electricity was gradually introduced
- fresh, piped water made cities cleaner
- Public Health Acts improved the situation
- MOHs insisted on improved sanitation
- Municipal Reform Acts improved streets
- municipal baths/wash-houses were provided
- details of improved conditions in council houses

(possible answers on Liberal Reforms; discovery of germs; improvements in working conditions)

## Unit II – Context A: 1790s – 1820s

### Section A

1. The candidate explains why British sailors were unhappy with life in Nelson's navy using **presented evidence** such as:
   - they endured dreadful conditions
   - pay had not increased in 150 years
   - deductions were made from their wages
   - ships' surgeons lacked skill
   
   and **recalled evidence** such as:
   - did not receive full value of wages/use of ticket system
   - bad quality of provisions (weevils/maggots in biscuits)
   - water supplies were often polluted
   - poor accommodation on board
   - disease (scurvy) was common
   - severe discipline enforced
   - harsh punishments
   - no official leave
   - desertion carried the death penalty
   - some had been press ganged
   - sailors were often commanded by young midshipmen.

2. The candidate assesses the importance of the Congress System using **presented evidence** such as:
   - not effective after 1827
   - established notion of settling disputes by agreement
   - held important conferences
   - helped to prevent major war for 40 years
   
   and **recalled evidence** such as:
   - found it hard to overcome issues of nationalism
   - British support became lukewarm
   - France was invited to cooperate after 1818
   - agreement was reached on protection of Jews
   - further successes included issue of Swedish debts in Denmark/treatment of Napoleon
   - divisions continued regarding intervention in internal disputes: revolts in Spain; Piedmont; Naples; Spanish colonies.

### Section B

3. The candidate evaluates Source C using evidence such as:
   - contemporaneity:
     primary source produced at the time (of Revolutionary Wars)
   - authorship:
     drawn by a cartoonist during Revolutionary Wars/with first-hand knowledge
   - content:
     shows detail of effects of the wars: high prices/lower wages
   - accuracy:
     cartoon has elements of exaggeration
   - purpose:
     to criticise the effects of the war/government action
   - limitation:
     one cartoonist's view doesn't show other effects of the war.

4. The candidate compares Sources C and D using evidence such as:
   Sources agree that there were high prices:
   **Source C** shows: price of basic foodstuffs
   **Source D** says: increased prices for bread/other food
   Sources agree that bread was particularly expensive:
   **Source C** shows: price of bread/butcher offering meat as a substitute
   **Source D** says: increased prices for bread
   Sources agree that wages were low:
   **Source C** shows: low wages for craftsmen
   **Source D** says: wages stayed low
   Only **Source D** mentions unemployment
   Only **Source D** says farmers benefited

5. The candidate assesses the completeness of Source E using **presented evidence** such as:
   - France was invaded
   - troops were conscripted
   - married men were forced to work
   - women had to work for the war effort
   - even children were involved
   - shortages of bandages
   
   and **recalled evidence** such as:
   - effects of British blockade
   - high food prices
   - food shortages
   - inflation/money lost value
   - assignats became worthless
   - effects of the Reign of Terror
   - wages kept low by law
   - rebellions against government (Girondins)
   - worry at war losses
   - rise of crime.

# History General Level 2007 (cont.)

## Unit II – Context B: 1890s – 1920s

### Section A

1. The candidate explains why soldiers were unhappy with life in the trenches using **presented evidence** such as:
   - mud was waist deep/soaked your boots
   - had to use a mess tin to bale out water
   - trench foot was disabling/toes nearly rotted off
   - you could catch trench fever

   and **recalled evidence** such evidence as:
   - rats were endemic
   - lice made life uncomfortable
   - weather could be extremely warm
   - lack of clean drinking water
   - food was monotonous
   - letters censored – post interrupted
   - daytime mostly boring, despite the constant dangers of trench life
   - latrines had to be cleaned
   - barbed wire had to be repaired
   - dangers of being shot/gassed
   - impact of seeing friends wounded or killed.

2. The candidate assesses how successful the League of Nations was in solving the world's problems using **presented evidence** such as:
   - solved various border squabbles during the 1920s
   - solved dispute over Aaland islands
   - improved people's lives

   and **recalled evidence** such as:
   - persuaded Serbia to remove troops from Albania
   - arbitrated over Mosul
   - helped in the Greece-Bulgaria dispute
   - arbitrated in 1923 Corfu incident
   - arbitrated in Silesian situation
   - created international port of Memel
   - chaired Kellogg Briand Pact
   - monitored British and French rule in ex German and Turkish colonies
   - established Health Organisation
   - international Labour Organisation established
   - legal disputes between countries to be established in Holland
   - attempt was made to stop drug smuggling
   - Nansen Passports helped solve the refugee problem
   - returned approximately 400,000 soldiers to their homes/P.O.W.s returned
   - campaigned against slavery/freed slaves in British-owned Sierra Leone
   - encouraged and promoted the Red Cross
   - fought the trade in young women and children
   - fought against leprosy and malaria

2. (continued)

   **BUT**
   - was seriously weakened without several leading countries/USA, Russia, Germany not members
   - dominated by Britain and France, many members resented this
   - international disputes continued
   - some member countries ignored League rulings
   - largely failed to get disarmament in the 1920s
   - no effective way of enforcing decisions
   - lack of its own army
   - needed decisions to be unanimous.

### Section B

3. The candidate evaluates Source C using evidence such as:
   - contemporaneity:
     primary source produced at the time (of the First World War)
   - authorship:
     official government poster
   - content:
     shows women as nurses/gives other possible occupations and destinations, e.g….
   - accuracy:
     many thousands of women did volunteer as nurses
   - purpose:
     to encourage women to help the war effort
   - limitation:
     only gives a few occupations employing women during the war/omits e.g….

4. The candidate assesses agreement between Sources C and D using evidence such as:
   Sources agree that women joined the Voluntary Aid Detachment:
   **Source C** shows: a poster encouraging women to join the VAD
   **Source D** says: the Voluntary Aid Detachment was an organisation set up to help the sick and wounded.
   Sources agree that women worked as nurses:
   **Source C** shows: three female nurses
   **Source D** says: women became nurses.
   Sources agree that women had the opportunity to work outside of Britain:
   **Source C** lists: various possible destinations abroad
   **Source D** says: some of these women had a chance to work abroad
   Only **Source C**: lists other occupations they did
   Only **Source D**: mentions the fact that women volunteered for unpaid work
   Only **Source D**: says they worked in military hospitals/army bases in Britain.

5. The candidate assesses the completeness of Source E using **presented evidence** such as:
   - people started to keep an allotment to grow food
   - the amount of farming land increased
   - contribution of the Women's Land Army
   
   and **recalled evidence** such as:
   - Prisoners of War and conscientious objectors were used to produce food
   - parks and tennis courts turned into vegetable plots
   - rationing was introduced for certain foodstuffs from 1917
   - substitute foods were used
   - posters discouraged people from wasting food
   - game such as rabbit was eaten, especially by country dwellers
   - food was eaten from the wild: crab apples; brambles; chestnuts
   - British Summer Time was introduced to give longer daylight hours
   - black market existed for those who could afford it
   - standard bread (using flour mixed with powdered potatoes/beans)
   - people had to queue to get some foods
   - on occasions food lorries hijacked.

## Unit II – Context C: 1930s – 1960s

### Section A

1. The candidate explains why Britain was less powerful after 1945 using **presented evidence** such as:
   - Britain was poorer than in 1939
   - war had cost a lot of money
   - war dug deep into the country's savings
   - great deal of the nation's trade had been lost
   - two new giants in 1945 were the USSR and the USA
   
   and **recalled evidence** such as:
   - it owed money to other countries, especially USA
   - it gave up much of its Empire, especially India
   - its armed forces, especially the Navy, had to be reduced
   - initially, it was not an atomic power like the USA
   - it had to rebuild its social and economic infrastructure
   - it was slow to join the reconstruction of mainland Europe
   - much of the old Empire and other areas looked to the USA
   - loss of confidence as world power.

2. The candidate assesses how successful the UN was as peacekeeper using **presented evidence** such as:
   - United Nations has not always succeeded in preventing conflicts
   - has provided a place for discussions
   - peacekeeping forces have limited minor wars
   - prevented escalation of trouble in Cyprus
   
   and **recalled evidence** such as:
   - USA/USSR and their interests have dominated the UNO
   - UNO also has other roles with UNESCO/refugees/human rights
   - UNO also has other roles with education/WHO/justice
   - part played in Korean War 1950-53
   - role in Berlin crises
   - role in Cuban crisis
   - were many major wars in which it had no influence: Vietnam
   - failed in many peacekeeping zones eg Middle East/Congo
   - effective use of sanctions against some countries
   - some success in many peacekeeping zones, e.g. Suez 1956
   - has been at the mercy of other International Alliances
   - lack of trust/quarrels at UN Debates/Great Power Vetoes.

### Section B

3. The candidate evaluates Source C using evidence such as:
   - contemporaneity:
     primary source produced at the time (of World War II)
   - authorship:
     official government poster
   - content:
     shows a woman working on a farm
   - purpose:
     to encourage women to join the Land Army
   - accuracy:
     agrees with other evidence, e.g. other female employment/many women did join Land Army
   - limitation:
     omits details on other war work done by women, e.g.... .

4. The candidate assesses disagreement between Sources C and D using evidence such as:
   Sources disagree over the enjoyment of war work:
   **Source C** shows: the woman is happy and smiling
   **Source D** says: not what we had looked forward to
   Sources disagree over the conditions in which women worked:
   **Source C** shows: the weather appears to be dry and warm
   **Source D** says: bitterly cold day
   Sources disagree over the type of work done by women:
   **Source C** shows: the woman is working easily with a horse

# History General Level 2007 (cont.)

### 4. (continued)

**Source D** says: we tried to kick parsnips out of the frozen earth
Sources disagree over the clothing provided to work on a farm:
**Source C** shows: the woman is well dressed
**Source D** says: a female colleague wearing an old, long coat
Sources agree that women joined the Land Army:
**Source C** says: join the Women's Land Army
**Source D** says: we both joined the Land Army

5. The candidate assesses the completeness of Source E using **presented evidence** such as:
   - people in towns had to be very careful not to show lights
   - cars drove without lights
   - house windows had to be screened with dark material
   - wardens had to patrol/spot illegal lights
   - bombs were dropped on towns/cities

   and **recalled evidence** such as:
   - extensive damage was caused
   - many people were killed/injured
   - anti aircraft guns were used against bombers
   - air raid shelters were built
   - underground stations were used as shelters
   - Anderson/Morrison shelters were built
   - morale of civilians was affected
   - many children had to be evacuated/separated from parents
   - injuries were caused by accidents in Blackout
   - fears of gas attacks
   - white lines painted on roadside
   - no street lights.

## Unit III – Context A: USA 1850 – 1880

### Section A

1. The candidate explains why slavery was opposed using **presented evidence** such as:
   - many subject to many rules and regulations/had no freedom
   - discipline was harsh
   - slave families often broken up/separated
   - slaves unable to visit family/friends in other plantations

   and **recalled evidence** such as:
   - slaves could be bought and sold
   - slaves worked long hours at hard work
   - whipping was common
   - runaway slaves were beaten/maimed
   - slaves needed permission to get married
   - slave marriages had no legal status
   - slave owners often named slave children
   - female slaves were sometimes sexually abused by owners/overseers
   - children born to a slave, fathered by a white owner were still slaves
   - pregnant slaves were expected to work until the child was born.

2. The candidate describes what happened at Fort Sumter using **presented evidence** such as:
   - General Beauregard demanded surrender of the fort
   - Major Anderson offered to leave (once supplies were exhausted)
   - Anderson's offer was rejected

   and **recalled evidence** such as:
   - Confederate troops opened fire
   - the fort was bombarded for 34 hours
   - the fort was severely damaged
   - Anderson was forced to surrender the fort
   - the 'battle' was bloodless – no lives lost
   - Anderson evacuated his men (by steamer to New York).

### Section B

3. The candidate assesses the attitude of Mrs Platt in Source C using **presented evidence** such as:
   - negative attitude to Reconstruction/refers to "terrible" days
   - angry that she could not raise hogs/feed livestock
   - upset that everything had gone to ruin
   - annoyed that there were no African Americans to work the farm
   - blames carpetbaggers for encouraging African American crime.

4. The candidate assesses the completeness of Source D using **presented evidence** such as:
   - Black Codes virtually preserved slavery
   - Black Codes imposed restrictions
   - homeless African Americans could be fined/sold into service
   - African Americans did get new rights

   and **recalled evidence** such as:
   - excellent work of the Freedmen's Bureau
   - other examples of Black Code restrictions
   - African Americans could not own farms
   - examples of White people treating African Americans as inferior/White people often gave African Americans the worst jobs
   - armed gangs stopped African Americans voting
   - Ku Klux Klan activities: lynchings; schools burned; murders; beatings
   - Jim Crow Laws: bans on inter-marriage, segregation.

## Unit III – Context B: India 1917 – 1947

### Section A

1. The candidate explains why Britain wanted to keep control of India using **presented evidence** such as:
   - India was Britain's most important colony
   - India was a huge market for British goods
   - India sent Britain a lot of cheap food
   
   and **recalled evidence** such as:
   - India provided good jobs in the civil service and army
   - examples of Indian foods sent to Britain
   - India bought a lot of British cotton
   - India provided vital raw materials like cotton
   - India provided Britain with many soldiers.

2. The candidate describes the British control of India using **presented evidence** such as:
   - 1500 British administrators ran the Civil Service
   - 3000 British officers were in charge of the army
   - Indians were given no/little power/say
   
   and **recalled evidence** such as:
   - Indians regarded as inferior
   - British determined and levied taxes
   - British lawyers/judges in charge of courts
   - controlled education
   - British businessmen in positions of power
   - British interests in charge of railways
   - Indian natural resources exploited
   - British used 'divide and rule' tactics
   - passed repressive laws – Rawlett Act
   - used violent repression: Amritsar.

### Section B

3. The candidate identifies the attitude of Muhammad Ali Jinnah in Source C using **presented evidence** such as:
   - supported partition/opposed to a united India
   - convinced Hindus and Muslims cannot live together
   - certain keeping India as one country will cause discontent
   - believes a united India will be destroyed by the tension.

4. The candidate assesses the completeness of Source D using **presented evidence** such as:
   - millions of people became refugees
   - Muslims fled to Pakistan
   - Hindus fled to India
   - the two parts of Pakistan were divided by India
   
   and **recalled evidence** such as:
   - refugee camps established
   - many refugees suffered from bad weather and food shortages
   - lots of killings/massacres
   - settlement of refugees caused huge problems
   - violence claimed life of Gandhi
   - special problems in Bengal.

## Unit III – Context C: Russia 1914 – 1941

### Section A

1. The candidate explains why many Russians disliked being ruled by the Tsar using **presented evidence** such as:
   - he was weak/controlled by his wife
   - his wife was German
   - the system gave the Tsar too much power
   - the army continued to do badly under his leadership
   
   and **recalled evidence** such as:
   - favoured family members
   - dislike of the Tsar's autocracy
   - his wife was seen as a German spy
   - many disliked Rasputin's influence
   - the Duma was undemocratic and weak
   - policy of repression
   - discontent among the armed forces
   - effects of the First World War on Russian civilians, e.g. severe shortages
   - heavy loss of soldiers.

2. The candidate describes the Bolshevik takeover using **presented evidence** such as:
   - key points in Petrograd were seized
   - bridges, railway stations and government offices were taken over by the Bolsheviks
   - capture of the Winter Palace
   
   and **recalled evidence** such as:
   - most Government troops melted away
   - weapons taken from government fortress
   - capture of banks, printers and power stations
   - Kerensky fled Petrograd
   - use of the cruiser Aurora
   - members of the Provisional Government arrested.

### Section B

3. The candidate assesses the completeness of Source C using **presented evidence** such as:
   - war weariness – 7 years of war
   - worst ever famine
   - food shortages in cities/cities had been abandoned
   - steel/coal production dropped
   
   and **recalled evidence** such as:
   - financial dislocation/inflation
   - transport was not working properly
   - farm production was down
   - crime was common
   - disease was widespread
   - free speech was not allowed.

4. The candidate identifies the attitude of the authors in Source D using **presented evidence** such as:
   - is against War Communism
   - unhappy workers don't control the factories
   - upset workers can't choose where to work
   - annoyed workers can't choose their work
   - angry at severe punishment of critics of War Communism.

# History General Level 2007 (cont.)

Unit III – Context D: Germany 1918 – 1939

## Section A

1. The candidate explains why the Germans hated the Treaty of Versailles, using **presented evidence** such as:
   - left Germany torn and tattered/badly damaged Germany
   - Germany wasn't allowed a say in the Treaty
   - she had lost German land
   - the peace was unacceptable/harsh

   and **recalled evidence** such as:
   - Germany was blamed for starting the war
   - felt it humiliated Germany
   - called it a 'Diktat': a dictated peace
   - armed forces were greatly reduced
   - argued it wasn't based on Wilson's Fourteen Points, e.g. no self-determination
   - examples of land lost
   - some Germans now lived under foreign rule
   - made to pay reparations
   - took away all Germany's overseas colonies
   - Allies ignored all German protests
   - with the Kaiser gone, Germans didn't believe they should be punished.

2. The candidate describes what happened during the Spartacist rising using **presented evidence** such as:
   - launched an uprising in Berlin
   - tried to overthrow Ebert/Provisional Government
   - Ebert used the Freikorps against the Spartacists
   - Freikorps violently/brutally/crushed the Spartacists

   and **recalled evidence** such as:
   - Spartacists seized public buildings
   - Government called for a general strike
   - Spartacists built barricades in the streets
   - role of Noske (Defence Minister)
   - hundreds of Spartacists killed
   - Freikorps regained control of other cities
   - Spartacist leaders Karl Liebknecht and Rosa Luxemburg were both killed.

## Section B

3. The candidate assesses the completeness of Source C using **presented evidence** such as:
   - Protestant churches pressured into forming a Reich Church
   - hundreds of Confessional Church ministers arrested
   - many put in concentration camps
   - youth organisation shut down

   and **recalled evidence** such as:
   - intimidated by Nazi/Hitler's threats
   - appointed a Nazi as Reich Bishop
   - censorship in press and radio
   - secret police used against them

3. (continued)
   - leader of Confessional Church, Martin Neimoller, arrested and imprisoned
   - Protestant youth movement taken over by Hitler Youth
   - Nazis signed Concordat with Catholic Church
   - Catholic Church agreed not to interfere in politics
   - Catholic bishops swore oath of loyalty to Hitler
   - Catholic church schools shut down
   - priests arrested and put in concentration camps
   - church property damaged
   - ministers and priests attacked
   - Jehovah's Witnesses imprisoned for refusing to fight.

4. The candidate identifies the attitude of the Confessional Church in Source D towards the Nazi Government using **presented evidence** such as:
   - critical of the Nazis/anti-Nazi
   - accuses Nazis of interfering in Church affairs
   - angry at Nazi ban on church youth organisation
   - alarmed at reduced Christian influence in media
   - ashamed about concentration camps.

# History Credit Level 2007

## UNIT I – Context A: 1750s – 1850s

### Section A

1. The candidate explains why the population of Scotland increased between 1750 and 1820, using evidence such as:
   - fall in the death rate: decrease in infant mortality/healthier mothers meant healthier babies
   - increase in the birth rate/earlier marriages led to larger families
   - some better housing eg New Town, model villages
   - better hygiene/greater use of soap
   - cheaper cotton led to cleaner clothes
   - advances in medical knowledge
   - some diseases disappeared, eg plague, malaria
   - farming improvements led to a better diet
   - no famines
   - immigration from Ireland
   - vaccination prevented disease.

2. The candidate describes housing in the countryside in the late 18th century using evidence such as:
   - most cottages were just hovels/huts
   - few rooms which tended to be small
   - built of stone or turf
   - thatch or turf roof
   - had earth/dirt floors which made houses damp and cold
   - low walls seldom more than 1.8 metres high
   - tended to be single storey
   - cooking done in open fire in middle of floor
   - chimney just a hole in the roof
   - inside of house tended to be dark and smoky
   - windows small, often unglazed
   - very little furniture apart from chests, stools and a dresser
   - sanitation poor or non-existent
   - accommodation often shared with animals
   - poorly ventilated
   - single, male workers lived in bothies
   - landlords lived in mansions or castles
   
   But
   - not all Lowland housing was poor
   - Improvers built substantial houses
   - built of stone and slate
   - wooden or stone floors
   - glass in windows
   - had fireplaces and chimneys
   - had other amenities such as barns for animals.

### Section B

3. The candidate evaluates the usefulness of Source A using evidence such as:
   contemporaneity:
   primary source written at the time of great change in agriculture
   authorship:
   official report; written by an eyewitness/a reputable minister
   content:
   details on the impact of the agricultural revolution, e.g....
   accuracy:
   matches other evidence presented by candidate, e.g....
   purpose:
   to inform people about changes in the countryside
   limitation:
   only refers to Inverkeithing/may be different elsewhere in Scotland.

4. The candidate identifies evidence from the sources for the issue such as:
   **Source A**
   - most available land was cultivated
   - wasteland was reclaimed
   - farmers given long leases
   
   **Source B**
   - better wages for remaining labourers
   - those remaining in countryside enjoyed a better standard of living
   
   **Source C**
   - landlords got higher rents.
   
   The candidate identifies evidence from the sources against the issue such as:
   **Source A**
   - loss of pasture
   - loss of common land
   - high rents
   
   **Source B**
   - many people driven away from the countryside/encouraged emigration
   - many cottages destroyed/workers evicted who were no longer needed
   - Small's plough halved the number of men needed to cultivate the land
   
   **Source C**
   - many farmers lost their farms and became farm/day labourers
   - no work for many day labourers
   - more people relied on the parish for help
   - great increase in poverty/poor families.

# History Credit Level 2007 (cont.)

5. The candidate offers a balanced conclusion on the issue using **presented evidence** such as that given in answer 4 and **recalled evidence** such as:
   **For the issue:**
   - new farm machinery meant that work could be done more quickly/easily; labour costs fell
   - more food was produced for Scotland/to feed workers in urban areas
   - ending of famines
   - abolition of balks released more land
   - long leases gave incentive to improve
   - allowed farmers to introduce new methods on farms, e.g. new crops and selective breeding
   - better yields – produced more/better crops
   - enclosure provided short-term work fencing and building
   - made it easier for farmers to run farms
   - many tenant farmers became rich
   - Scottish lairds got wealthier
   - increased wealth helped to improve standard of living: housing, clothing etc
   - emigration was beneficial for some
   
   and **Against the issue**:
   - some areas especially in the Highlands, experienced few benefits
   - wages dropped for some workers
   - farm labourers forced to move to find work in dirty mill towns
   - some Scots villages became deserted
   - many Scots reduced to begging
   - families ties were broken
   - some farm machinery could lead to accidents.

## UNIT I – Context B: 1830s – 1930s

### Section A

1. The candidate explains reasons for the population of Scotland growing between 1830 and 1920's using evidence such as:
   - increased birth rate (until 1870s)
   - early marriages led to larger families
   - decrease in the death rate, especially infant mortality
   - improvements in medicine eg use of anaesthetics
   - better understanding of the causes of disease – use of antiseptics
   - better training for doctors/better hospitals
   - improved personal hygiene/use of soap
   - cleaner water supply
   - improved sanitation, eg drains and sewers
   - better housing/slums demolished/less overcrowding
   - immigration, eg Irish
   - improved/healthier diet
   - disappearance of killer epidemics, eg smallpox, cholera
   - rising standard of living/higher wages
   - better cotton clothing.

2. The candidate describes housing in the countryside in the late 19th century using evidence such as:
   - improvements had been made but much poor housing still remained
   - some cottages were just hovels/huts
   - few rooms/tended to be small
   - built of stone or turf
   - thatch or turf roof
   - earth/dirt floors which made houses damp and cold
   - tended to be single storey
   - cooking done on open fire
   - chimney just a hole in the roof
   - inside of house tended to be damp and smoky
   - lighting was still oil-based
   - few had indoor/flush toilets
   - accommodation still shared with animals in some areas
   - poorly ventilated
   - single, male workers lived in basic bothies/chaumers
   
   **But**
   - considerable improvement had been made
   - Improvers built substantial houses
   - some houses had a second storey added
   - more built of stone and brick
   - slate was replacing thatch roofs
   - wooden or stone floors
   - glass in windows
   - had fireplaces and chimneys
   - running water being installed
   - flush toilets/septic tanks beginning to be installed
   - kitchen equipment/ranges were also improving
   - had other amenities such as barns for animals.

### Section B

3. The candidate evaluates the usefulness of Source A using evidence such as:
   contemporaneity:
   primary source from the period when railways were being built
   authorship:
   eyewitness account; first-hand experience of someone involved in building railways
   content:
   details of how railways impacted on an area, e.g.…
   accuracy:
   matches other evidence as demonstrated by candidate, e.g.…
   purpose:
   to relate his experiences of the difficulties involved in railway development
   limitation:
   experience of just one man, in one situation/does not give a balanced account.

4. The candidate selects evidence for the issue from the sources such as:
   **Source A**
   - supplied cheap travel
   
   **Source B**
   - reduced transport costs
   - encouraged competition in business/trade/manufacturing
   - brought prices of some goods down/brought in cheaper clothing
   
   **Source C**
   - new railway hotels were built/with modern facilities
   - industries in Inverurie benefited.
   
   The candidate selects evidence against the issue, such as:
   **Source A**
   - cheap travel brought together an objectionable variety of people
   - railways would frighten grouse
   - 'floaters' would no longer be required
   
   **Source B**
   - local manufacturers suffered/loss of monopoly/prices dropped
   - employment for some became less certain
   - traditional (Kinross) industries suffered/went out of business
   
   **Source C**
   - navvies caused alarm
   - other transport (coaching) was affected
   - coaching inns closed down.

5. The candidate reaches a balanced conclusion using **presented evidence** such as that given in answer 4 and **recalled evidence** such as:
   **For the issue**:
   - coal industry benefited
   - agriculture benefited
   - newspaper industry benefited
   - specialised industries (eg Dundee jam) had a nationwide market
   - new employment opportunities: on the railways; building railways
   - iron and steel industries were boosted
   - tourist trade was boosted
   - opportunities for travel/holidays/commuting
   - fresh food could be delivered quicker
   - fishermen could transport fresh fish
   - mail/newspapers could be delivered
   - standardised time adopted
   
   and **Against the issue**:
   - stage coaches became obsolete
   - canal industry declined
   - road engineers lost jobs
   - toll operators were affected
   - landscape/countryside was affected/blighted
   - farmers were worried about effect on livestock
   - complaints about Sunday travel
   - some doctors feared effects on health.

## UNIT I – Context C: 1880s – Present Day

### Section A

1. The candidate explains the reasons for the growth in Scotland's population between 1880 and 1939 using evidence such as:
   - increased birth rate: earlier marriages led to larger families
   - fewer women died in childbirth
   - contraception not widely available
   - decline in infant mortality
   - increased life expectancy
   - rising living standards: more money for food
   - improved diet: better farming/trade/transport
   - impact of Liberal Welfare Reforms: free school meals; medical inspection: pensions
   - improved public health: clean water; sewers
   - better housing: demolition of slums/new council houses
   - improved domestic facilities in houses
   - improvements in hygiene: soap; disinfectant; personal cleanliness
   - medical improvements: X rays; vaccinations; antibiotics; new medicines
   - better medical facilities: hospital staff; improved surgery; new equipment
   - cures/preventions for childhood diseases: TB; polio; measles
   - killer epidemics disappeared: cholera; typhoid; diphtheria; smallpox
   - National Insurance Act: free medical care for workers
   - immigration from abroad, eg Ireland, Poland, Italy.

2. The candidate describes rural housing conditions using evidence such as:
   - but and ben housing
   - farm-workers' rows/many cottages badly built/earth floors
   - miners' rows – variable in quality
   - few rooms to a house: overcrowding common
   - some houses with no piped/running water; proper bath; mains drainage
   - some cottages lit by oil/paraffin
   - piped water/inside toilets were slowly being introduced
   - electricity was slowly being installed by 1930
   - beaten earth floors being replaced by stone/wood
   - slate tiles replacing thatch/some rural housing still thatched
   - from 1920s council housing was being built in rural towns and villages
   - some crofters houses in the islands still of the 'black house' type
   - some Highland and Island dwellings still with peat fire in centre of room
   - some dwellings with low doors, no/few windows; shared with livestock
   - existence of bothies/chaumers – mostly for single men
   - bothy life was basic: built in wooden beds; kist for belongings.

## History Credit Level 2007 (cont.)

### Section B

3. The candidate evaluates the usefulness of Source A using evidence such as:
   contemporaneity:
   primary source from post-war period/when yards were forced to close down
   authorship:
   eyewitness account; first hand experience
   content:
   information on the decline of shipbuilding, e.g....
   accuracy:
   matches other evidence as demonstrated by candidate, e.g....
   purpose:
   to give his own views of causes of shipyard decline
   limitation:
   management view/one person's view/not a balanced opinion.

4. The candidate selects evidence for the issue from the sources such as:
   **Source A**
   - in other countries one man worked four machines
   - in Britain one man worked one machine/took longer
   
   **Source B**
   - only yards which adopted modern technology survived
   
   **Source C**
   - Britain's rivals modernised/introduced latest technology
   - British yards were slow to adopt new technology.
   
   The candidate selects evidence against the issue such as:
   **Source A**
   - Trade Union attitudes to progress regrettable/British shipyard workers objected to automatic machinery/new technology
   - collapse of shipbuilding was the fault of trade unions
   
   **Source B**
   - British government gave less encouragement/fewer subsidies than others
   - industrial relations between men and management were poor
   - frequent disputes/stoppages led to late deliveries
   - Britain/Scotland's reputation as a shipbuilder was damaged
   - Even yards that introduced new technology (Yarrow's) laid off men
   
   **Source C**
   - World slump after World War Two
   - industrial disputes resulted in strikes
   - demarcation disputes
   - attempts to introduce labour saving devices led to disputes.

5. The candidate reaches a balanced conclusion on the issue using **presented evidence** such as that given in answer 4 and **recalled evidence** such as:
   **For the issue**:
   - Germany and Japan modernised their shipbuilding
   - overseas countries (USA; Scandinavia; Korea) introduced mass production/prefabrication
   - Scottish yards failed to introduce dry docks/roof berths
   - expansion of air travel (new aeronautical technology) reduced demand for passenger ships
   
   **Against the issue**:
   - Clyde was too narrow to build tankers/container ships
   - inability to compete with cheaper foreign competition
   - overseas shipyards delivered faster
   - Clyde specialised in passenger ships and people were turning to air travel
   - sites of many Scottish yards made it difficult to enlarge/adapt
   - Scottish yards were very weather-dependent
   - poor management of personnel
   - bad management practices
   - outdated working processes
   - low pay increases demoralised workers
   - rising costs in Scotland
   - difficulties in obtaining steel
   - Scottish reputation for over-expensive ships.

### UNIT II – Context A: 1790s – 1820s

### Section A

1. (*a*) The candidate assesses the importance of Coalition strengths as a factor in bringing victory using evidence such as:
   - combined power of the Third Coalition: Russia; Austria; Sweden; Britain
   - Napoleon defeated each separately, but threat of renewed hostilities remained
   - Britain was undefeated and won at Trafalgar
   - Fourth Coalition was strong: made up of Britain, Prussia, Austria, Russia
   - Prussian strength increased due to modernisation and feelings of nationalism
   - Austria joined Coalition and defeated French at Leipzig
   - capture of Paris in 1814 led to Napoleon's abdication
   - Napoleon attacked from all sides
   - British naval blockade/naval strength affected France
   - British ability to control trade
   - Generalship of Wellington, Blucher.

1. (b) The candidate assesses the importance of French weaknesses as a factor in bringing victory to the Coalition using evidence such as:
    - heavy losses in the Russian campaign
    - defeat by Wellington in the Peninsular War – 'Spanish ulcer'
    - Napoleon's image of invincibility was crushed after Leipzig
    - loss of allies: Sweden deserted to the Coalition because of Continental System
    - French armed forces smaller than Coalition's – France became exhausted of manpower
    - Napoleon took on too much; past his best
    - French weaknesses at home: food prices; inflation
    - inability to beat British naval blockade.

## Section B

2. The candidate evaluates the completeness of Source A using **presented evidence** such as:
    - attracted widespread Scottish newspaper coverage
    - viewed by some as a threat to social order
    - worry by British government that Edict of Fraternity would incite revolution

   and from **recalled evidence** such as:
    - initially widespread support
    - writers like Thomas Paine championed the revolution
    - poets like Wordsworth and Burns applauded it
    - some opposition from the start: Edmund Burke
    - Reform societies grew: Society of the Friends of the People/Thomas Muir
    - government reaction was to crush reform
    - fear of threat of invasion
    - reaction to execution of King Louis XVI.

3. The candidate discusses the attitude of William Pitt using evidence such as:
    - believes action must be taken against France
    - believes France had no right to interfere over the Scheldt
    - believes France will break treaties
    - believes England (Britain) was right to stand up to France over Antwerp
    - believes aggressive French policies are a threat.

4. The candidate compares Sources B and C using evidence such as:
   Sources agree that the French threatened the River Scheldt:
   **Source B** says: French had no right to interfere in River Scheldt
   **Source C** says: French sent naval warships down Scheldt.
   Sources agree that French would break/had broken treaties:
   **Source B** says: no right to cancel laws/other treaties
   **Source C** says: broke Treaty of Utrecht.
   Sources agree that French had threatened Holland:

4. (continued)
   **Source B** says: Holland applied for help over Antwerp
   **Source C** says: Dutch neutrality was ignored.
   Sources agree that peace in Europe was threatened:
   **Source B** says: French were intent on destroying England/Europe
   **Source C** says: war between Britain and France was certain.
   Only **Source C** mentions the threat posed by Decrees of November 1792.

## UNIT II – Context B: 1890s – 1920s

## Section A

1. (a) The candidate assesses the contribution of Allied technology in the defeat of Germany during the First World War using evidence such as:
    - development of the Dreadnought
    - new naval technology used in blockading German ports/defeating U-boats
    - use of chemical warfare/gas
    - development of the tank
    - development of machine guns
    - developments in artillery
    - increasing air-power
    - development in troop transport: trains; motor vehicles
    - new methods of communication: telephone; wireless
    - developments in range-finding techniques

   and other possible factors such as:
    - failure of the German Schlieffen Plan in 1914
    - Germany's failure to defeat the enemy in the field
    - failure of the German Spring Offensive
    - failure of U-boats to starve Britain into surrender
    - actions which brought US into the war
    - failure to find a breakthrough weapon
    - surrender of Germany's Allies from September 1918
    - strengths of British Home Front: rationing; women making munitions, etc
    - morale boost of US entry into the war
    - industrial strength and manpower of the US
    - huge manpower contribution: soldiers from the British Empire
    - success of the 1918 Allied offensive.

   (b) The candidate assesses the collapse of the German home front as a reason for defeat in the First World War using evidence such as:
    - results of British naval blockade
    - food shortages/turnip winter/use of ersatz foods
    - German agriculture could not supply enough
    - German industry could not supply enough weapons

# History Credit Level 2007 (cont.)

1 (b). (continued)
- inability of national government to cope with 4 years of industrialised warfare
- need for army manpower affected industrial potential
- German naval mutinies at Kiel
- strikes and demonstrations in certain German cities
- morale-lowering effect of German defeats/loss of life/collapse of allies
- collapse of German morale/war weariness/ increasing unwillingness to face sacrifices
- civilian opposition to state bureaucracy
- Berlin government in turmoil.

## Section B

2. The candidate discusses the attitude of the author of Source A using evidence such as:
   - openly hostile towards Austria
   - convinced that war between Serbia and Austria is inevitable
   - believes Serbia will not allow itself to be conquered by Austria
   - believes Serbia is fighting for fellow Slavs against Austria
   - believes Serbs should be united in its forthcoming war with Austria
   - believes that the Austrians are 'aliens'.

3. The candidate assesses the agreement between Sources A and B using evidence such as:
   Sources agree that war was likely between Serbia and the Austro-Hungarian Empire
   **Source A** says: the war between Serbia and Austria is inevitable
   **Source B** says: assassination an excellent excuse for taking action against Serbia.
   Sources agree that the Southern Slavs were a cause of tension in the Austro-Hungarian Empire:
   **Source A** says: this war must bring about everlasting freedom of Serbia, of the South Slavs
   **Source B** says: it was accused of encouraging unrest among the Southern Slavs inside the Austro-Hungarian Empire.
   Sources disagree on who is the aggressor/the cause of tension:
   **Source A** says: our whole race must stand together to halt the onslaught of these aliens from Austria
   **Source B** says: Serbia was disliked as and seen as a direct threat to the Austro-Hungarian Empire.
   Only **Source A**: mentions that Serbia's honour is at stake.
   Only **Source A**: mentions that Serbia is fighting for traditions/culture.
   Only **Source B**: mentions the assassination of the Archduke Franz Ferdinand.

4. The candidate evaluates the completeness of Source C using **presented evidence** such as:
   - Dual Alliance signed between Germany and Austria-Hungary in 1879.
   - Triple Alliance signed between Germany, Austria-Hungary and Italy in 1882
   - alliance between France and Russia in 1893
   - Anglo-Japanese Alliance in 1902
   
   and from **recalled evidence** such as:
   - Entente Cordiale between Britain and France, 1904
   - increasing military/naval understanding between Britain and France
   - Anglo-Russian Entente between Britain and Russia, 1907
   - Triple Entente of Britain, France and Russia
   - Europe divided into two 'armed camps'
   - Russian/Serbian understanding
   - German/Turkish understanding.

## UNIT II – Context C: 1930s – 1960s

### Section A

1. (a) The candidate assesses the importance of Allied technology as a reason for victory in World War Two using evidence such as:
   - development of rifles, eg M1 Garand
   - development of the tank
   - development of anti-tank technology (rockets; bazookas)
   - development of heavy bombers used to destroy German targets
   - German civilian morale was affected by the bombing and the British naval blockade
   - 'bouncing bomb' attack on German dams
   - development of fighter aircraft
   - use of radar
   - use of 'window'/metal foil
   - use of decoding machines/Ultra; Enigma
   - use of Atomic bombs
   - development of naval technology: aircraft carriers
   - anti-submarine devices: Huff Duff; ASDIC/Sonar; Leigh Light; Sonobuoys.

   (b) The candidate assesses the importance of British civilians' efforts as a reason for victory in World War Two using evidence such as:
   - war production was good/out-produced Germany
   - part played by food rationing/Dig for Victory
   - role of air-raid wardens/fire-watchers
   - part played by the Women's Land Army
   - role of women, eg in industry/munitions
   - participation/co-operation in air raid precautions
   - British morale was not broken by the Blitz/endurance and resilience of civilians
   - contribution of the Merchant Navy
   - part played by the post-raid emergency services

## 1. (b) (continued)

- bombing caused little voluntary absenteeism from work
- willingness to accept government regulation, e.g. Emergency Powers Act; evacuation; ID cards; conscription
- labour mobility was good
- part played by the Home Guard
- contributions to war loans/salvage schemes

**and other possible reasons such as:**

- Britain defeated Germany in the Battle of Britain 1940 – ensured survival
- by 1941, Britain was linked to the resources of the USA/USSR/Empire
- after initial German successes, the War on the Eastern Front by 1945 had broken the German Army
- Soviet Industries remained beyond the Urals and out of German range
- from 1942, Soviet generals had more freedom on military strategy
- Hitler's declaration of war on the USA brought in the "arsenal of democracy"
- Lend Lease Law/Military Resources to Britain 1941
- offering hope to Liberation Movements/moral resistance in occupied Europe
- Allied agreements about the best way to fight the war
- Allied victories in North Africa
- Allied invasions of D Day
- ultimate success of the invasion of Germany
- failure of Germany to defeat Britain before invasion of USSR
- Germany had to fight a two-front war from 1941
- German military and industrial resources declined after 1943
- German Generals had less freedom on military strategy/Hitler's later tactics wrong
- Nazi policies provoked resentment/resistance in occupied Europe
- Germany and its Allies did not always agree about the best way to fight the war
- failure of the 'wonder weapons' of 1945 to defeat Britain
- failure of Italy to win control of Mediterranean or North Africa
- failure of some Italians to fight the war/overthrow of Mussolini in 1943
- less effective use of civilians in Germany and its allies' wartime Industries
- German military and territorial losses were severe by 1945
- Japan did not fight alongside Germany: did not declare war on Russia.

## Section B

**2.** The candidate discusses the attitude of Hitler with reference to evidence such as:
- wants Germany to be master of/rule Europe
- wants Germany to be independent (of other nations)
- wants Germany to have its military strength restored
- wants Germany to have mastery in the East
- determined to expand the nation to the West
- prepared to attack various countries to make Germany strong
- demands an Empire like Britain's.

**3.** The candidate compares Sources A and B using evidence such as:

Sources agree over the possibility of a war over territory:
**Source A** says: he was prepared to take over/attack various countries
**Source B** says: policies of territorial expansion.
Sources agree over the rebuilding of Germany's Armed forces:
**Source A** says: must restore Germany's military strength
**Source B** says: compulsory military service/increase its navy/Luftwaffe.
Sources agree that Hitler wanted a war:
**Source A** says: if this means war, so be it
**Source B** says: war was a price Germany would pay.
Sources agree over desire for German expansion:
**Source A** says: Greater Germany will include Austria; Sudetenland
**Source B** says: pursuit of greater German Empire.
Sources disagree over relationship with Britain:
**Source A** says: Hitler wanted to be a colonial power equal to that of Britain
**Source B** says: agree an increase in naval strength with Britain
Only **Source A** says: Hitler was determined to expand to the East.

**4.** The candidate assesses the completeness of **Source C** using **presented evidence** such as:
- attack began on September 1st, 1939 (at 4.45am)
- Germans used blitzkrieg tactics
- Germans tore through Polish military forces
- by the end of September, Poland had surrendered

and from **recalled evidence** such as:
- pretext for war was fabricated
- German gunboat opened fire (on Polish Post Office) in Danzig harbour
- German units entered from East Prussia, Silesia and Slovakia
- Germans used 40 infantry divisions and 4 motorised divisions
- Germans used over 2000 tanks (11 divisions)
- Germany used over 1200 planes (850 bombers; 400 fighters)

## History Credit Level 2007 (cont.)

**4. (continued)**
- Germans commanded by General von Brauchitsch
- Russians attacked in the East
- Poles had 11 inefficient cavalry divisions
- Poles had only 360 aircraft: many obsolete
- Germans crossed the Vistula after just 5 days
- Warsaw bombed on 24th September, encircled and surrendered on September 28th.

### UNIT III – Context A: USA 1850 – 1880

#### Section A

1. The candidate assesses the importance of slavery as a cause of tension between the North and South using evidence such as:
   - slavery was essential to the Southern economy/South depended on slave labour
   - South feared for its distinct way of life
   - South feared social problems/revolts if slaves were set free
   - attacks on slavery by Northern abolitionists worried South
   - Northern abolitionists believed slavery was an evil and should be ended
   - opponents of slavery did not want it to expand
   - background slavery issues played a part: Senate involvement in slave/non-slave states; Fugitive Slave Laws; 1854 Kansas Nebraska Act; 1857 Dred Scott Case; 1859 John Brown's raid
   - Northern wage payers objected to free slave labour in the South
   - Slavery was seen in the North as an affront to democracy
   
   **and other possible factors such as:**
   - indebtedness of slave-owning South to Northern banks
   - disagreement about tariffs
   - movement towards Secession in the South/belief in States' rights
   - election of Lincoln perceived as a threat by the South.

2. The candidate describes the main aims of the Republican Party using evidence such as:
   - reflect political and economic interests of the North
   - stand for the Union/against Secession
   - support high tariffs
   - belief in justice/equal opportunities/freedom
   - promote the idea of slavery as an evil/against American values of equality
   - stop the spread of slavery on moral grounds
   - prevent extension of slavery as threat to 'free labour'
   - not to interfere where slavery existed
   - ambivalent official line on social equality of African Americans
   - in favour of the Homestead Bill
   - committed to trans-continental railroad.

#### Section B

3. The candidate evaluates the usefulness of **Source A** using evidence such as:
   contemporaneity:
   primary source drawn at the time of settlers going west
   authorship:
   artist based it on first hand experience
   content:
   shows Native Americans attacking a wagon train
   accuracy:
   agrees with other evidence, eg many native Americans were hostile/attacked wagon trains
   purpose:
   to portray 'Indians' as hostile/cruel/barbaric
   limitation:
   one-sided/dramatised/soldier's view/doesn't show peaceful Native Americans such as the Cherokee.

4. The candidate assesses the completeness of **Source B** using **presented evidence** such as:
   - opposition to White men building a road to the gold mines (Bozeman Trail)
   - feared bison (buffalo) would be scared off/hunting grounds disturbed
   - wanted to stop others flooding in
   - believed road building would lead to loss of homeland
   - believed army presence would lead to extermination of Native Americans
   - distrust of the army/thinks White men are scheming against the Sioux
   
   and **recalled evidence** such as:
   - Bozeman Trail was cause of conflict and triggered the war
   - Trail passed through Yellowstone River – heart of Sioux hunting grounds
   - 'Indians' believed US government had broken Treaty of Fort Laramie/Black Hills had been promised to the Sioux for 'as long as the grass grows'
   - Custer provoked the war by leading an expedition into the Black Hills
   - Custer's discovery of gold in the Black Hills brought thousands of miners in
   - Black Hills were sacred Sioux territory
   - miners offered $200 per 'Indian' scalp
   - railroad companies sent in hunters to kill buffalo
   - Army tried to build a series of forts to protect travellers
   - Native Americans feared loss of freedom/hated idea of Reservations
   - Native Americans feared destruction of their way of life/culture
   - Native Americans regarded farming as women's work
   - Native American belief that land could not be bought or sold
   - US government failed to provide a decent life on Reservations
   - tribes feared loss of power: government did not see them as 'nations'
   - US government over-exaggerated power of chiefs to control warriors.

## UNIT III – Context B: India 1917 – 1947

### Section A

1. The candidate assesses the importance of economic factors as a cause of discontent using evidence such as:
   - competition from British factories pauperised Indian artisans
   - taxation, eg Salt Tax
   - use of Indian natural resources
   - restrictions on trade/Indian needs sacrificed to those of the British economy
   - British businessmen in powerful positions
   
   and the possible importance of other factors such as:
   - British control of law and order
   - discrimination against Indians
   - use of English language
   - control of education
   - suppression of Indian culture
   - British policy of repression.

2. The candidate describes the aims of the Congress Party using evidence such as:
   - more self-government (until 1929)
   - full independence from Britain (after 1929)
   - keep India united as one country
   - wanted India to be a secular state with tolerance for non-Hindus
   - reduce social divisions among Indians
   - mostly believed in non-violent methods
   - some extremists aimed to use force.

### Section B

3. The candidate evaluates the usefulness of **Source A** using evidence such as:
   contemporaneity:
   primary source produced at the time of opposition to the Salt Tax
   authorship:
   photograph giving eye-witness evidence
   content:
   shows Indians defying the Salt Tax law
   accuracy:
   possibility of photo being posed by the Congress Party
   purpose:
   to stress the strength of Indian opposition to British taxes
   limitation:
   doesn't give the views of all Indians/not a balanced account.

4. The candidate assesses the completeness of **Source B** using **presented evidence** such as:
   - the mission failed
   - more terrorism and rebellion
   - return of Gandhi to prison
   
   and **recalled evidence** such as:
   - attacks on railways and post offices
   - army put down the 'Quit India' campaign
   - more than one thousand people killed
   - 60, 000 arrests
   - activities of Bose's Indian National Army
   - Muslim League co-operative with Britain.

## UNIT III – Context C: Russia 1914 – 1941

### Section A

1. The candidate assesses the importance of the First World War as a cause of discontent using evidence such as:
   - Russians were war-weary
   - continuing war made it harder to deal with other problems
   - more defeats/failure to pull out of war caused unrest
   - heavy casualties
   - unrest in the armed forces
   - caused food/fuel shortages
   - breakdown of rail network
   
   and the possible importance of other factors such as:
   - delay in land redistribution
   - growing anarchy alarmed middle and upper classes
   - Bolshevik propaganda
   - failed Kornilov coup.

2. The candidate describes the aims of the Bolsheviks using evidence such as:
   - end of Russian participation in the First World War
   - provide food for the people
   - share out land among the peasants
   - give workers control of industry
   - end class distinctions/create a communist state
   - improve the position of women
   - provide better housing
   - provide education and healthcare
   - establish absolute control of Russia
   - crush other political parties.

### Section B

3. The candidate evaluates the usefulness of **Source A** using evidence such as:
   contemporaneity:
   primary source from period of collectivisation
   authorship: official government photograph
   eyewitness photographer
   content:
   shows peasants supporting collectivisation
   accuracy:
   probably posed by the government/biased
   purpose:
   to show that the peasants wanted collectivisation/justify purge of kulaks/encourage peasants to join collectives
   imitation:
   doesn't show the kulaks' reaction to collectivisation.

# History Credit Level 2007 (cont.)

4. The candidate assesses the completeness of **Source B** using **presented evidence** such as:
   - use of show trials
   - victims were leading Communists
   - victims were accused of/confessed to trying to overthrow the government
   - many victims were innocent
   - use of torture/fake promises to get confessions
   - use of death penalty
   - use of labour camps for other party members

   and **recalled evidence** such as:
   - began with Kirov's murder in 1934
   - some charged with supporting Trotsky
   - threats made to family members
   - show trials broadcast live
   - about 10 million killed
   - many army officers killed.

## UNIT III – Context D: Germany 1918 – 1939

### Section A

1. The candidate assesses the importance of economic problems in making the Weimar Government unpopular by 1923 using evidence such as:
   - unemployment and shortages at the end of the war
   - burden of reparations
   - rising inflation after 1918
   - hyperinflation in 1923
   - money lost its value/prices rose rapidly
   - savings became worthless/pensions lost value
   - wages rose more slowly than prices
   - industrialists made huge profits _ caused resentment
   - living standards fell/growing poverty among working and middle classes

   and possible other factors such as:
   - blamed for losing World War One
   - associated with the hated Treaty of Versailles
   - seemed unable to control outbreaks of violence
   - criticised for weak coalition governments/weak leadership
   - criticised by nationalists for giving in to foreign powers
   - desire for dictatorship/strong leadership
   - criticised for French invasion of Ruhr.

2. The candidate describes the appeal of the Nazi Party using evidence such as:
   - Hitler appeared to offer Germany strong leadership
   - offered solutions to Germany's economic problems
   - promised to provide jobs for the unemployed
   - Nazi rallies, eg Nuremberg, impressed people
   - promised to overthrow the Treaty of Versailles

## 2. (continued)
   - Hitler was a superb speaker
   - effective use of propaganda to get over his message
   - Hitler had a clear, simple message which appealed to many people
   - promised support for the farmers, shopkeepers, etc
   - businessmen were attracted by Hitler's promise to destroy trade unions
   - young people were attracted to the Hitler Youth
   - promised to restore Germany as a world power
   - appeared to be Germany's best defence against Communism
   - discipline of the SA impressed people
   - widespread support from nationalists for his racial theories/anti-Semitism
   - people were tired of the chaos of the Weimar Government and wanted a change.

### Section B

3. The candidate evaluates the usefulness of **Source A** using evidence such as:
   contemporaneity:
   primary source from the time of the Nazi persecution of the Jewish people
   authorship:
   photograph taken by an eyewitness of the event
   content:
   shows SA/SS enforcing the boycott of Jewish shops
   accuracy:
   agrees with other evidence on treatment of Jews, e.g. lost Government jobs
   purpose:
   to inform people what was happening in Germany/Nazi propaganda
   limitation:
   only one shop, in one place in Germany/one example of Nazi persecution, does not mention, e.g.... .

4. The candidate assesses the completeness of **Source B** using **presented evidence** such as:
   - annual mass rallies at Nuremberg
   - military parades/men marching past Hitler
   - events were staged with military precision
   - banners and flags

   and from **recalled evidence** such as:
   - many organisations used military style uniforms
   - use of drums and military marching bands
   - in schools images of armed forces were everywhere
   - military situations introduced into school subjects, e.g. maths
   - Hitler Youth based on militarism
   - boys taught military skills in Hitler Youth, e.g. marching, shooting, fighting

## 4. (continued)

- organisations set up for most groups, eg teachers, each with its own uniform, insignia
- festivals regularly held with marches, military uniforms and music
- military fly-pasts
- Hitler ordered massive rearmament programme
- new armed forces displayed to people in great parades and displays
- Nazis spent 73, 000 million Reichmarks on armed forces between 1933 and 1939
- war was glorified as a means of making Germany great again
- all Germans expected to conform … eg salute Hitler to military ideals of discipline, obedience and loyalty to Führer
- suspected pacifists sent to concentration camps
- military-type discipline vital to Hitler's rule, imposed through fear
- Germans were expected to sacrifice personal interests for the good of the state.

# General History 2008

### UNIT I - Context A: 1750s - 1850s

### Section A
In answering questions in Section A, candidates are required to carry out the appropriate process and to use relevant presented evidence. In order to obtain full marks for a question, candidates must in addition use recalled evidence in their answer.

1. The candidate describes the improvements made to rural housing using **presented evidence** such as:
    - two storey houses built with slate roofs
    - houses are now built by good builders using mortar
    - the outside of the houses are finished with lime
   
   and from **recalled evidence** such as:
    - wooden or stone floors
    - glass in windows
    - had fireplaces and chimneys
    - had other amenities such as separate barns for animals.

2. The candidate assesses the importance of new technology in the British textile industry using **presented evidence** such as:
    - the Mule could produce a thread that was both soft and strong
    - by 1790 this machine could spin 300 threads at once
    - after 1790 many of the Mules were steam driven
    - a steam driven Mule needed only one operator to control a total of 1,200 spindles at the same time.
   
   and from **recalled evidence** such as:
    - factories built to house large machinery
    - decline of cottage/domestic system
    - details of Hargreave's Spinning Jenny
    - details of Arkwright's Water Frame
    - James Watt's Steam Engine replaced muscle/water power
    - details of Cartwright's power loom
    - vast quantities of cheap goods produced
    - growth of factories employing hundreds of workers.

### Section B
In answering questions in Section B, candidates are required to carry out the appropriate process and to use relevant presented evidence and recalled evidence where appropriate. Where **recall is required** in an answer this is stated in the question paper.

3. The candidate evaluates the usefulness of **Source C** using **evidence** such as:
    - contemporaneity:
      a primary source written at/near the time
    - authorship:
      eyewitness account of changes in food supply
    - content:
      detailed information of increased food supply eg …
    - accuracy:
      matches candidate's knowledge/knowledge of other areas of the country eg … /an official statistical account, unlikely to be biased

## General History 2008 (cont.)

**3. (continued)**

- purpose:
  to give information about the increased food supply
- limitation:
  only applies to one area of Scotland/omits eg …

**4.** The candidate selects **evidence** from **Source C** that improved diet and food supply caused population growth such as:
- well supplied with water
- well supplied with butcher meat
- food supplies have increased very much.

The candidate selects **evidence** from **Source D** that other factors caused population growth such as:
- improvements in personal hygiene
- cheap soap which kept people cleaner
- better water supplies: clothes washed
- better housing conditions led to less disease.

**5.** The candidate comes to a conclusion on the issue using **presented evidence** as outlined above and **recalled evidence** such as:

- **For the issue**
  - details on Agricultural Revolution/Enclosure Movement/scientific farming methods
  - revolution in agriculture helped to feed urban population/increased food production helped population growth
  - fertility of mothers increased as a result of improved diet
  - babies born healthier/decline in infant mortality as a result of improved diet
  - railways transported fresh food/milk to towns
  - growth of overseas trade meant that more food could be imported if necessary.

- **Against the issue**
  - mass immigration from Ireland due to the potato famine
  - some advances in medical knowledge, eg Dr. Jenner's smallpox vaccinations
  - some diseases declined/disappeared, eg scurvy
  - improved standard of midwifery led to fewer mothers and babies who died in childbirth
  - earlier marriage with more childbearing years/people were marrying younger and having larger families
  - lack of effective contraception
  - high tax on alcohol reduced deaths from gin drinking
  - cotton clothes became more common

**UNIT I – Context B: 1830s – 1930s**

### Section A

In answering questions in Section A, candidates are required to carry out the appropriate process and to use relevant presented evidence. In order to obtain full marks for a question, candidates must in addition use recalled evidence in their answer.

**1.** The candidate describes the improvements made to rural housing using **presented evidence** such as:
- small windows became common
- fireplaces had a proper chimney
- front doors were made
- the door through to the byre was blocked up/people no longer had to share with animals.

and from **recalled evidence** such as:
- running water was introduced
- indoor sanitation introduced/piped water/flush toilets/septic tanks
- tiled roofs replaced thatch
- wooden floors introduced
- houses were extended to add another storey or kitchen
- stoves or ranges introduced to kitchens
- houses better constructed/sandstone/brick walls

**2.** The candidate assesses the importance of new technology in the development of railways using **presented evidence** such as:
- steel rails replaced iron rails
- block signalling was introduced
- travelling became safer and faster
- the design of locomotives made them more powerful and reliable

and from **recalled evidence** such as:
- development of steam locomotives eg more efficient boilers
- new fuels eg diesel (first used in 1933)
- streamlined engines
- better carriages: heating/sleeping cars/restaurant cars/lavatories
- Dead Man's Handle
- continuous braking system
- construction of railway bridges: Tay, Forth
- telegraph used in signalling from 1845
- electric operated signals in early 20th century

BUT other factors
- standardised gauge
- 1844 Railway Act: penny a mile fares
- Standard Time – standardised timetables.

### Section B

In answering questions in Section B, candidates are required to carry out the appropriate process and to use relevant presented evidence and recalled evidence where appropriate. Where **recall is required** in an answer this is stated in the question paper.

**3.** The candidate evaluates the usefulness of **Source C** using **evidence** such as:
- contemporaneity:
  a primary source written at/near the time
- authorship:
  first hand knowledge/eyewitness account
- content:
  details of improved diet/food supply eg …
- accuracy:
  matches candidate's knowledge/knowledge of other areas of the country eg … /memories may have changed/been embellished/facts forgotten over time
- purpose:
  to give information on changes in past 50 years

## 3. (continued)

- limitation:
  only applies to one person's experience/only relates to Glasgow/1900, later in period/omits eg ...

4. The candidate selects **evidence** from **Source C** that improved diet and food supply caused population growth, such as:
   - food is now more varied
   - fresh fruit is available all year round
   - milk is much cleaner

   The candidate selects **evidence** from **Source D** that other factors caused population growth:
   - great expansion of linen trade/spinning mills brings workers to area
   - extension of harbour attracts workers
   - early marriages led to larger families
   - Irish immigrants

5. The candidate comes to a conclusion on the issue using **presented evidence** as outlined above and **recalled evidence** such as:
   - **For the issue**
     - clean water
     - cheaper food/cheaper imports
     - railways transport fresh food/milk to towns
     - revolution in agriculture helped to feed urban population/increased food production helped population growth
     - detail on Agricultural Revolution/Enclosure Movement/scientific farming methods
     - fertility of mothers increased as result of improved diet
     - infant mortality dropped/babies born healthier as a result of improved diet.
   - **Against the issue**
     - improvements in town conditions
     - improved medical knowledge eg Lister-antiseptics and Simpson-anaesthetics
     - better welfare provisions eg Liberal Welfare Reforms
     - lack of effective contraception
     - improved standard of living
     - improvements in hygiene/soap and public water supplies
     - vaccinations
     - improvements in clothing
     - decline of killer diseases eg cholera

## UNIT I – Context C: 1880 – Present Day

### Section A
In answering questions in Section A, candidates are required to carry out the appropriate process and to use relevant presented evidence. In order to obtain full marks for a question, candidates must in addition use recalled evidence in their answer.

1. The candidate describes improvements in housing in the countryside after 1880 using **presented evidence** such as:
   - a second storey of two bedrooms was added
   - piped water
   - a flush toilet with septic tank.

   and **recalled evidence** such as:
   - solid, stone or brick cottages built
   - stone or wood floors
   - slate roofs
   - proper fireplace/chimney
   - electricity
   - council houses built in countryside

2. The candidate assesses the importance of new technology in the development of the motor car industry using **presented evidence** such as:
   - the car industry could use mass production methods
   - it produced a large number of cars cheaply and quickly
   - machinery made the parts to the same quality
   - output rose

   and **recalled evidence** such as:
   - the use of robots
   - the use of computer control
   - use of assembly line
   - huge presses stamping out large sections of car in single process

### Section B
In answering questions in Section B, candidates are required to carry out the appropriate process and to use relevant presented evidence and recalled evidence where appropriate. Where **recall is required** in an answer this is stated in the question paper.

3. The candidate evaluates the usefulness of **Source C** using **evidence** such as:
   - contemporaneity:
     a primary source written at/near the time
   - authorship:
     eyewitness account/a well informed reporter
   - content:
     gives detail about link between food supply/diet and population growth eg ...
   - accuracy:
     matches candidate's own knowledge/knowledge of other areas of the country eg ... /an official statistical account, unlikely to be biased
   - purpose:
     to inform people about life changes in Scotland
   - limitation:
     only covers one parish in Perthshire/only considers one reason for growth towards later part of period/omits eg ...

4. The candidate selects **evidence** from **Source C** that improved diet and food supply caused population growth such as:
   - people have a more varied diet
   - school meals are provided
   - increased pre-packing of food
   - refrigeration means greater variety of fresh food throughout the year.

# General History 2008 (cont.)

**4. (continued)**

The candidate selects **evidence** from **Source D** that other factors caused population growth such as:
- infant mortality rate fell
- better housing/removal of slums
- higher standards of cleanliness
- medical improvements.

5. The candidate comes to a conclusion on the issue using **presented evidence** as outlined above and **recalled evidence** such as:
   - **For the issue**
     - clean water supply
     - people spent more money on food
     - free school milk
     - uncontaminated milk available
     - improved transportation of food
   - **Against the issue**
     - better health care, eg health visitors and child welfare clinics
     - vaccination campaigns
     - NHS meant free medical treatment
     - higher wages/improved living standards
     - improvements in working conditions
     - better public health, eg drains and sewers
     - increased use of soap and disinfectant
     - immigration
     - creation of welfare state
     - more cures for childhood diseases: polio; measles

## UNIT II – Context A: 1790s – 1820s

### Section A
In answering questions in Section A, candidates are required to carry out the appropriate process and to use relevant presented evidence. In order to obtain full marks for a question, candidates must in addition use recalled evidence in their answer.

1. The candidate assesses the importance of the fear of revolution as a cause of war using **presented evidence** such as:
   - French government wanted to spread the revolution
   - the possible use of force was a worry for countries
   - the British government were scared of a rebellion by the lower classes
   - increasingly hostile relationship between Britain and France.

   and from **recalled evidence** such as:
   - execution of Louis XVI horrified many
   - concern for the monarchy in Britain
   - speed of revolution outside France caused anxiety
   - French control of Austrian Netherlands alarmed many
   - opening of the River Scheldt seen as a threat

2. The candidate explains why the Congress of Vienna maintained the peace of Europe using **presented evidence** such as:
   - decisions made were wise
   - France was not unfairly treated
   - France had no reason for revenge/grievances

**2. (continued)**
   - there was a balance of power between nations
   - congresses would solve problems in the future.

   and from **recalled evidence** such as:
   - there was no European war for forty years
   - monarchs across Europe were restored to their thrones
   - barriers against future French aggression were created
   - Prussia takes over Rhine provinces
   - the Netherlands territory was expanded
   - France suffered an army of occupation for 3-5 years
   - Russia, Austria, Prussia and Britain agree to maintain an alliance against France

### Section B
In answering questions in Section B, candidates are required to carry out the appropriate process and to use relevant presented evidence and recalled evidence where appropriate. Where **recall is required** in an answer this is stated in the question paper.

3. The candidate evaluates the usefulness of **Source C** using **evidence** such as:
   - contemporaneity:
     a primary source written at/near the time
   - authorship:
     eyewitness account/a ship's crew member
   - content:
     details of naval battle methods, eg …
   - accuracy:
     matches other evidence on naval warfare eg …
   - purpose:
     to indicate problems encountered during naval battles
   - limitation:
     refers only to the experiences of one ship/one battle/omits eg …

4. The candidate compares **Sources C** and **D** using **evidence** such as:
   - Sources agree that sails/rigging were damaged in battle:
     **Source C** says: yards, sails and masts were disabled
     **Source D** shows: rigging was broken/sails were ripped
   - Sources agree that naval combat was often broadside to broadside:
     **Source C** says: that their ship lay at the side of their enemy
     **Source D** shows: that each ship was facing each other sideways
   - Sources agree that during battle a great deal of smoke was created:
     **Source C** says: that they could not see where they were firing due to the amount of smoke
     **Source D** shows: that there was a large cloud of smoke around the ships

## 4. (continued)

- Sources agree that sailors could fall off ships:
  **Source C** says: that some sailors went into the water
  **Source D** shows: that there are men holding onto masts in the sea

5. The candidate evaluates the completeness of **Sources C** and **D** using **presented evidence** such as:
   - ships fought at close range
   - rigging was often destroyed
   - sailors were the target of enemy fire
   - ships were often damaged beyond repair.
   
   and **recalled evidence** such as:
   - 'splitting the line' was one of Nelson's tactics
   - cannons were often used
   - sailors boarding the enemy ship was common
   - carronades were introduced as a weapon
   - destroying a ship's hull by 'raking' occurred

## UNIT II – Context B: 1890s – 1920s

### Section A

In answering questions in Section A, candidates are required to carry out the appropriate process and to use relevant presented evidence. In order to obtain full marks for a question, candidates must in addition use recalled evidence in their answer.

1. The candidate assesses the importance of the Alliance System in causing the First World War using **presented evidence** such as:
   - Britain felt threatened by the system of alliances
   - Europe was divided into two separate alliances
   - France's humiliating defeat by the Germans in 1871 led to her desire for revenge
   
   and from **recalled evidence** such as:
   - Suspicion between members of the two rival alliances (Triple Alliance/Entente)
   - Austria-Hungary, Germany and Italy formed the Triple Alliance
   - Entente powers only promised to be on good terms/friendly
   - naval race between Britain and Germany
   - arms race between two armed camps
   - colonial rivalry
   - economic rivalry
   - nationalism in the Balkans
   - assassination at Sarajevo
   - alliance obligations caused the war to spread

2. The candidate explains why the Treaty of Versailles could be criticised using **presented evidence** such as:
   - the Treaty would eventually prove disastrous
   - economic terms criticised
   - reparations could never work
   - the Treaty would cripple Germany
   - a poor Germany would mean a poor Europe.
   
   and **recalled evidence** such as:
   - German protests about the unfair nature of the Treaty
   - Germany argued that the Treaty was a Diktat
   - German territorial losses: Alsace and Lorraine returned to France, Polish Corridor - led to sense of injustice

## 2. (continued)

- War Guilt Clause, Article 231, gave Germany sole responsibility for causing the First World War
- German army reduced to 100,000 men – hurt military pride
- no tanks allowed/no airforce/6 battleships allowed/no submarines, felt vulnerable
- France argued that the Treaty was too lenient on Germany
- many Americans believed that the Treaty had been too severe on Germany

### Section B

In answering questions in Section B, candidates are required to carry out the appropriate process and to use relevant presented evidence and recalled evidence where appropriate. Where **recall is required** in an answer this is stated in the question paper.

3. The candidate evaluates the usefulness of **Source C** using **evidence** such as:
   - contemporaneity:
     a primary source written at the time
   - authorship:
     eyewitness, written by a soldier who fought in the First World War
   - content:
     technical information about the capability of the Vickers machine gun eg …
   - accuracy:
     matches candidate's own knowledge/evidence eg …
   - purpose:
     to inform others about how deadly the machine gun was
   - limitation:
     only one British soldier's experience of a machine gun/omits eg…

4. The candidate compares **Sources C** and **D** using **evidence** such as:
   - Sources agree that the machine gun was mounted on a tripod:
     **Source C** says: the gun was fixed on the tripod
     **Source D** shows: the Vickers machine gun on the tripod.
   - Sources agree that the rate of fire was 600 bullets per minute:
     **Source C** says: in good condition the rate of fire was 600 bullets per minute
     **Source D** shows: 600 bullets per minute.
   - Sources agree about the weight of the gun:
     **Source C** says: "weighed 28lbs without water"
     **Source D** shows: "weighed about 28lbs without water".
   - Sources agree that the machine gun required water:
     **Source C** says: the gun itself weighed 28 lbs without water
     **Source D** shows: that water was used to keep the gun cool.

# General History 2008 (cont.)

**4. (continued)**
- Sources agree that the use of front and rear sights helped accuracy:
  - **Source C** says: the use of front and rear sights increase the accuracy
  - **Source D** shows: that the use of front and rear sights increased accuracy.

5. The candidate assesses the completeness of **Sources C and D** using **presented evidence** such as:
   - Vickers gun proved to be a successful weapon/highly efficient
   - Vickers machine gun could fire 600 bullets per minute
   - accurate weapon
   - machine guns killed thousands of men
   
   and **recalled evidence** such as:
   - types and effects of poison gas: phosgene, chlorine, mustard
   - flame throwers were used to clear out enemy trenches/cross "No-man's land"
   - tanks were used to break through enemy trenches/cross muddy terrain
   - aircraft were used for reconnaissance/combat/bombing
   - shrapnel shells were used to attack enemy trenches
   - railway mounted artillery was introduced to ease transportation
   - trench mortars were used to attack enemy trenches
   - howitzers were used to bombard trenches
   - grenades were used to attack/clear out enemy trenches
   - lorries were used to ease transportation

## UNIT II – Context C: 1930s – 1960s

In answering questions in Section A, candidates are required to carry out the appropriate process and to use relevant presented evidence. In order to obtain full marks for a question, candidates must in addition use recalled evidence in their answer.

1. The candidate assesses the importance of Hitler's attack on Poland as a cause of the Second World War by using **presented evidence** such as:
   - Britain and France could no longer give in to Germany
   - Britain and France gave Poland their full support/ready to go to war if attacked by Germany
   - Hitler thought he could get away with force as Britain and France wanted to avoid a war
   - France and Britain issued an ultimatum to Germany
   
   and **recalled evidence** such as:
   - appeasement was not working
   - details of Nazi Soviet pact
   - Hitler breaking terms of the Treaty of Versailles eg…
   - German rearmament
   - conscription introduced in Germany
   - occupation of Rhineland
   - takeover of Czechoslovakia
   - alliance building in Europe

2. The candidate explains why the building of the Berlin Wall caused a crisis, by using **presented evidence** such as:
   - it divided Berlin into two
   - any Berliner who tried to cross the wall got shot, which angered the Americans
   - President Kennedy tried to get the wall pulled down, but he failed
   - raised tension
   
   and **recalled evidence** such as:
   - built on existing suspicion eg … (refer to previous tension)
   - many felt the event might spark a nuclear war
   - Kennedy wanted to exercise his authority (as a new leader)
   - Kennedy was determined to achieve success following the disastrous "Bay of Pigs"
   - Kennedy wished to show his support for Berliners and the principles of Western democracy
   - many East Germans continued to escape which embarrassed the Soviet Union
   - the West believed the Soviet Union used the wall to oppress people against capitalism
   - showed the lengths the Soviet Union would go to prevent people escaping.

## Section B

In answering questions in Section B, candidates are required to carry out the appropriate process and to use relevant presented evidence and recalled evidence where appropriate. Where **recall is required** in an answer this is stated in the question paper.

3. The candidate evaluates the usefulness of **Source C** using **evidence** such as:
   - contemporaneity:
     primary source written at the time
   - authorship:
     eyewitness/survivor who experienced the event
   - content:
     details about the effect of the A bomb on Japan eg …
   - accuracy:
     matches candidate's own knowledge/other evidence eg …
   - purpose:
     to inform others about what was happening in Hiroshima
   - limitation:
     only one person's viewpoint/only one area/ omits eg …

4. The candidate compares **Sources C and D** using **evidence** such as:
   - Sources agree that many people were killed:
     **Source C** says: many were killed instantly
     **Source D** says: 78,150 were killed
   - Sources agree that there was a huge blast:
     **Source C** says: a wave of wind swept away everything in its path
     **Source D** says: a blast of 500 miles per hour

## 4. (continued)

- Sources agree that many people were injured:
    **Source C** says: others lying on the ground screaming in agony
    **Source D** says: 9,428 were seriously injured.
- Sources agree that housing was destroyed:
    **Source C** says: housing was completely destroyed
    **Source D** says: 176,487 were homeless

    **Only Source C** mentions a glaring pinkish light.
    **Only Source C** mentions a huge tremor that followed.
    **Only Source D** mentions many people were missing.
    **Only Source D** mentions sickness after-effects

5. The candidate evaluates the completeness of **Sources C** and **D** using **presented evidence** such as:
    - huge tremor
    - many were killed
    - blast swept everything away
    - injured/burned thousands
    - housing completely destroyed/thousands made homeless
    - factories destroyed
    - sickness after-effects
    - many people were missing

    and **recalled evidence** such as:
    - use of radar which acted as early warning system
    - bouncing bomb which destroyed dams
    - anti-aircraft guns which shot down enemy planes
    - searchlight batteries which detected enemy planes
    - V1/V2 Rocket which could reach London and long-range targets.
    - use of aircraft revolutionised naval warfare

## UNIT III – Context A: USA 1850 – 1880

### Section A
In answering questions in Section A, candidates are required to carry out the appropriate process and to use relevant presented evidence. In order to obtain full marks for a question, candidates must in addition use recalled evidence in their answer.

1. The candidate explains the problems affecting Native Americans as a result of Westward expansion using **presented evidence** such as:
    - hunters wiped out the buffalo
    - traditional Native American way of life was almost destroyed
    - Native Americans were treated badly on reservations

    and from **recalled evidence** such as:
    - loss of homeland
    - decrease of Native American population
    - increasing economic dependence on Whites
    - loss of traditional skills
    - gold mined in Sioux-Dakota territory
    - cheated by whisky salesmen
    - settlers spread disease, eg smallpox, which killed many.

## 1. (continued)
- importance/uses of buffalo: food; shelter; clothing
- White disregard for sacred land

2. The candidate describes the treatment received by the Mormons using **presented evidence** such as:
    - Mormons were mocked/ridiculed
    - organised gangs burned their houses
    - they were forced from their homes
    - such mistreatment was ignored by the government

    and from **recalled evidence** such as:
    - non-Mormons did not accept Mormons as part of their community
    - Mormons were distrusted and criticised for their beliefs
    - propaganda in the form of posters and cartoons was used to ridicule Mormons
    - Mormons were accused of losing non-Mormons money (after the Mormon Bank failed)
    - Mormons were forced to flee from Ohio
    - Mormons beaten up/whipped
    - the State Governor of Missouri declared Mormons should be treated as enemies
    - Mormon leaders were sent to jail in Missouri
    - Mormons were driven out of Missouri and Illinois
    - Joseph Smith, the Mormon leader, was killed by a mob
    - mobs looted Mormon homes and workshops
    - the US government refused to let Mormons have their state

### Section B
In answering questions in Section B, candidates are required to carry out the appropriate process and to use relevant presented evidence and recalled evidence where appropriate. Where **recall is required** in an answer this is stated in the question paper.

3. The candidate evaluates the attitude of the Southerners towards the election of Lincoln using **presented evidence** such as:
    - Southerners were **unhappy** that Lincoln had been elected (**holistic**)
    - **few** Southerners **supported/wanted to vote** for Lincoln
    - Southerners **felt** they **could tolerate no more** after the election of Lincoln: final straw
    - Southerners were **worried**/felt **threatened** Lincoln would end slavery
    - Southern honour was **offended** by Lincoln becoming President

4. The candidate compares **Sources C** and **D** using **evidence** such as:
    - Sources agree that Lincoln was the Presidential candidate for the Republican Party:
        **Source C** says: in the 1860 election, Abraham Lincoln was the Republican Party candidate
        **Source D** says: in 1860 the Republican Party leaders asked Lincoln to run for President.

# General History 2008 (cont.)

**4. (continued)**

- Sources agree that the South did not support Lincoln:
  **Source C** says: only a handful of Southerners voted for Lincoln
  **Source D** says: he had little support in the South.

- Sources agree that the South believed slavery would come to an end with the election of Lincoln:
  **Source C** says: Southerners believed slavery would become extinct
  **Source D** says: plantation owners in the South were terrified that slavery would die out.

- Sources agree that Lincoln's election would threaten their way of life:
  **Source C** says: (He) seemed a threat
  **Source D** says: (He wanted to) make them poor.

- Sources disagree about Lincoln's intention towards slavery:
  **Source C** says: (He would) lead slavery's extinction
  **Source D** says: (He) did not insist on ending slavery

## UNIT III – Context B: India 1917 – 1947

### Section A
In answering questions in Section A, candidates are required to carry out the appropriate process and to use relevant presented evidence. In order to obtain full marks for a question, candidates must in addition use recalled evidence in their answer.

1. The candidate explains why Britain benefited from ruling India, by using **presented evidence** such as:
   - India paid for the British Army which was used in other parts of the world
   - the army provided many important jobs for British people
   - Britain traded a lot with India/India bought Lancashire cloth
   
   and **recalled evidence** such as:
   - Britain benefited by fixing high taxes to suit themselves
   - India was Britain's largest single market
   - Indian goods sold to British people at a cheap rate – tea, jute, cotton, rice, wheat etc
   - British employers in India benefited from low wages paid to Indian workers eg tea plantations
   - use of Indian army in both World Wars
   - many British products were sent to/sold in India – heavy engineering products, cotton etc.

2. The candidate describes the way in which the Untouchables were treated using **presented evidence** such as:
   - Untouchables are outside their caste system
   - Untouchables had to do jobs no one else would do eg toilet cleaning
   - Untouchables have separate entrances to buildings

**2. (continued)**
   - not allowed to drink from the same well as others
   
   and from **recalled evidence** such as:
   - bear the mark of their caste
   - cannot move from their caste
   - forced to live apart from others
   - not allowed into the same temples
   - no inter-marriages allowed
   - had to live in slums

### Section B
In answering questions in Section B, candidates are required to carry out the appropriate process and to use relevant presented evidence and recalled evidence where appropriate. Where **recall is required** in an answer this is stated in the question paper.

3. The candidate evaluates the attitude to Ghandi using **presented evidence** such as:
   - **holistic** view is that he was **liked/admired**
   - **thinks** that Ghandi is a **special** man: **different** from anybody else
   - **believes** that Ghandi is a **man of principle: patriot/great leader**
   - **recognises** that Ghandi has done much to **prevent violence**
   - **thinks** that Ghandi has the **respect** of his opponents.

4. The candidate assesses points of agreement between **Sources C** and **D** about the appeal of Ghandi using **evidence** such as:

   - Sources agree that Ghandi could relate to different groups in India:
     **Source C** says: even those who hold different views from you look up to you as a man of saintly ideals
     **Source D** says: Ghandi attracted people of different kinds

   - Sources agree that Ghandi was admired by the population:
     **Source C** says: in the eyes of millions of your countrymen, you are a great patriot and a great leader
     **Source D** says: Ghandi got on so well with the Indian masses

   - Sources agree that Ghandi was special:
     **Source C** says: you are different from any other person I have tried
     **Source D** says: I have come across no-one like him in my life.

   **Only source C** mentions Ghandi was against violence

## UNIT III – Context C: Russia 1914 – 1941

### Section A
In answering questions in Section A, candidates are required to carry out the appropriate process and to use relevant presented evidence. In order to obtain full marks for a question, candidates must in addition use recalled evidence in their answer.

1. The candidate explains why the Provisional Government faced difficulties in 1917 using **presented evidence** such as:
   - shortage of food because the railways could not bring enough to the cities
   - many Russian soldiers had decided to desert
   - factory workers went on strikes
   
   and **recalled evidence** such as:
   - the needs of the Army at war took away many of the farm workers and livestock which also caused food shortages
   - there were shortages of fuel for industrial and domestic needs
   - the increase in the cost of living caused industrial trouble
   - the distribution of goods was poor and caused many street queues
   - the poor quality of Russian roads caused difficulties
   - some factories closed which led to unemployment
   - factory workers feared that the employers might cut their wages
   - the government was distracted by the decision to continue the War
   - prices were soaring ever higher because the government simply printed money
   - the government were slow at collecting taxes and could not meet its expenses
   - growing demand for Russia to get out of the war
   - political threat from the Bolsheviks.

2. The candidate describes the ways in which Stalin treated the Kulaks using **presented evidence** such as:
   - he introduced the policy of collectivisation, which meant that their farms should become collective farms
   - Stalin's soldiers shot peasants who resisted collectivisation
   - Stalin encouraged poor peasants to denounce these wealthier peasants as Kulaks
   - any Kulak could be sent to prison
   
   and from **recalled evidence** such as:
   - the Kulaks lost all they had worked for in their lives
   - 1.5 million were transported to Siberia
   - many died from cold/hunger/disease/forced labour

## Section B

In answering questions in Section B, candidates are required to carry out the appropriate process and to use relevant presented evidence and recalled evidence where appropriate. Where **recall is required** in an answer this is stated in the question paper.

3. The candidate evaluates the attitude of Sukhanov using **presented evidence** such as:
   - he is **supportive** of Lenin's actions inside Russia (**holistic**)
   - he **thinks** that Lenin was a **very important** person in communist history: created Communist Party
   - he **praises** Lenin's important decisions: saved with bold actions
   - he **credits** Lenin with introduction of N.E.P
   - he **thinks** that Lenin was **responsible** for making Russian Communism a world force
   - he **thinks** that Lenin was **not a vain** person: never boasted

3. (continued)
   - he **thinks** his achievements were **great**
   - he was **sad** when Lenin died.

4. The candidate compares **Sources C** and **D** using **evidence** such as:
   - Sources agree that he created the Communist Party:
     **Source C** says: he created the Communist Party
     **Source D** says: the Communist Party that he created.
   - Sources agree that Lenin brought in the New Economic Policy:
     **Source C** says: introducing the New Economic Policy in 1921
     **Source D** says: the man who brought in the New Economic Policy.
   - Sources agree that Lenin had a world role for Communism:
     **Source C** says: Lenin made Communism a world force
     **Source D** says: he had made Communism a world force.
   - Sources agree about the reaction to his death/that he was much loved:
     **Source C** says: thousands mourned his death
     **Source D** says: thousands of sad Russians queued for hours in the biting cold of Moscow.
   
   **Only Source C** mentions: he took bold action to keep Communists in power.
   **Only Source C** credits: him with signing an unpopular peace treaty.
   **Only Source C** says: he was modest about his achievements.

## UNIT III – Context D: Germany 1918 – 1939

### Section A

In answering questions in Section A, candidates are required to carry out the appropriate process and to use relevant presented evidence. In order to obtain full marks for a question, candidates must in addition use recalled evidence in their answer.

1. The candidate explains why hyperinflation caused hardship in Germany using **presented evidence** such as:
   - prices rose but pensions stayed the same
   - people's savings in the bank lost their value
   - workers had to spend their wages immediately before prices went up
   
   and **recalled evidence** such as:
   - people were starving because they couldn't afford the high price of food
   - money became worthless causing great suffering
   - working class suffered a fall in their standard of living
   - people sold items of value to buy necessities
   - those on fixed benefits suffered badly eg unemployed
   - many people were reduced to poverty due to soaring prices

## General History 2008 (cont.)

**1. (continued)**
- people couldn't afford clothes and fuel due to high prices
- workers struggled as wages didn't keep up with prices
- cleanliness suffered as people couldn't afford soap etc
- to survive people had to barter/exchange items
- health problems increased as a result of shortages caused by hyperinflation.

2. The candidate describes the way Hitler treated the Jews before 1939 using **presented evidence** such as:
   - restrictions imposed on Jews
   - sacked Jews from the Civil Service and legal profession
   - Jewish doctors couldn't work for the state

   and from **recalled evidence** such as:
   - boycott of Jewish shops
   - Nuremberg Laws banned marriages between Jews and non-Jews
   - Jews lost German citizenship/no vote
   - Jewish children humiliated at school
   - Law Against Overcrowding of German Schools restricted the number of Jewish students in any one school/university to 5% of the total
   - Jews forbidden to join army
   - all Jews had to take on a new first name – Israel and Sarah
   - attacks on Jewish properties
   - removal of human and civil rights
   - anti-Jewish propaganda
   - violence was used against Jews
   - sent to concentration camps
   - Kristallnacht

### Section B

In answering questions in Section B, candidates are required to carry out the appropriate process and to use relevant presented evidence and recalled evidence where appropriate. Where **recall is required** in an answer this is stated in the question paper.

3. The candidate evaluates the attitude of the author of **Source C** using **presented evidence** such as:
   - **very impressed** by Hitler's speech (holistic)
   - **spellbound/hypnotised** by Hitler
   - **felt** very **emotional**
   - **inspired** to take action against Germany's enemies

4. The candidate compares **Sources C** and **D** using **evidence** such as:
   - Sources agree about how the crowd reacted when Hitler arrived:
       **Source C** says: when Hitler arrived onto the platform there was not a sound to be heard
       **Source D** says: when Hitler moved onto the stage, 100,000 people became silent.

**4. (continued)**
- Sources agree that at the start of his speech Hitler spoke very quietly:
    **Source C** says: then he began to speak, quietly at first
    **Source D** says: Hitler started his speech very quietly
- Sources agree his voice rose to a scream:
    **Source C** says: his voice had risen to a hoarse shriek
    **Source D** says: by the end he was yelling at the crowd
- Sources agree that Hitler had the audience spellbound:
    **Source C** says: he was holding the masses, and me ... under a hypnotic spell
    **Source D** says: the crowd were hypnotised by Hitler
- Sources agree that Hitler criticised the Treaty of Versailles in his speeches:
    **Source C** says: spoke of the disgrace of Versailles
    **Source D** says: spoke of how awful the Treaty of Versailles was

    **Only Source C** says: his speeches inspired patriotism in the audience.

# Credit History 2008

## UNIT I – Context A: 1750s – 1850s

### Section A

In answering questions in Section A, candidates are required to carry out the appropriate process and to use relevant recalled knowledge.

1. (a) The candidate fully explains the impact of the Highland Clearances on people's lives using **evidence** such as:
    - many Highlanders moved to the Lowlands/issues of housing
    - had to learn new trades/take employment in factories
    - many Highlanders were forcibly evicted/horrible experience
    - landlord authority used directly to impose expulsion
    - the Highland landowners gained control of the land resources for development for sheep/deer/sporting estates
    - the Highland landowners controlled the sizes of crofts and the passing on of land to the next generation
    - the loss of much of the old ways of living
    - the loss of Gaelic/clan culture/language
    - families were split up
    - younger Highlanders tended to be emigrants/older people left behind
    - pace of emigration grew as people lost relatives
    - some emigrants died on the journeys out of Scotland/impact on relatives
    - tension/bitterness between Highlanders and the traditional clan chiefs/new landowners
    - view that it drew away "the life blood of the nation"
    - moved to coastal areas: often fishing related/kelp collecting

    BUT
    - most of the forced clearances were finished by 1860
    - many Highlanders were encouraged/persuaded to leave
    - some Highlanders saw it as an opportunity/adventure/voluntary migration
    - it did ease the overcrowding and lack of jobs in some Highland areas
    - it eased the poor relief system in Highlands but put pressure on Lowlands
    - helped to deal with the potato famine in Highlands/Islands in 1836 and 1840s
    - the balance of "Highland/Scottish" identity altered as immigrants from outside Scotland arrived

   (b) The candidate fully explains the impact of overseas emigration on people's lives using **evidence** such as:
    - generally made a deep mark on their adopted homelands in USA/Canada/South Africa/Australia/New Zealand
    - growth of English as language of adopted homelands

1. (continued)
    - much of Gaelic/clan culture/language now stayed alive in Canada
    - export of "Caledonian/tartan" culture
    - economic contributions to the agricultural and industrial growth of adopted homelands
    - the USA had the greatest lure for Scots – impact on development of USA society, politics and Westward expansion
    - important to retain links back to relatives in Scotland
    - adopted homelands gained skilled workers/professional people
    - emigrants suffered hardships crossing oceans
    - some emigrants had difficulty settling in/were unprepared for conditions
    - overseas they faced hardships/hostile land and crowded cities
    - many Scots missed by family and friends back home
    - some emigrants were not made welcome
    - some emigrants got low wages and struggled to survive
    - strange diseases killed immigrants
    - areas of Scotland became depopulated

    BUT
    - Scottish links with Native American Indians – both negative in sense of land grab and positive in some cases – "Glencoe and the Indians"
    - involvement in gold rush exploitation of "native" peoples in USA/Australia
    - involvement in land grabs of "native" peoples in Australia/South Africa
    - Scots roles/images/experience in the British Empire as seen by local peoples
    - better living prospects abroad/opportunities for a better future/escape poor living conditions in Scotland
    - emigration offered chance to escape hardship/poverty of life in Scotland
    - cheap farmland available overseas
    - greater freedom overseas
    - Scots try and retain Scottish identity – use Scottish place names/traditional music

### Section B

In answering questions in Section B, candidates are required to carry out the appropriate processes and to use relevant presented evidence and recalled knowledge where appropriate. Where **recall is required** in an answer this is stated in the question paper.

2. The candidate makes a balanced evaluation of **Source A** using **evidence** such as:
    - contemporaneity:
      a primary source written at the time of Radical unrest
    - authorship:
      eyewitness account of the Radical unrest/involved observer
    - content:
      details of the Radicals and Government actions eg …

# Credit History 2008 (cont.)

2. (continued)
   - accuracy:
     supports many other views on the events at Peterloo eg …/ matches candidate's own knowledge eg …
   - purpose:
     to give the Radical views on what happened at Peterloo
   - limitation:
     may be biased as a radical view/only one man's experience, but he was a leading Radical. Only tells us about Peterloo, nothing about eg …

3. The candidate selects and organises **evidence to support the view that there was little support for the militant Radicals** using evidence such as:

   **Source A**
   - peaceful meeting
   - the crowd gathered in an orderly fashion
   - many singing hymns
   - sabres hacked naked hands/defenceless heads

   **Source B**
   - a **small** crowd of men and **boys** met up with the troops
   - a whole company of loyal volunteers took 5 of the rebels to Greenock jail

   **Source C**
   - attracted only a handful of Radicals, mainly from a few weaving areas
   - protest by a dying craft rather than a working class rebellion
   - the propertied classes strongly supported the authorities

   The candidate selects and organises **evidence against the issue** using evidence such as:

   **Source A**
   - the cavalry could not break through the demonstrators

   **Source B**
   - the authorities became alarmed
   - whole company sent to guard prisoners
   - crowd increased considerably on route
   - mob attacked the jail and released the Radicals

   **Source C**
   - the government could not guarantee control of many areas
   - large numbers of armed men drilling openly worried the authorities

4. The candidate offers a **balanced conclusion** on the issue using **presented evidence** such as that given in Answer 4 and **recalled evidence** such as:
   - **For the issue:**
     - transportation sentences for convicted Radicals
     - no real popular support for revolution/many people supported the authorities
     - landowner support for the government
     - government use of spies/agent provocateurs/surveillance

4. (continued)
   - the government had the real power
   - little support in Scotland for physical force
   - some rise in living standards took minds away from reform ideas
   - children present at Peterloo: peaceful
   - only 30 Radicals engaged in the Battle of Bonnymuir
   - **Against the issue:**
     - Glasgow Radicals/general strike of 60,000 in Glasgow
     - many weavers were unemployed and unhappy
     - a party of Radicals tried to march to Carron to get weapons: Bonnymuir Riots
     - the Government was worried enough to send 2,000 soldiers to Glasgow
   ALSO
   - details on: Strathaven Rising; planned armed revolt of the United Scotsmen etc

## UNIT I – Context B: 1830s – 1930s

### Section A

In answering questions in Section A, candidates are required to carry out the appropriate process and to use relevant recalled knowledge.

1. (a) The candidate fully explains the impact of Irish immigration on people's lives using **evidence** such as:
   - contributed to population growth
   - contributed particularly to growth of cities like Glasgow and Dundee
   - many employed in textile trade – settled in Paisley, Lanark etc
   - Irish provided unskilled workers for road/canal/railway building
   - provided seasonal workers in agriculture
   - did dirty work/jobs Scots reluctant to do eg sugar factories
   - Irish worked for lower wages/caused resentment amongst native population (in 1840s)
   - most of the Irish immigrants were Catholics
   - after 1870s many Irish immigrants were Protestants from Ulster: increased Protestant/Catholic divide
   - conflict between native Protestant population and Irish Catholic population led to Orange Order marches/physical violence occurred (Orange and Green Riots)
   - Irish community stuck together and formed own football teams eg Edinburgh Hibernian (1875), Glasgow Celtic (1888) and Dundee Hibernian (1909) – later Dundee United
   - arrival of large numbers of Irish immigrants increased housing problems/contributed to overcrowding
   - arrival of Irish was a burden on parish poor rates
   - some Irish resorted to begging/sought solace in alcohol
   - employment as strike-breakers in coalmining led to resentment/accusations of lowering wages

## 1. (continued)

- by 1880s Irish were prominent in trade unions helping to push up wages
- after 1872 Catholic Irish attended denominational schools since school boards would not guarantee the religious character of schools

(b) The candidate fully explains the impact of Scottish Emigration upon people's lives using **evidence** such as:

- emigrants suffered hardships crossing oceans
- some emigrants had difficulty settling in/were unprepared for conditions
- overseas they faced hardships/hostile land and crowded cities
- many emigrants returned home
- many Scots missed by family and friends back home
- Scots missed their homeland/culture – export of "Caledonian/tartan" culture
- some emigrants were not made welcome
- some emigrants got low wages and struggled to survive
- strange diseases killed emigrants
- sense of clan loss/culture breakdown/decline of Gaelic
- areas of Scotland became depopulated
- few jobs on arrival
- inhospitable climate

BUT

- better living prospects abroad/opportunities for a better future/escape hardship, poverty and poor living conditions in Scotland
- lots of employment especially for skilled workers/adopted homelands gained skilled workers/professionals
- chance of better jobs/escape unemployment back home
- family and friends already there/welcomed them
- chance of better/more regular schooling abroad
- cheap farmland available overseas
- greater freedom overseas
- many Scots did very well/rose to high positions eg Andrew Carnegie
- some emigrants made a fortune eg by finding gold
- less class prejudice abroad/everyone treated more equally
- Scots try and retain Scottish identity – use Scottish place names/traditional music
- Scottish links with Native American Indians – both negative in sense of land grab and positive in some cases – "Glencoe and the Indians"
- involvements in gold rush, exploitation of "native" peoples in USA/Australia
- involvements in land grabs of "native" peoples in Australia/South Africa.

## Section B

In answering questions in Section B, candidates are required to carry out the appropriate processes and to use relevant presented evidence and recalled knowledge where appropriate. Where **recall is required** in an answer this is stated in the question paper.

2. The candidate makes a balanced evaluation of **Source A** using **evidence** such as:

- contemporaneity:
  a primary source written near to/during period of Suffragette campaigns
- authorship:
  leading figure in WSPU/informed eyewitness
- content:
  details on reactions to militant campaigns eg weakened public support
- accuracy:
  matches candidate's own knowledge eg … but as autobiography memories may have changed/been embellished/facts forgotten over time
- purpose:
  to record the history of the Suffragette movement/to give the Suffragette view on militant action
- limitation:
  may be biased towards her own personal view/only the view of one Suffragette who differed from other leading Suffragettes/omits eg…

3. The candidate selects and organises **evidence for the issue** using evidence such as:

### Source A
- the militants were heroes
- people recognised government reaction left women with no alternative
- people recognised women were simply using similar means men had used in past franchise struggles

### Source B
- self-sacrifice has moved people who would otherwise sit still and do nothing
- reporters were impressed

### Source C
- bravery of suffragettes won them admiration
- they had support from women and men of all classes
- dockers acted as bodyguards for Mrs Pankhurst
- some men formed a movement to support the Suffragettes

The candidate selects and organises **evidence against the issue** using evidence such as:

### Source A
- deeply unhappy with new policy of militancy
- public sympathy would be weakened
- fire raising lost them support/opposition increased

### Source B
- militancy is detested by majority of Suffragists
- no triumphs have been won by physical force
- press ridiculed Suffragettes

### Source C
- militancy provoked ridicule and hostility
- militant suffragettes should have their heads shaved

## Credit History 2008 (cont.)

4. The candidate offers a **balanced conclusion** on the issue using **presented evidence** such as that given in Answer **4** and **recalled evidence** such as:

- **For the issue (helped):**
  - activities increased pressure on government
  - non-militant tactics had not achieved as much in 60 years/little attention paid to cause until 1905 when militancy began
  - Emily Davison became a martyr for the Cause
  - Cat and Mouse Act attracted sympathy
  - membership of suffrage societies grew
  - actions embarrassed the government
  - actions encouraged insurance companies to lobby government
  - actions showed determination
  - many were horrified at force-feeding
  - Conciliation Bill suggested Suffragettes were having an effect
  - got publicity
  - raised awareness

- **Against the issue (harmed):**
  - Government determined not to give in to violence
  - made women appear foolish/irresponsible/irrational/damaged Suffragist argument that women were mature, sensible enough to deserve the vote
  - law breaking strengthened the view that women could not be trusted/did not deserve the vote
  - Suffrage Movement split
  - details of violence which disgusted people eg slashing artwork
  - Suffragettes arrested
  - Asquith determined not to back down
  - death of Emily Davison shocked many and militant Suffragettes faced hostile crowds
  - gave government a reason/excuse not to grant the vote
  - alienated the would-be supporters
  - alienated previously sympathetic MPs eg Winston Churchill
  - led to concerns about law and order
  - failed to win vote up to 1914

- **Other factors**
  - peaceful methods eg petitions helped win support
  - war work/effort won respect for women: WRAF/nurses/munitions

## UNIT I – Context C: 1880s – Present Day

### Section A
In answering questions in Section A, candidates are required to carry out the appropriate processes and to use relevant recalled knowledge.

1. (a) The candidate fully explains the impact of the immigration into Scotland upon people's lives using **evidence** such as:
   - contributed to population growth
   - immigrants contributed to multi-culturalism eg language, customs
   - Irish contributed to railway/canal development
   - Irish play an important role in Trade Unions/contribute to improved wages
   - Irish Catholics formed own football teams eg Edinburgh Hibernian (1875), Glasgow Celtic (1888) and Dundee Hibernian (1909) – later Dundee United
   - many Lithuanians and Poles settle in Lanarkshire and find work in iron/coal industry
   - some Lithuanians recruited by mine owners to break strikes
   - Lithuanians establish own communities in Lanarkshire – own shops, churches, newspapers
   - Jews establish communities in Glasgow/Edinburgh
   - Jews start small businesses eg furniture makers, tailors, shoe makers, pawnbrokers
   - many Italians establish cafes and chip shops
   - from 1950s many Commonwealth immigrants eg Indians, Pakistanis, Afro-Caribbeans and Hong Kong Chinese arrive to take up employment
   - Asians performed valuable jobs in factories and public transport
   - success of immigrant workers provides jobs for others
   - many brought new skills which benefit Scotland
   - Scottish hospitals depend upon immigrant doctors and nurses to care for public
   - immigrants brought new foods eg fish and chips, pasta, curries which now form part of Scottish diet
   - recent immigrants – Asylum Seekers
   - migrant workers from Eastern Europe work in hotel/fish processing industry
   
   BUT
   - many immigrants felt they were worse off and wanted to return home – suffered homesickness
   - native Scots accuse immigrants of lowering wages
   - immigrants sometimes blamed for increasing racial tension
   - arrival of large groups of immigrants could worsen an existing housing shortage
   - immigrants forced to live in poor housing
   - established Protestant and Catholic churches were hostile to Jews

## 1. (continued)

- immigrants sometimes worsened sectarian divide
- Irish accused of drinking too much and causing violence
- Italians criticised for breaking the Sabbath by opening cafes on a Sunday.

(b) The candidate fully explains the impact of Scottish Emigration upon people's lives using **evidence** such as:

- emigrants suffered hardships crossing oceans
- some emigrants had difficulty in settling in/were unprepared for conditions
- overseas they faced hardships/hostile land and crowded cities
- many emigrants returned home
- many Scots missed by family and friends back home
- Scots missed their homeland/culture – export of "Caledonian/tartan" culture
- some emigrants were not made welcome
- some emigrants got low wages and struggled to survive
- strange diseases killed emigrants
- sense of clan loss/culture breakdown/ decline of Gaelic
- areas of Scotland became depopulated
- Scottish links with Native American Indians – both negative in sense of land grab and positive in some cases – "Glencoe and the Indians"
- involvements in gold rush exploitation of "native" in USA/Australia
- involvements in land grabs of "native" peoples in Australia.

BUT

- better living prospects abroad/ opportunities for a better future/escape poor living conditions in Scotland
- lots of employment especially for skilled workers/adopted homelands gained skilled workers/professionals
- chance of better jobs/escape unemployment back home
- family and friends already there/welcomed them
- chance of better/more regular schooling abroad
- emigration offered chance to escape hardship/poverty of life in Scotland
- cheap farmland available overseas
- greater freedom overseas
- many Scots did very well/rose to high positions eg Andrew Carnegie
- some emigrants made a fortune eg by finding gold
- less class prejudice abroad/everyone treated more equally
- Scots try and retain Scottish identity – use Scottish place names/traditional music

## Section B

In answering questions in Section B, candidates are required to carry out the appropriate processes and to use relevant presented evidence and recalled knowledge where appropriate. Where **recall is required** in an answer this is stated in the question paper.

2. The candidate makes a balanced evaluation of **Source A** using **evidence** such as:
   - contemporaneity:
     a primary source written near to/during period of Suffragette campaigns
   - authorship:
     leading figure in WSPU/informed eyewitness
   - content:
     details on reactions to militant campaigns eg weakened public support
   - accuracy:
     matches candidate's own knowledge eg … but as autobiography memories have changed/been embellished/facts forgotten over time
   - purpose:
     to record the history of the Suffragette movement/to give the Suffragette view on militant action
   - limitation:
     may be biased towards her own personal view/only the view of one Suffragette who differed from other leading Suffragettes/omits eg…

3. The candidate selects and organises **evidence for the issue** using **evidence** such as:

   **Source A**
   - the militants were heroes
   - people recognised government reaction left women with no alternative
   - people recognised women were simply using similar means men had used in past franchise struggles

   **Source B**
   - self-sacrifice has moved people who would otherwise sit still and do nothing
   - reporters were impressed

   **Source C**
   - bravery of suffragettes won them admiration
   - they had support from women and men of all classes
   - dockers acted as bodyguards for Mrs Pankhurst
   - some men formed a movement to support the suffragettes

   The candidate selects and organises **evidence against the issue** using evidence such as:

   **Source A**
   - deeply unhappy with new policy of militancy
   - public sympathy would be weakened
   - fire raising lost them support/opposition increased

   **Source B**
   - militancy is detested by majority of Suffragists
   - no triumphs have been won by physical force
   - press ridiculed Suffragettes

   **Source C**
   - militancy provoked ridicule and hostility
   - militant suffragettes should have their heads shaved

## Credit History 2008 (cont.)

4. The candidate offers a **balanced conclusion** on the issue using **presented evidence** such as that given in Answer 4 and **recalled evidence** such as:

    - **For the issue (helped):**
        - activities increased pressure on government
        - non-militant tactics had not achieved as much in 60 years/little attention paid to cause until 1905 when militancy began
        - Emily Davison became a martyr for the Cause
        - Cat and Mouse Act attracted sympathy
        - membership of suffrage societies grew
        - actions embarrassed the government
        - actions encouraged insurance companies to lobby government
        - actions showed determination
        - many were horrified at force-feeding
        - Conciliation Bill suggested Suffragettes were having an effect
        - got publicity
        - raised awarenes

    - **Against the issue (harmed):**
        - Government determined not to give in to violence
        - made women appear foolish/irresponsible/irrational/damaged Suffragist argument that women were mature, sensible enough to deserve the vote
        - law breaking strengthened the view that women could <u>not</u> be trusted/did not deserve the vote
        - Suffrage Movement split
        - details of violence which disgusted people eg slashing artwork
        - Suffragettes arrested
        - Asquith determined not to back down
        - death of Emily Davison shocked many and militant Suffragettes faced hostile crowds
        - gave government a reason/excuse not to grant the vote
        - alienated the would-be supporters
        - alienated previously sympathetic MPs eg Winston Churchill
        - led to concerns about law and order
        - failed to win vote up to 1914

    - **Other factors**
        - peaceful methods, petitions helped win support
        - war work/effort won respect for women: WRAF/nurses/munitions

### UNIT II – Context A: 1790s – 1820s

#### Section A
In answering questions in Section A, candidates are required to carry out the appropriate process and to use relevant recalled knowledge.

1. The candidate describes how the events after the Edict of Fraternity led to the outbreak of war using **evidence** such as:
    - French conquest of the Austrian Netherlands alarmed many

1. (continued)
    - French violation of Dutch neutrality contributed
    - opening of the River Scheldt concerned Britain
    - building up of the port of Antwerp to rival London
    - British public horrified at attacks on French upper classes
    - the September Massacres appalled many
    - the Reign of Terror had become extreme
    - the execution of Louis XVI
    - France declared war on 1st February 1793

2. The candidate explains the degree of success in dealing with the problems faced by the Congress system after 1815 using **evidence** such as:

    **Success**
    - no major wars
    - France brought back into the international system quickly

    **Difficulties**
    - Metternich intended it to have very limited functions
    - Sovereign power took precedence over Congress power
    - Sovereign rulers exercised their own wishes first
    - difficulties with interfering in the internal affairs of one state: Troppau; Verona
    - little regard was paid to the wishes of national groups
    - many delegates were more interested in stamping out revolution
    - difficulties in dealing with the Carbonari uprising in Italy
    - distrust among Congress members eg Russian expansion worries etc
    - problems over Greek independence

#### Section B
In answering questions in Section B, candidates are required to carry out the appropriate processes and to use relevant presented evidence and recalled knowledge where appropriate. Where **recall is required** in an answer this is stated in the question paper.

3. The candidate makes a balanced evaluation of **Source A** using **evidence** such as:
    - contemporaneity:
      primary source produced at the time of the Continental System
    - authorship:
      British cartoonist with first hand knowledge/contemporary observer
    - content:
      details of effects of Continental System eg…/tells us Britain's trade and commerce are doing well despite Continental System
    - accuracy:
      matches candidate's own knowledge eg…/but example of British propaganda and biased against Napoleonic Blockade
    - purpose:
      to show that Britain was not defeated by the Continental System

3. (continued)
- limitation:
  only shows one view/misses out the ways Britain suffered during the blockade eg …

4. The candidate compares **Sources A** and **B** using **evidence** such as:
- Sources agree ships were still trading with Britain.
  **Source A** shows: ships arriving in Britain.
  **Source B** says: the Baltic Sea was kept open to shipping.
- Sources agree Britain was determined to beat the Continental System.
  **Source A** shows: a barrel full of British "spirit".
  **Source B** says: the Continental System failed to break Britain's will to resist.
- Sources agree Napoleon traded with Britain.
  **Source A** shows: British goods being "sent" to Napoleon.
  **Source B** shows: Napoleon's army was supplied with British goods.

  **Only Source B** mentions: Britain increased her trade with America and India.
  **Only Source B** mentions: French controlled Europe was not allowed to trade with Britain.

5. The candidate assesses the completeness of **Sources A** and **B** using **presented evidence** such as:
- Britain had to gain control of the Danish fleet to keep shipping routes open
- Britain continued to import goods
- Britain increased her trade with America and India
- Britain even traded with Napoleon
- Britain's commerce was doing well

and **recalled** evidence such as:
- British Orders in Council 1807 had an impact in keeping trade open
- disruption to fishing
- some businesses depressed
- low wages for many workers
- unemployment
- agricultural change required to feed the nation: good and bad
- prices of basic foods rose
- taxes increased to pay for the war
- new taxes introduced (window tax, income tax)
- political censorship increased
- Radical movements suppressed
- new restrictive laws introduced: against sedition; anti-combinations etc
- Corn Laws passed
- Speenhamland System introduced

## UNIT II – Context B: 1890s – 1920s

### Section A
In answering questions in Section A, candidates are required to carry out the appropriate process and to use relevant recalled knowledge.

1. The candidate describes the slide to war after the assassination at Sarejevo using **evidence** such as:
   - assassinations in Bosnia blamed on Serbia
   - Austria-Hungary used assassinations as an excuse to deliver an ultimatum to Serbia which Serbia was unlikely to accept
   - Serbia refused to accept all points
   - Austria-Hungary declares war on Serbia
   - Russia mobilises in support of Serbia
   - Austria-Hungary/Russia rivalry in the Balkans
   - alliance system comes into play
   - Germany, part of the Triple Alliance, declares war on Russia
   - Germany declares war on France
   - invasion of Belgium by Germany in line with Schlieffen Plan
   - Britain declares war on Germany following violation of Treaty of London/ultimatum

2. The candidate explains the degree of success in dealing with the difficulties faced by the League of Nations using **evidence** such as:

**Difficulties/Failures**
- Germany not allowed to join (joined 1926)
- USSR not permitted to join
- USA was unwilling to join
- League did not possess an army
- failure of League to impose sanctions
- flaws in the Covenant
- need to get unanimous agreement before it would act
- members not committed to the League
- disagreement between member nations
- could not get countries to disarm
- failure to act over Fiume
- failed to get Poland to leave Vilna
- failure to get its own members to follow the instructions of the League over the Ruhr
- failure to act over Corfu.

**Successes**
- no major war
- commissions dealing with drugs, slavery, refugees, minorities etc
- help given to poor countries eg health
- mandate system for colonies
- minor disputes resolved eg Aaland Islands

### Section B
In answering questions in Section B, candidates are required to carry out the appropriate processes and to use relevant presented evidence and recalled knowledge where appropriate. Where **recall is required** in an answer this is stated in the question paper.

# Credit History 2008 (cont.)

3. The candidate makes an evaluation of **Source A** using **evidence** such as:
   - contemporaneity:
     primary source taken during the early years of the First World War
   - authorship:
     eyewitness/photographic account from a contemporary observer
   - content:
     gives details of damage/destruction eg devastation to shops, houses and bomb damaged street
   - accuracy:
     matches candidate's own knowledge eg .../ agrees with other aerial attacks on Britain which caused fatalities/damage eg ...
   - purpose:
     to inform of dangers posed/damage done by German Zeppelins/to encourage hostility towards the Germans
   - limitation:
     only one part of the country ie London but also eg ... /omits eg ...

4. The candidate evaluates the degree of agreement between **Sources A** and **B** using **evidence** such as:

   - Both sources agree that shops had been hit.
     **Source A** shows: that several shops have been damaged.
     **Source B** says: several shops were badly damaged.

   - Both sources agree that houses were badly bombed.
     **Source A** shows: a number of bomb damaged houses.
     **Source B** says: many houses were destroyed, windows were broken.

   - Both sources agree roofs were damaged/blown off.
     **Source A** shows: a building without a roof.
     **Source B** says: roofs blown off.

   - Both sources agree that the road had been cratered.
     **Source A** shows: a huge crater in the road.
     **Source B** says: the power of the bombs was illustrated by the large crater one bomb made in the road.

   **Only Source A** shows rescuers/bomb damage being repaired.
   **Only Source B** says the number of fatalities (22) caused by the bombs.
   **Only Source B** says the financial cost of the damage (£500,000).
   **Only Source B** says that massive warehouse fires broke out.
   **Only Source B** says that two packed buses were hit.

5. The candidate evaluates the completeness of **Sources A** and **B** using **presented evidence** such as:
   - buses hit
   - civilians were killed in London by Zeppelins
   - property (houses and shops) were badly damaged

5. (continued)
   - expensive to repair property
   - warehouses on fire

   and from **recalled evidence** such as:
   - suffering from starvation
   - German naval attacks on the east coast of England, Scarborough
   - bombs dropped by German Gotha bombers from 1917 killed more civilians than Zeppelins
   - men away at war
   - mourning, huge number of soldiers killed
   - many women forced to nurse wounded soldiers
   - blackout
   - DORA restrictions/censorship
   - food shortages/rationing
   - Black Market
   - more women working: Land Army, munitions factories
   - conscription
   - propaganda eg posters on rationing, enlistment etc.

## UNIT II – Context C: 1930s – 1960s

### Section A

In answering questions in Section A, candidates are required to carry out the appropriate process and to use relevant recalled knowledge.

1. The candidate describes the events after the Munich Agreement which led to the outbreak of the Second World War using **evidence** such as:
   - Czech troops withdrew from their frontier and left the country without adequate defence
   - Hitler claimed the Sudetenland was his last territorial claim
   - German troops marched into Sudetenland unopposed
   - Hitler had access to the Skoda arms factory and the Brno works which increased German military strength
   - Germany planned to invade Moravia and Bohemia, claiming they were ill-treated by the Czechs
   - when Slovakia claimed its independence, Czechoslovakia began to fall apart
   - appeasement was now dead and British attitude to Nazi Germany hardened
   - Britain began rearming at an accelerated rate
   - Hitler turned his attentions to Poland (Polish Corridor, Danzig and all Polish areas where German minorities lived)
   - France and Britain promise to guarantee Polish security if attacked
   - Hitler gave secret orders to his armed forces to be ready to invade Poland by 1st September 1939
   - Britain and France approached the Soviet Union to assist in stopping Hitler/negotiations to form an anti-Nazi Alliance dragged on
   - German-Soviet non-aggression pact signed. This made war inevitable
   - details of Nazi-Soviet Non-Aggression Pact
   - Germany invaded Poland on 1 September 1939
   - Britain and France honour their guarantee to Poland on 3rd September 1939

2. The candidate explains the degree of success in dealing with the problems faced by the United Nations Organisation after the Second World War using **evidence** such as:

**Difficulties/Failures**
- vetoing of proposals
- the UNO failed to stop war/minor wars continued
- limited success during Berlin Crisis
- tension continued between nations often despite UNO intervention
- difficulties over arms control/disarmament
- difficulties over role of observers/peace keepers (Middle East, Belgian Congo)
- difficulties over aspects of Cold War
- difficulties over Human Rights in some member states
- accusations of the UNO being bureaucratic/prone to corruption
- accusation of not acting within its Charter/acting outside the intended limits
- not all members were whole hearted supporters (eg contributions, following agreed policy)
- problems with national security remained
- difficulties in North Korea
- limited success in imposing sanctions

**Successes**
- no major world war
- successes of various UN Special Agencies eg UNESCO, WHO, UNICEF etc.

## Section B

In answering questions in Section B, candidates are required to carry out the appropriate processes and to use relevant presented evidence and recalled knowledge where appropriate. Where **recall is required** in an answer this is stated in the question paper.

3. The candidate evaluates the usefulness of **Source A** using **evidence** such as:
   - contemporaneity:
     primary source from the time of the Clydebank Blitz (13/14 March 1941)
   - authorship:
     eyewitness/photographic account from a contemporary observer
   - content:
     gives details of damage/destruction to Clydebank eg devastation to houses/tenements, shops and bomb damaged street
   - accuracy:
     matches candidate's own knowledge eg …/ agrees with/similar factual evidence such as eg …
   - purpose:
     to inform others about the damage done to Scottish cities by Germany/to encourage hostility towards Germans
   - limitation:
     snapshot – only one scene/location ie Clydebank but also eg … /omits eg …

4. The candidate assesses the degree of agreement between **Sources A** and **B** using **evidence** such as:

   - Sources agree that buildings had been destroyed.
     **Source A** shows: widespread damage to buildings.
     **Source B** says: the big house and tenement blocks close by had been bombed.
   - Sources agree there was much debris.
     **Source A** shows: debris and rubble all around/man walking on debris.
     **Source B** says: we were running on a carpet of broken glass and debris and I could feel it crunching under my feet.
   - Sources disagree on water supplies after the Blitz.
     **Source A** shows: water coming from hoses.
     **Source B** says: there was no water, the mains supply being ruptured.
   - Sources disagree about dousing out fires
     **Source A** shows: two firemen putting out fires/members of the fire brigade
     **Source B** shows: there were no fire brigades to put out other fires.

     **Only Source B** refers to people being killed.
     **Only Source B** refers to shops without windows

5. The candidate assesses the completeness of **Sources A** and **B** using **presented evidence** such as:
   - buildings destroyed
   - much debris scattered around
   - water supplies affected
   - many people were killed
   - shops damaged (no windows)

   and from **recalled evidence**:
   - bomb attacks united people/more determined to win
   - introduction of invasion precautions
   - wartime restrictions/disruptions to daily life
   - everyone had to carry gas masks which were uncomfortable
   - blackout to prevent German bombers getting through which caused accidents
   - evacuation of children to safe areas split many families up
   - shelters made available to British civilians – brought disruption to their everyday life
   - air raid sirens – many false alarms
   - men away at war
   - war casualties and loss of loved ones
   - use of propaganda eg posters on rationing, war work and spies
   - women taking over men's jobs/joining services
   - rationing and its effects
   - utility products disliked
   - Black Market
   - Home Guard.

# Credit History 2008 (cont.)

UNIT III – Context A: USA 1850 – 1880

## Section A
In answering questions in Section A, candidates are required to carry out the appropriate process and to use relevant recalled knowledge.

1. The candidate describes the lack of rights for slaves on Southern plantations before 1860 using **evidence** such as:
    - many subject to strict rules and regulations/had no freedom
    - slaves could be bought and sold/seen as property
    - worked long hours at hard work with only short breaks
    - subject to harsh/inhuman discipline eg whipping common
    - runaway slaves were beaten/maimed: use of dogs to hunt runaways
    - slaves needed permission to get married
    - slave marriages had no legal status
    - slave owners often named slave children
    - slave families often broken up/separated
    - slaves unable to visit family/relatives on other plantations
    - female slaves sometimes sexually abused by owners/overseers
    - children born to a slave, fathered by white owner, were still slaves
    - pregnant slaves were expected to work until the child was born.

2. The candidate explains the importance of the discovery of gold in causing tension between the Native Americans and the white settlers using **evidence** such as:
    - Bozeman Trail was cause of conflict/triggered war: Native Americans opposed white men building road to gold mines
    - Trail passed through Yellowstone River/heart of Sioux hunting grounds
    - feared destruction of bison/buffalo herds: reliance on buffalo for all needs
    - railroad companies sent in hunters to kill buffalo
    - Custer's discovery of gold in Black Hills brought thousands of miners
    - miners offered $200 per "Indian" scalp
    - Custer provoked war by leading an expedition into the Black Hills: Black Hills were sacred Sioux territory
    - Native Americans felt betrayed/believed US government had broken Treaty of Fort Laramie: Black Hills had been promised to the Sioux "for as long as the grass grows"
    - Native Americans feared extinction/destruction of way of life/culture
    - railroads caused tension with Native Americans: opened up West/encouraged white settlers to buy prairie lands

2. (continued)
    - Native Americans and Whites brought into conflict over use of prairies: Native Americans wanted freedom to roam/hunt; Whites wanted to farm/Native Americans believed Great Spirit created land for their care; Whites had a "property attitude"
    - Manifest Destiny/White belief in civilising the wilderness: Native Americans regarded as inferior/"savages", tribes not seen as a nation
    - Native Americans feared white invasion: loss of homelands/removal to reservations

## Section B
In answering questions in Section B, candidates are required to carry out the appropriate processes and to use relevant presented evidence and recalled knowledge where appropriate. Where **recall is required** in an answer this is stated in the question paper.

3. The candidate discusses the attitude of the author in **Source A** using **evidence** such as:
    - the Ku Klux Klan **hated** Black Americans (**holistic**)
    - it was **wrong** for Black Americans to worship as they pleased
    - **hostility** towards Black American education
    - **warned off/intimidated** Black Americans who held public office
    - **believed** Black Americans **should be punished** violently/whipped
    - didn't accept Black Americans were **equal** to white people
    - held a **racist** attitude.

4. The candidate compares **Sources A** and **B** using **evidence** such as:
    - Sources agree that teachers were targeted by the KKK.
        Source A says: hostility was shown to teachers.
        Source B says: teachers were frequently intimidated.
    - Sources agree that violence was used against Black Americans.
        Source A says: they were whipped/school houses burned down.
        Source B says: violence was directed at black people/Black Americans were beaten, mutilated and murdered.
    - Sources agree that night was a dangerous time.
        Source A says: that the KKK gave warnings at night.
        Source B says: that attacks usually took place at night.

    **Only Source A** mentions Black American religion was threatened.
    **Only Source B** mentions that Klansmen were dressed in white clothes and left behind burning crosses.
    **Only Source B** mentions that Black Americans did not resist their treatment at the hands of the KKK.

# UNIT III – Context B: India 1917 – 1947

## Section A
In answering questions in Section A, candidates are required to carry out the appropriate process and to use relevant recalled knowledge.

1. The candidate describes the lack of rights for Indian people during British rule by using **evidence** such as:
   - suppression of 'native culture'
   - control of school/use of English language and culture
   - violent repression eg Amritsar massacre
   - repressive laws eg Rowlett Act – took away many civil liberties
   - all meetings and processions banned
   - discrimination against Indians – no opportunities for Indians to rise in powerful positions eg Simon Commission (1927) returned no Indians to its rank
   - restricted entrance to civil service – entrance exam, sit exam in Britain etc
   - Government of India Act 1919 gave limited diarchy to Indians, but Britain could still over-rule
   - limited attempts to improve voting rights
   - voting rights largely limited – based on wealth
   - problems associated with the Caste system – jobs, lack of political rights.

2. The candidate explains the importance of Ghandi's non-violent actions in putting pressure on Britain to grant India more freedom using **evidence** such as:

### Ghandi
   - Ghandi's actions encouraged other Indians to break the law eg Indians staged acts of non-violence around the country (eg making salt)
   - His actions showed Britain that India was not governable without Indian co-operation/ publicity forced many people in Britain to realise they could not hold India by force
   - Ghandi's simple and symbolic acts received massive publicity through newspapers and newsreels
   - regular imprisonment of Indians including Ghandi brought huge embarrassment to Britain/publicity harmed Britain's reputation and image as a humane world power
   - while in jail, Ghandi learned of plan to divide India's voters on the basis of religion; Ghandi announced he would fast to death unless Britain backed down – Britain feared him dying a martyr, so they withdrew their plans.

### Other factors
   - many were shocked at Britain's heavy handed response to the non-violent protest
   - some British politicians began to think in terms of Indian self-government
   - Indians now believed they could win their independence
   - Britain needed Indian support during World War II, so did not press for Indian independence: in return, the India Commission planned to give India independence after the war
   - political parties/figures pressurised/negotiated with Britain eg Nehru/Jinnah/Muslim League.

## Section B
In answering questions in Section B, candidates are required to carry out the appropriate processes and to use relevant presented evidence and recalled knowledge where appropriate. Where **recall is required** in an answer this is stated in the question paper.

3. The candidate discusses the attitude of the author towards events in **Source A** using **evidence** such as:
   - overall **displeasure/fear** at scenes witnessed (**holistic**)
   - people were beginning to **panic** about the situation
   - killing was **relentless**: "butchered"
   - killers were displaying **no mercy**/killing **indiscriminately**
   - **desperation** to leave the city.

4. The candidate compares **Sources A** and **B** using **evidence** such as:
   - Sources agree that people were frightened.
     **Source A** says: a marked feeling of panic … has been a feature.
     **Source B** says: terrified groups of people.
   - Sources agree that there were many dead bodies.
     **Source A** says: dead bodies were everywhere.
     **Source B** says: hundreds of corpses were lying in the gutters.
   - Sources agree that the scene was reminiscent of a battlefield.
     **Source A** says: Calcutta was beginning to look like a battlefield.
     **Source B** says: General claimed that areas were as bad as anything he saw when he was a soldier on the Somme.
   - Sources agree that troops were brought in.
     **Source A** says: the troops were called out of their barracks.
     **Source B** says: troops were called out.
   - Sources agree that many people left.
     **Source A** says: lines of refugees lined the streets and Howrah railway station became a seething mass of people desperate to get out.
     **Source B** says: people left in search of safer areas.

   **Only Source A** mentions: the train being stopped and looted.
   **Only Source B** mentions: the gangs.
   **Only Source B** gives: specific details about casualties eg 4,000 killed/3,000 injured.

# UNIT III – Context C: Russia 1914 – 1941

## Section A
In answering questions in Section A, candidates are required to carry out the appropriate process and to use relevant recalled knowledge.

1. The candidate describes the limited rights of the Russian people under the Tsar before 1917 using **evidence** such as:
   - restrictions eased on the right to vote/demonstrate/freedom of speech/from arrest

# Credit History 2008 (cont.)

## 1. (continued)

- demands for a national parliament led to an elected duma
- promise of constitutional monarchy
- political parties legalised – had been illegal/secret

BUT
- Russia really an autocracy/Tsar had unlimited power
- majority of population denied voting rights/favoured landowners
- books and newspapers were censored
- universities were tightly controlled
- secret Police/Okhrana operated eg intercepted mail
- people imprisoned/exiled for political beliefs
- minority nationalities were discriminated against
- Russification as policy in schools/religion, with 'native languages' not used while Russian was the instrument of teaching in schools.
- workers were denied trade union rights
- peasants remained under control of landowners/redemption payments continued
- army used to put down anti-government demonstrations

2. The candidate explains the importance of the weaknesses of the Provisional Government in the success of the Bolshevik Revolution in October 1917 using **evidence** such as:

**The weaknesses of the Provisional government**
- failure to solve food shortages
- they had continued the war and were losing popular support
- they had not been elected/no speedy arrangements for elections had been made
- they failed to organise their military forces
- they had allowed the Bolsheviks to recover from the July days
- they had been weakened during the Kornilov revolt
- Kerensky left to find loyal troops but never returned
- many Russians did not care/were indifferent/little resistance.
- failure to organise land transfer for peasants
- role of Soviets – idea of 'Dual Government'.

**The strengths of the Bolsheviks**
- Bolsheviks were armed
- the skills of Lenin and Trotsky in organising a military takeover
- Red Guards tightly organised group
- the seizure of key points in Petrograd/power stations/telephone exchanges/railway stations/bridges
- Trotsky's role in getting Peter and Paul fortress support
- cruiser Aurora and artillery attack on Winter Palace
- storming of Winter Palace
- arresting of Provisional Government
- support for Bolshevik ideas of "peace, bread, land"
- Bolsheviks also won control in Moscow

## Section B

In answering questions in Section B, candidates are required to carry out the appropriate processes and to use relevant presented evidence and recalled knowledge where appropriate. Where **recall is required** in an answer this is stated in the question paper.

3. The candidate discusses the attitude of the survivor to the Purges using **evidence** such as:
   - he was **distressed/worried** by the techniques used in the Purges (**holistic**)
   - **believed** mistreated men were **innocent**
   - he was **relieved** not to be included
   - confusion was **terrible; frantic** running/**sad** farewells
   - he was **upset** by executions
   - he was **glad** to survive

4. The candidate compares **Sources A** and **B** using **evidence** such as:

   - The sources agree that people were killed.
     **Source A** says: they were executed.
     **Source B** says: seven million of them were executed/tens of thousands of Party members were killed.

   - The sources agree that people were arrested.
     **Source A** says: whole columns of prisoners.
     **Source B** says: over 40,000 were arrested in Leningrad/almost a million in the country/Stalin sent many others of his fellow citizens to prisons.

   - The sources agree that the Secret Police were involved.
     **Source A** says: the Secret Police had been ordered.
     **Source B** says: also executed by the Secret Police.

   - The sources agree prisoners were sent to camps.
     **Source A** says: forced everyone out of their cells in the camp.
     **Source B** says: millions were sent to Labour camps.

## UNIT III – Context D: Germany 1918 – 1939

### Section A

In answering questions in Section A, candidates are required to carry out the appropriate process and to use relevant recalled knowledge.

1. The candidate describes the rights people were given in the Weimar Republic using **evidence** such as:
   - all men and women over 20 had the vote
   - all Germans were equal before the law
   - people had the right to vote by secret ballot
   - everyone had the right of freedom of speech/to express opinions freely and openly
   - freedom of association/people had the right to hold peaceful meetings
   - freedom of press
   - everyone had the right of freedom of religion
   - letters and correspondence could not be opened and read

## (continued)

- no one could be arrested without good reason/unless they broke the law
- people had the right to join trade unions and societies
- no one could be imprisoned without trial
- rights of privacy/people had the right of privacy in their own homes
- people had the right to form political parties.

The candidate explains the importance of the Munich Putsch in causing Hitler and the Nazis to lose support in the 1920s using **evidence** such as:
- Nazi supporters dispersed by police: violence discredited as criminal
- Hitler revealed as a "hot-head": putsch ill-planned
- realised support overestimated: majority of support still in Bavaria
- Hitler found guilty of high treason and sentenced to 5 years' imprisonment: isolated from political scene/party suffered loss of leadership
- Nazi party/newspaper banned until 1925: effectively censored
- even when Hitler released and party reorganised, support fell away eg only 12 seats/delegates 1928.

BUT
- 16 Nazis who were killed became martyrs
- Hitler gained national publicity from trial: his words were read by millions/ propaganda weapons
- judge sympathetic: received short prison sentence – only served 9 months of 5 years
- imprisonment in Landsberg Castle made Hitler a hero/well-known
- Hitler wrote "Mein Kampf" in prison, allowing Nazi ideas to be publicised

**ALSO OTHER REASONS**
- 1925-1929 Weimar government strong and popular: unemployment low/period of relative prosperity until Wall Street Crash
- Germany benefited from policies of Gustav Stresemann: withdrawal of French and Belgian troops from Ruhr; new currency, Rentenmark; Dawes Plan
- financial crisis in America 1929 allowed Nazis to seize power
- Nazis won more seats in Reichstag as economic depression got worse eg 1928-12/1930-107/1932-230
- fear of Communism led many industrialists/middle class to support Nazis
- Nazis propaganda/Hitler's oratory had greater appeal in 1930s

**Section B**

In answering questions in Section B, candidates are required to carry out the appropriate processes and to use relevant presented evidence and recalled knowledge where appropriate. Where **recall is required** in an answer this is stated in the question paper.

3. The candidate discusses the attitude of **Source A** using **evidence** such as:
   - a very **positive** view/**supported** Hitler's actions (**holistic**)
   - praised Hitler for being **courageous**
   - made Hitler a **hero** in the eyes of many Germans
   - strong **approval/understanding/sympathy** for what he did
   - credited with wanting to restore order and **decency** in Germany
   - **satisfaction** that he acted **decisively**
   - **relief** that he had removed the threat of the SA.

4. The candidate compares **Sources A** and **B** using **evidence** such as:

   - Sources agree that Hitler acted decisively.
     **Source A** says: in taking decisive action/Hitler has acted so decisively.
     **Source B** says: welcomed the decisive action.

   - Sources agree Hitler's actions increased his popularity.
     **Source A** says: made him a hero in the eyes of many ordinary Germans.
     **Source B** says: Hitler's personal popularity soared.

   - Sources agree Germans supported his actions.
     **Source A** says: he has won strong approval …
     **Source B** says: express my most grateful thanks and that of the German people.

   - Sources agree that the SA was a threat.
     **Source A** says: against the serious threat posed by Rohm and the SA.
     **Source B** says: saved the German nation from serious danger.

   **Only Source A** says that Hitler acted to restore order and decency to Germany.
   **Only Source B** says the SA was disliked for its arrogance and corruption.
   **Only Source B** praises Hitler for his brave personal intervention.

Official SQA answers to ISBN 978-1-84372-635-7
2006–2008